MW00478338

THE SEEDS OF
SECULARIZATION

Calvinism, Culture, and Pluralism in America, 1870-1915

Gary Scott Smith

**CHRISTIAN
UNIVERSITY
PRESS**

A subsidiary of Christian College Consortium
and Wm. B. Eerdmans Publishing Company,
Grand Rapids, Michigan

To Patty
For all your encouragement, support, and love

Available from Wm. B. Eerdmans Publishing Co.
255 Jefferson Ave. S.E., Grand Rapids, Mich. 49503

Library of Congress Cataloging in Publication Data

Smith, Gary Scott, 1950-
  The seeds of secularization.

  Includes index.
  1. Calvinism — United States — History. 2. Secularism
— United States — History. 3. United States — Civilization
— 1865-1918. I. Title
BX9422.2.S65 1985   285.7 73   84-25998

ISBN 0-8028-0058-0

Chapter VII, "Tracing the Roots of Modern Morality," first
appeared in the *Westminster Theological Journal* 44
(1982):327-51, and is used by permission.

CONTENTS

ACKNOWLEDGMENTS

In the five years that I have worked on this book, I have received help and wise counsel from numerous people. The encouragement and constructive criticism offered by many scholars has been of immense benefit. My deepest appreciation goes to several of my colleagues at Grove City College who provided helpful suggestions on various chapters: James Bibza, James Dixon, Marvin Folkertsma, Diane Grundy, W. Andrew Hoffecker, Alan Rice, Mary Sodergren, John Sparks, David Valle, John Van Til, and Kathy Van Til. Special thanks also go to Anne Dayton of Slippery Rock State University, Robert Vande Kappelle of Washington and Jefferson College, James Smylie, editor of the *Journal of Presbyterian History,* John Higham of Johns Hopkins University, and to members of the board of the Christian University Press, especially David Moberg of Marquette University. Suggestions from George Marsden of Calvin College helped me to restructure my book and to develop its main themes more clearly. My greatest debt is to Timothy Smith of Johns Hopkins University. He directed my research for this book and the writing of its first two drafts. His criticisms on both style and substance were invaluable, and he served for me, as he has for countless others, as a model of scholarship and Christian love. I also wish to thank Sandra Nowlin of Eerdmans for her painstaking work in editing this book, Carolyn Wood, Barbara Longnecker, and Diane Anderson for laboring long hours to type various drafts, Jane Gilliland and Susan Browne for their help in proofreading, and Everett DeVelde and Jane Christner for assisting with the indexing. To all these people I am very grateful.

ABBREVIATIONS

BRPR	*Biblical Repertory and Princeton Review*
BT	*Banner of Truth*
Cath P	*Catholic Presbyterian*
CI	*Christian Intelligencer*
CO	*Christian Observer*
CP	*Central Presbyterian*
Ind	*Independent*
L	*Leader*
NAR	*North American Review*
PB	*Presbyterian Banner*
POS	*Presbyterian of the South*
PQ	*Presbyterian Quarterly*
PQPR	*Presbyterian Quarterly and Princeton Review*
PR	*Presbyterian Review*
Pres	*Presbyterian*
Proceedings: General Council	*Proceedings of the [no.] General Council of the World Alliance of Reformed Churches*
PRR	*Presbyterian and Reformed Review*
PSt	*Presbyterian Standard*
PTR	*Princeton Theological Review*
SP	*Southern Presbyterian*
SPR	*Southern Presbyterian Review*
SWP	*South West Presbyterian*
UP	*United Presbyterian*

INTRODUCTION

During the 1920s many began to recognize that a profound shift in American attitudes, values, and beliefs was occurring. Orthodox Christianity had principally sustained American cultural ideals from the Puritans of the seventeenth century to the Progressives of the early twentieth century. Belief in the Bible had provided the foundation for much of America's political, social, economic, and educational life for three centuries; the worldview taught there had long shaped the thinking and behavior of most Americans. While Americans had often disagreed about how to interpret and apply scriptural principles, only after 1870 did significant numbers of them begin to challenge the idea that the Bible's teachings should be the basis for public as well as private life.

By the 1920s, however, a new spirit filled the air. Theological debate between fundamentalists and modernists, controversies over evolution, increasing religious, ethnic, and cultural heterogeneity, and the emergence of secular humanism had combined to diminish the cultural influence of historic Christianity. These new currents repeatedly battered America's biblical foundations and increasingly eroded familiar ramparts. By the end of the 1920s many intellectuals and growing numbers of common folk agreed with prominent literary critic Joseph Wood Krutch that "no foundation in authority for ideas of right and wrong" remained. "Both our practical morality and our emotional lives are adjusted to a world that no longer exists."[1] The "acids of modernity," stated political commentator Walter Lippmann, had dissolved the traditional understanding of the universe that previously had enabled human beings to explain all their relevant experience. For the first time in history "fixed and authoritative belief" had become "incredible to large masses of men."[2] Both humanism and hedonism stood ready to replace evangelical Christianity as the predominant shaper of American culture.[3]

The new cultural perspectives and directions that blossomed in the 1920s and have borne fruit during the past sixty years have roots that lie in earlier periods of our history. In this book I hope to elucidate the origins and evolution of secular thought and values in America during the years from 1870 to 1915 and to show how developments during this period prepared the way for the increasing secularization of American public life after 1930. During the late nineteenth and early twentieth centuries strong challenges were mounted to the traditional biblical basis of American politics and government, education and morality, science and technology, business and industry, entertainment and the arts, and marriage and the family. The predominant evangelical culture planted in America by the Puritans, firmly established by the First and Second Great Awakenings, and maintained by countless crusades to reform public and private moral practice during the nineteenth century did not simply collapse under secular onslaughts. Rather, theists struggled valiantly to stem the tide of secular ideas and influences that after 1870 flowed with increasing force. No group worked more fervently to build dikes against secular currents during the years between the Civil War and World War I than Christians who belonged to Calvinist or Reformed denominations.

Many today consider Calvinism a historical relic that is best left buried in a graveyard of obscurity. True, it was the dominant expression of evangelical Christianity in America from the arrival of the Mayflower to the outbreak of the Revolution. But after the War for Independence its influence began to wane, and during the postbellum years this theology was supposedly crushed by an avalanche of Methodist piety, liberal theology, and naturalistic materialism that descended upon the nation.[4] Many applaud Calvinism's supposed demise because its advocates primarily promoted predestination and capitalism, two ideologies out of phase with modern thought. Contrary to this common perspective, however, during the years between 1870 and 1915 Reformed orthodoxy attracted hundreds of thousands of followers. Moreover, its advocates in the late nineteenth century continued strongly to defend a biblical worldview and worked to shape civilization as their forefathers had done for three centuries.

The postbellum years brought stiff challenges to the Christian civilization that Protestants had attempted to construct in America. Doctrines of scientific and social Darwinism, labor unrest produced by industrialization and Marxist doctrines, problems arising from urban poverty, and especially the naturalistic understanding of life and culture promoted by Charles Darwin, Karl Marx, Herbert Spencer, Auguste Comte, and many others in the nineteenth century all threatened Protestant dominance of society. Although religion prospered institutionally in America from 1870 to 1915 (and has continued to ever since), opponents increasingly pressed theists to surrender their influence over the public dimensions of life —

politics, economics, education, and social relationships — and to limit their role to private aspects of individual morality, family customs, and leisure.

Calvinists played a major role in theists' attempts to rest American culture more firmly upon biblical principles and patterns. They argued that other theistic approaches to the relationship between religion and culture, whether Catholic, Jewish, Pietist, Wesleyan, Anabaptist, or dispensationalist, did not fully recognize that the aim of all cultural activity was to glorify God and to advance his kingdom on earth. By laboring diligently to build American society upon biblical teachings, Reformed Christians strongly affected the attitudes and approaches that other Protestants took toward cultural issues.

Many Calvinists warned that the most dangerous force battering America's biblical foundations was secular humanism. Long before Walter Lippmann, John Dewey, Harry Elmer Barnes, and others systematized and popularized this philosophy, heirs of the Genevan Reformation argued that its influence would be pernicious. They identified its principal sources as scientific and literary naturalism, philosophical materialism, and theological liberalism. As a theology that exalted God's sovereignty and abased man's goodness and pride, Calvinism offered from 1870 to 1915 unrelenting opposition to humanist doctrines that declared human beings capable of achieving both individual fulfillment and a good society by their own efforts, without recourse to God's grace.

During the late nineteenth century Calvinists repeatedly warned that accepting a naturalistic worldview would inevitably produce disillusionment, cynicism, pessimism, and despair. As the stock market collapsed, Joseph Wood Krutch, though a naturalist himself, complained that this philosophy had produced precisely these results. He protested that naturalism discouraged efforts to improve humanity or society; it claimed the scientific method could solve all problems and thus depreciated other valid remedies; and, most significantly, it undermined traditional moral and social values without providing a replacement.[5]

Between the Civil War and World War I, Calvinists who sought to thwart the advance of secularism were by no means confined to the South, although they were most numerous there, or to Princeton University, as is generally held. The battle raged from the Atlantic to the Pacific and from Maine to Texas, but was especially heavy in the East and Midwest.

Nor were Calvinists confined to any specific denomination. Until 1915, nearly all Presbyterian and Reformed denominations

(Northern, Southern, United, Reformed, and Associate Reformed Presbyterians, as well as two denominations of Dutch background — the Reformed Church of America and the Christian Reformed Church) strongly maintained orthodox doctrines. But Calvinists also flourished among Northern and Southern Baptists, Congregationalists, Reformed and other Episcopalians, and Welsh Calvinistic Methodists.

For the purposes of this study, we will define a Calvinist as one who adheres to the theology of John Calvin primarily as set forth in his *Institutes of the Christian Religion*. This theology is popularly summarized in five points often referred to by the acronym TULIP — Total depravity, Unconditional election, Limited (or definite) atonement, Irresistible grace, and Perseverance of the saints. These points were not formulated by Calvin but by the Synod of Dort in 1619 about fifty years after his death, in response to the challenges of Jacob Arminius to his teachings. Calvin's system is based primarily on the doctrines of God's sovereignty and human depravity. To be a Calvinist is, above all, to believe in the supremacy and all-sufficiency of God both in the universe as a whole and in the process of salvation. Calvin's admirers in the late nineteenth century continually asserted that he did not invent this theological system in the sixteenth century. Rather, it is rooted in the writings of St. Augustine, the towering theologian of the fourth century, and ultimately in the teachings of the apostle Paul and Jesus Christ.

Two factors will be used to determine who among American Christians during the years under consideration were adherents of John Calvin: their own definition of themselves and the testimony of other avowed Calvinists. If groups or individuals maintained that they belonged in this company and others who made the same confession recognized them as conforming to orthodox, historic Calvinism, then they will be accepted as such. I make no effort to draw fine distinctions between debated points of Reformed theology. My purpose is not to clarify the precise nature and variations of that theology in America after the Civil War but to identify its central principles and to describe Calvinists' interaction with American culture and society.

What seemed during the 1920s to persons such as Walter Lippmann to be a new beginning replete with spectacular possibilities has borne bitter fruit. American philosopher Will Durant has described the demise of the sacred that has so profoundly affected many aspects of our national life during the past sixty years:

God, who was once the consolation of our brief life and refuge in bereavement and suffering, has apparently vanished from the scene; no telescope, no microscope discovers him. Life has become . . . a fitful pullulation of human insects on the earth; nothing is certain except defeat and death. . . . Faith and hope disappear; doubt and despair are the order of the day. . . . It seems impossible any longer to believe in the permanent greatness of man, or to give life a meaning that cannot be annulled by death. . . . The great question of our time is . . . whether man can bear to live without God.

During the past half-century we have discovered that emancipation from transcendent absolutes destroys the truly human. Human autonomy produces self-centeredness rather than freedom. The desacralization of the world has not enabled human beings to reach their fullest potential, as secular humanists promised it would. Instead it has produced frustration and hopelessness.[6] As Americans have rejected God's authority over cultural life, flagrant immorality, militant amorality, growing materialism, and pervasive despair have resulted. Law has lost its majesty and moral chaos is widespread.

Many today believe that America is adrift socially, morally, politically, and spiritually. Millions lament the seeming collapse of our ideals, the failure of our institutions, the corruption of our leaders, and the greed of our people. Although numerous Americans declare themselves to be evangelical Christians, and their influence on our nation's culture seems to be growing, we live in a largely secular age where an evangelical religious consensus no longer undergirds our values, life-styles, and public institutions.

Understanding the roots of the secularization of American culture is especially significant today when so many Christians once again appear eager to transform American culture into the kingdom of God—or at least to arrest the moral, political, and cultural decay they believe is destroying our civilization. Contemporary Christians generally agree that our nation's slide into the secular abyss can only be prevented by reinstituting the biblical values Americans cherished for three centuries. Few, however, adequately understand the nature and history of secularization in our country, or how Christ's followers in earlier periods of American history responded to secular trends, or which strategies are most likely to restore biblical values to our cultural life. The Christian's ultimate model for building social life is, of course, not history but the Scriptures. As pervasive as biblical values were during America's first 250 years, our public institutions and practices have never been uniformly or even consistently Christian. In numerous ways the public life developed by the Puritans and their evangelical Christian successors in the eighteenth and nineteenth centuries fell short of scriptural standards.[7] Although history cannot provide us with a perfect blueprint for designing sociocultural life, it can help us to evaluate what social models and strategies are most likely to be effective in our own day.

Such a study can aid us in two ways. It can help us to understand the sources and process of secularization in America, and it can enable us to avoid faulty strategies employed in the past to halt this development. Many of the secular seeds planted between 1870 and 1915 have borne mature fruit only in our time. We are reaping a harvest sown by an earlier generation. Only by examining the roots can we completely understand the fully grown plant. Moreover, remarkable parallels exist between our day and a century ago. Current debates about the earth's origins, the nature and direction of the public schools, the relationship between religion and government, what principles, if any, underlie public morality, which economic system and structures most advance human welfare, and which economic policies and social programs best help the poor — all were waged in strikingly similar ways in the late nineteenth century. Perhaps past experience can help us better to comprehend and work to remedy today's pressing and perplexing social problems.

While Calvinists closely watched the development of secularism in the late nineteenth century and sharply criticized its premises, their basic strategy against this philosophy was, in the final analysis, inappropriate and ineffective. Throughout the years of our study, Calvinists mistakenly believed that a Christian worldview should and could continue to dominate America's political, educational, and moral institutions and practices. In so doing, they misinterpreted New Testament teachings about the relationship between the gospel and the world, and they failed to recognize that the changing cultural circumstances of these years were making it impossible for Christians to control public life.

Calvinists believed that alternative ideologies to Christianity had no right to exist in the public arena; thus, they sought to prevent proponents of non-Christian worldviews from participating in public questions of politics, education, and morality. They wished to force those who disagreed with their Christian values nevertheless to live under these values as citizens of the state, especially in the education of their children and in observing the Christian Sabbath. Today, Christians often claim that the reverse is true. Humanism, the argument goes, has so pervaded American culture that Christians cannot exercise liberty of conscience in such areas as education and politics.

If Calvinists and other Protestants had not tried to force their values on society during the late nineteenth century and instead had supported the concept of cultural pluralism, the contours of contemporary American culture might be quite different. Advocates of cultural pluralism insist that all groups with different worldviews should have equal opportunity under the law both to teach their understandings of life and to develop associations — schools, labor unions, political parties, businesses, voluntary organizations, and the like — and to promote the same. According to this view, all ideologies should be recognized in public life, and public policies should be hammered out by compromise among various groups. All groups should not have to live under a public order controlled by one worldview, as Christians sought to mandate in earlier American history and humanists strive to accomplish today.

SETTING THE STAGE: CALVINISM AND THE DENOMINATIONS

By 1870 many American churchmen were beginning to realize that the Civil War marked a cultural divide in their country's history. New challenges were emerging that would require great effort to meet. Evolutionary theories, biblical criticism, and utilitarian ethical systems raised questions about traditional views of human origins, scriptural authority, and absolute moral standards. Dramatic industrial and economic changes were transforming society. Urbanization, technology, labor strife, and massive immigration were uprooting familiar ways of life. The new age threatened their persistent determination to build a Christian America; it challenged their notion of cultural homogeneity by demanding pluralism; and it threatened to tear the nation's intellectual and moral leadership from their hands.

Indeed, looming on the horizon of the new era was a whole new view of life and reality that discerning persons realized would soon engage Christianity in a struggle for cultural supremacy. The situation was similar to the geological theory of plate tectonics. According to this theory, giant "plates" lying deep beneath the earth's surface keep it rigid and stable. Sometimes these massive geologic formations, which constantly grind against one another, shift their positions. These plates are so immense that even small shifts along their fault lines cause volcanoes and earthquakes on the surface.[1] During the late nineteenth century the "giant plates" of American culture were beginning to shift. Deep below the surface the ground was moving, thereby transforming the landscape above so that familiar, comforting landmarks were vanishing. Those living closest to society's cultural fault lines, those most aware of new intellectual developments, were the first to notice these changes. In America, Calvinists' educational, cultural, and professional hegemony placed them in a position to feel the tremors of social change before most other Christians.

In 1870 two of the most influential religious leaders of the nineteenth century, Charles Hodge, professor of systematic theology at Princeton Seminary from 1828 until 1878, and Lyman Atwater, professor of moral philosophy and political science at Princeton College from 1854 until 1881, announced the arrival of new cultural conditions. As coeditors of the *Biblical Repertory and Princeton Review* they wrote:

> The minds of men are unsettled; multitudes are drifting away from the faith of their fathers; the profoundest verities of the Word are questioned. . . . The moral, political and social world is astir. . . . A new era of thought, of investigation, of doubting, of testing everything has dawned. . . . Error is rife, and science, falsely so called, is arraying itself against the truth. . . . The agencies of hell and of an ungodly world are leagued in every conceivable form to lead men astray.[2]

Yet, at the same time that they recognized these problems, they rejoiced because sowers of the gospel were multiplying and human hearts were becoming increasingly receptive to its planting.

Such Reformed evangelicals found the post–Civil War years both alarming and exciting. More than most other Christians, they were sensitive to the rise and significance of secular ideologies that began to reshape American society. Their historic position as cultural leaders and their effort to see all of life through the spectacles of a consistent biblical worldview led them to resist vigorously the secularizing trends and philosophies that increasingly affected America after 1870. Examining the strength and contours of the Calvinist community in America in the late nineteenth century and its response to cultural developments during these years can help us better to understand our present society.

Calvinists had much reason to enter the postbellum era with confidence, despite views such as that of Winthrop Hudson, who called the late nineteenth century the "Methodist Age" in America. Many others contend that Calvinism was a dying and decaying theology during these years.[3] The evidence indicates, however, that Calvinism remained a vibrant and influential religious movement until at least World War I. Although their proportional strength among American churches had been steadily diminishing since the Revolutionary era, in the aggregate they were stronger numerically, financially, and institutionally than ever before. A reading of both theirs and the general religious literature of the period sustains the estimates given in chart A of the number of Calvinists in the United States around 1870; chart B shows the number of institutions Calvinists controlled (see pp. 12, 13).

In 1870 Hodge and Atwater were very encouraged by the reunion the previous year between the Old and New Schools of the Presbyterian Church, U.S.A. They saw God's blessing in the size, wealth, ministry, and creed of the communion and believed it even stronger than its numbers suggested. Presbyterians' commitment to an educated ministry helped them attract "the thinking, thrifty, and influential class in each community." No other group of clergymen could match Presbyterian ministers in dedication, thorough training, theological understanding, or reasoned, persuasive preaching. Presbyterian strength, the editors continued, rested not only upon their devoted laity and their outstanding clergy but upon their theological unity and doctrinal standards. Although the "world disrelishes it," and "a liberal Christianity seeks its overthrow," they wrote, the Westminster Confession, the finest Calvinistic creed, remained intact.[6] In the 1870s Calvinists of all denominations agreed with Hodge and Atwater that their doctrinal heritage was indeed the source of their power and the ground of their hope of building a better tomorrow.

A debate in 1873 between Presbyterians and Methodists was typical of numerous discussions about how many soldiers marched under the Reformed banner. Presbyterian minister Robert Aikman responded to a Methodist editorial that had declared that "the Arminian revolution of opinion" had "nearly eliminated Augustinian theology" and that few American clergymen acknowledged "Calvin's *Institutes* as their theological standard."[7] Aikman argued that significant numbers of Episcopalians, Southern and Northern Baptists, Congregationalists, and Presbyterians still accepted the Genevan theology. Even after making due allowance for those who did not profess to hold their doctrinal creed in any strict way, Aikman concluded that at least half the members and ministers of evangelical denominations in America affirmed the doctrines of the Westminster Confession.[8]

While seeming to concede Aikman's claims about clergymen and denominational creeds, the editors of the *Methodist Quarterly* argued that he was focusing on the wrong kind of evidence. The crucial issue was not what theological seminaries taught, nor what doctrines pastors believed, but what the laity actually heard and accepted. "If all the Arminians in the Presbyterian pews were to

CHART A
Number of Calvinists in America ca. 1870[4]

Denomination	Members	Proportion of Members Deemed Calvinists	Number of Calvinists
Presbyterian Church in the United States of America	472,023	90%	425,000
Presbyterian Church in the United States	93,903	100%	93,903
United Presbyterian Church North America	73,452	100%	73,452
Reformed Presbyterian Church in North America	8,752	100%	8,752
Reformed Presbyterian Church of North America	10,009	100%	10,009
Associate Reformed Presbyterians and other minor bodies	30,000	90%	27,000
Total Number of Presbyterian Calvinists			638,116
Reformed Church of America	67,123	100%	67,123
Christian Reformed Church	10,000	100%	10,000
Reformed Church in the United States (German Reformed)	130,299	20%	26,000
Total Number of Reformed Calvinists			103,123
Regular Baptists (Northern and Southern)	1,585,232	70%	1,110,000
Anti-Mission Baptists	40,000	100%	40,000
Total Number of Baptist Calvinists			1,150,000
Congregationalists	318,916	50%	159,000
Episcopalians	239,218	25%	60,000
Welsh Calvinistic Methodists	2,000	100%	2,000
Total Number of other Calvinists			221,000
Grand Total			2,112,000
Total Number of Evangelical Protestants*			7,399,888

Thus about 30 percent of American Evangelicals were Calvinists in 1870.

*I am using "evangelical" in the broad nineteenth-century sense as referring to those who held to the divine inspiration and absolute authority of Scripture, the deity and bodily resurrection of Jesus Christ, and the necessity of a new-birth experience.

Number of Colleges and Theological Seminaries
Controlled by Calvinists[5] (Using the same percentages)

Denomination	Number of Colleges	Percentage of Calvinists	Number of Calvinist Colleges
Congregationalists	21	50%	10
Episcopalians	18	25%	4
Baptists	38	70%	26
Presbyterian	31	90%	27
Dutch and German Reformed	6	60%	3

Total Number of Calvinist Colleges: 70

Total Number of Evangelical Colleges: 194
Thus Calvinists sponsored about 36 percent of America's evangelical colleges around 1870.

Denomination	Number of Seminaries	Percentage of Calvinists	Number of Calvinist Seminaries
Congregationalists	8	50%	4
Episcopalians	12	25%	3
Baptists	22	70%	15
Presbyterians	19	90%	17
Lutheran and German Reformed	21	10%	2

Total Number of Calvinist Seminaries: 41

Total Number of Evangelical Seminaries: 97

Thus Calvinists sponsored about 42 percent of America's Theological institutions around 1870.

evacuate," the editors asserted, "they would leave a decidedly thinned church." Many laymen remained in Presbyterian congregations, they asserted, because the sermons never challenged their Arminian convictions.[9]

Although Aikman was a former New School Presbyterian pastor who early in his ministry was the assistant to one of that movement's more Arminian leaders, N. S. Beman of Troy, New York, he disagreed with these Methodist critics. He insisted that the vast majority of Presbyterians accepted the Reformed doctrine of salvation as taught in Charles Hodge's recently published *Systematic Theology*; Hodge had trained hundreds of Presbyterian ministers, and most of the denomination's seminaries taught his strict Augustinian theology. Furthermore, the decrees of predestination, which were the foundation of the Calvinist system, were best taught not through sermons but through catechism and Sunday School classes.[10]

The creation in 1875 of the "Alliance of Reformed Churches Throughout the World Holding the Presbyterian System" by the various Reformed denominations to promote cooperation in both foreign and home missions bolsters Aikman's argument. The records of the Alliance's conferences, held every four years beginning in 1876, and its publication, the *Catholic Presbyterian*, testify to the strength and persistence of Calvinism among Reformed communions.[11]

Although a gradual decline in the number of those Americans holding consistently Reformed doctrines was apparent after 1890, Calvinism continued to inspire many Christians. In 1897 Calvinists celebrated the 250th anniversary of the formulation of the Westminster Confession with great hope and expectation. After years of effort by Northern Presbyterians to revise the Confession, in 1903 only a few verbal changes were accepted. And Calvinists noted that Presbyterian and Reformed denominations alone claimed about twenty-five million adherents worldwide, making them the largest Protestant denominational family in the world, while many Baptists, Congregationalists, and German Reformed also accepted the Genevan theology.[12]

In 1901 the English Methodist Frederic Platt, writing in the *London Quarterly Review*, predicted "the renaissance of Calvinism," after surveying "certain conditions of life and thought," including several recently published Reformed works. Platt concluded that a theology which illuminated the path of all Presbyterian denominations and many Congregationalist, Baptist, and Anglican congregations could not be considered dead; moreover, many signs indicated that this star would achieve its former magnitude.[13] In America, many Presbyterians agreed with Platt that there were valid historical, philosophical, and biblical reasons for expecting Reformed orthodoxy once again to dominate theology and culture as it had in the sixteenth and seventeenth centuries.[14]

CONSISTENTLY CALVINIST

Although Calvinism never did achieve its earlier historical influence,[15] in the years between 1890 and 1915 its proponents repeatedly used its worldview to resist alternative secular ideals that attempted to transform American politics, education, morality, and social relationships. During these years those denominations with Calvinistic roots and Reformed creeds could be divided into three groups, according to their actual adherence to the five points of

Calvinism. The first group — Southern, United, Reformed and Associate Reformed Presbyterians, and the Christian Reformed Church — were almost totally Calvinist in belief and practice in 1890 and remained so through 1915. They continued to defend their confessional statements — the Westminster Standards for Presbyterians and the Heidelberg Catechism for the Christian Reformed — against all who opposed them. Before World War I their Calvinistic armor contained few chinks.

A leading contemporary historian of the Southern Presbyterians, largest of the five bodies in this first group, described them during this period as "strongly Calvinistic and remarkably homogeneous in outlook and belief."[16] From pulpit and press, Southern Presbyterian ministers argued that accepting Calvinistic principles would produce the most aggressive congregations and the best social order.[17]

Reformed, United, and Associate Reformed Presbyterians were also rigorously Calvinistic. All three denominations were descendants of the Covenanter or Seceder Branch of the Presbyterian Church of Scotland. All sang only Psalms without instrumental accompaniment in worship, attempted to emulate closely the New Testament pattern of worship, and practiced strict church discipline. In faith, usage, and spirit these groups were virtually one.[18]

Reformed Presbyterians divided into two branches in 1833 over differing views of whether their members could vote and hold political office in the United States. While both branches held that all nations must explicitly confess Jesus Christ's headship over them, the Reformed Presbyterian in North America branch refused to allow members to serve as government officials or to vote in nations — like the United States — that failed to acknowledge legally Christ's dominion. Although small (it had reached about 11,000 members in 1890), the communion exerted a force well beyond its numbers. In 1864 its leaders helped to organize the National Reform Association, which worked to pass a constitutional amendment declaring Christ's authority over the government of the United States. Reformed Presbyterians also labored to aid the poor, reduce drunkenness, resolve labor problems, and promote peace.[19]

The much more numerous United Presbyterians, about 130,000 strong in 1905 and centered primarily in Pennsylvania, Ohio, and New York, were also active social reformers and staunch Calvinists. Like Reformed Presbyterians, most of them supported the National Reform Association and urged the American government to recognize Christ's lordship. They promoted women's suffrage, racial equality, a more just distribution of wealth, better factory conditions, civil service reform, and more harmonious international relations.[20]

Springing from the same Scottish origins, Associate Reformed Presbyterians numbered about 15,000 members in 1910. Located primarily in North and South Carolina, their beliefs and practices were very similar to Reformed and United Presbyterians.[21]

Members of the Christian Reformed Church also consistently affirmed Calvinism during these years. The CRC was the product of an 1857 schism within the Reformed Church of America, whose roots lay in colonial New York. Because the majority of the membership was nineteenth-century Dutch immigrants living in Michigan and Iowa, before 1890 it was, due to its Dutch language and culture, largely isolated from other American Reformed bodies. After 1890, however, its members' social and economic advancement and the repercussions in America of the Calvinistic revival in the Netherlands under Abraham Kuyper combined to produce more social interaction.[22] By the 1890s the Christian Reformed and United Presbyterian communions were very similar in theology, church government, and religious practice; but efforts to secure cooperative union failed because of differences in national background, history, and language.[23]

In the years between 1870 and 1915, then, these four Presbyterian denominations and the Christian Reformed Church strongly defended and promoted Reformed principles.

CONSIDERABLY CALVINIST

A second group of denominations, although containing some adherents who accepted Arminian principles and others who embraced liberal theology, remained generally, but not unanimously, Calvinistic. This group includes the Reformed Church of America, Northern Presbyterians, Southern Baptists, and Northern Baptists, listed in order of their members' decreasing faithfulness to the Westminster Confession.

Despite Christian Reformed protests that the Reformed Church of America had modified its theological heritage, the witness of RCA leaders and of other Calvinist communions indicates its continuing orthodoxy during this time. The call of an influential New York City pastor for organic union between the Reformed Church and Southern Presbyterians illustrates this testimony. The pastor claimed that both denominations' theological standards "represented the same type of Calvinism" and were, except in form of expression, "conceded to be substantially identical."[24] Although a few Southern Presbyterians opposed union on theological grounds, many of them pronounced the Reformed Church "just as sound" theologically as their own.[25]

Because of its size and English Puritan heritage, the Northern Presbyterian Church (formally called the Presbyterian Church in the United States of America) influenced all American Calvinists. In 1889, however, fourteen years of controversy began in that body over a proposal to revise its doctrinal standard, the Westminster Confession. The revision accomplished in 1903 was in fact moderate in tone and substance, but the conflict revealed widespread desire for a less strict theological standard. Lefferts Loetscher has argued that the entire history of Presbyterianism in America reflects a "broadening" movement toward a more inclusive and hence less Calvinistic theology. It is true, as many late-nineteenth-century Presbyterians noted, that the denomination contained two ethnic parties with different ideological orientations. Those from Scottish and Scotch-Irish ancestry exalted rationality, championed precise theological formulas, and supported orderly and authoritarian church government. Those of English and Welsh heritage, most of them of New England background, emphasized spontaneity, adaptability, and warm, vital piety.[26] Twice these parties divided over issues of theological emphasis, evangelistic methods, and social or cultural matters: in the New Side/Old Side schism of 1741–1759, and in the New School/Old School division of 1837–1869, in which the slavery issue played some part. Yet this picture is easily overdrawn, for many representatives of the New School party, such as Henry B. Smith and Edward D. Morris, were vigorously rational and desired careful, consistent theological statements. And such Old Schoolers as Charles and A. A. Hodge and B. B. Warfield deeply valued warm hearts as well as committed minds.[27]

Too many complex factors were at work for us to assume, as some historians have, that the attempt to revise the Confession was simply the logical flowering of either the quasi-Arminian or crypto-liberal views of New School Presbyterianism, and that a gradual and logical progression of these views led to theological liberalism and finally to modernism. George Marsden has shown that New Schoolers became increasingly conscious of their historical, denominational, and Calvinistic heritage in the years after 1837 when they were ousted from the denomination. By the time of reunion of 1869, the vast majority of Old Schoolers considered the New School theologically sound.[28]

Since such theological detectives as Charles Hodge, who opposed reunion, vigorously worked to uncover significant doctrinal errors and found practically none, it is incorrect to believe that desire for unity, increased size, and strength muted arguments over what constituted sound doctrine. Those who supported reunion certainly aimed to extend the mission of the church and to re-cement a major historical tradition. But reunion did not so much ignore theological differences as celebrate the discovery of growing theological agreement. Edward Morris, a professor at Lane Theo-logical Seminary in Cincinnati, insisted that the reunion involved "no compromise, no ignoring of an essential element in the com-mon Calvinism. Both parties, having adhered to the same standards during their separation, adopted the standards anew." The docu-ments of reunion gave less room, rather than more, he wrote, "for a man who is not in heart and brain a Calvinist."[29]

For the first two decades after 1869 the denomination enjoyed theological harmony amid firm affirmations of loyalty to Calvin-ism. A spirit of unity and concentration on practical ministry prompted rapid growth. Despite the celebrated trial of David Swing of Chicago for theological heterodoxy in 1873 and the much pub-licized debates over biblical inspiration that involved Charles Briggs, B. B. Warfield, A. A. Hodge, and Henry Green in the pages of the *Presbyterian Quarterly and Princeton Review* a decade later, in the years between 1870 and 1890 most Northern Presbyterians con-tinued to affirm Calvin's five points.[30] During this period the sys-tematic theologies of such staunch Calvinists as Charles and A. A. Hodge, W. G. T. Shedd, and Henry B. Smith were widely used in the Northern Presbyterian's seminaries and its pastors' studies.

Theological discontent became apparent, however, in calls for revision of the Westminster Confession in 1889, and it erupted the following year when Charles Briggs gave his inaugural address as professor of biblical theology at Union Seminary in New York.[31] The immediate result of the public controversy was favorable to conservatives. Their opponents, Briggs and Henry Preserved Smith of Lane Seminary, were expelled from the Presbyterian ministry; and A. G. McGiffert of Union Seminary chose to withdraw rather than face a trial. The 1903 revision was so minimal as to seem not to affect the integrity of the Westminster system. Conservatives controlled the denomination's educational institutions, its period-icals, and the majority of its chief pulpits outside of New York City, dominated the General Assemblies, and seemed to have wide support from the laity.[32]

The pervasiveness of Calvinism within Baptist circles during the years from 1870 to 1915 is difficult to judge precisely. How-ever, Baptist confessions of faith, the testimony of contemporary observers, the theology of A. H. Strong, and the instruction at Southern Baptist Theological Seminary all suggest that many American Baptists affirmed Reformed orthodoxy.

Unlike Presbyterian and Reformed denominations, Baptists did not require their ministers to subscribe formally to creeds. Yet in the late nineteenth and early twentieth centuries their two most widely accepted confessions — the Philadelphia and the New Hampshire Confessions of Faith — were Calvinistic.[33]

Testimony by those both inside and outside the Baptist tradition further indicates that Baptist allegiance to Genevan theology was widespread. Northern Presbyterians regarded most Baptists as Calvinists, as strong allies against Arminianism on the one hand, and rationalism and humanism, on the other.[34] In 1892 two Baptist journals, *The Standard of Chicago* and the *Western Recorder* (published in Louisville), debated the precise nature of their tradition's commitment to Reformed orthodoxy; yet both recognized the strength of that commitment.[35]

Furthermore, the powerful impact from 1872 until 1912 of A. H. Strong, president and professor of theology at Rochester, the leading Northern Baptist Seminary, and the significant influence of many who taught at the Southern Baptist Seminary in Louisville during the late nineteenth century also suggest that many Baptists were Calvinists. Although Strong changed his position radically after 1900, until that date he viewed those who denied the five points of Calvin as outside the main current of Baptist orthodoxy.[36] Strong helped shape the theological convictions of many Baptist ministers and his *Systematic Theology,* first published in 1886 and widely used in Baptist schools, underwent seven editions by 1906.[37] Such outstanding professors at the Southern Baptist seminary in Louisville as James P. Boyce were also staunch Calvinists. Boyce taught theology at the seminary, was the chairman of the faculty from 1859 to 1887, and in 1888 became its president. He was also repeatedly elected president of the Southern Baptist Convention. Several other Southern Baptist seminaries used his *Abstract of Systematic Theology,* published in 1882.[38] Testifying to Boyce's impact, one Southern Baptist wrote, "though the young men were generally rank Arminians when they came to the Seminary, few went through this course under him without being converted to his strong Calvinistic views."[39]

SOMEWHAT CALVINIST

In addition to those communions that were almost completely Calvinistic and to the Reformed Church in America, Northern Presbyterians, and Northern and Southern Baptists, which were largely so, five American denominations, which were not officially Reformed, contained significant numbers who accepted Genevan theology. Listed in order of the estimated descending percentage of their Calvinist adherents, these were Congregationalists, Reformed Episcopalians, German Reformed, Episcopalians, and Cumberland Presbyterians.

The theology of Congregationalists in the period from 1870 to 1915 is an intricate tapestry with threads of decided and moderate orthodoxy, evangelical Arminianism, New Theology, and even universalism. Although the waning of Puritan orthodoxy in Congregational circles began around 1800,[40] a significant Calvinist influence still remained in the communion long after 1870. Like Baptists, Congregationalists historically adopted creeds, but because of their independent polity, these were not binding on ministers or local congregations. The major creeds, such as the Savoy Confession and the Saybrook Platform, were distinctively Reformed.

Changes in Congregationalist theological views are evident in the actions of the National Councils held in 1865 and 1871. These councils replaced the adjective "Calvinist" with "evangelical" to describe Congregationalist doctrinal beliefs.[41]

Moreover, Calvinist views were gradually eliminated at Congregationalist seminaries at Andover, Yale, Oberlin, Chicago, and Bangor. As conservative professors at these institutions retired or died, they were replaced by men holding more liberal views. By 1905, all Congregational seminaries were propagating the New Theology, a moderate form of theological liberalism.[42]

Some decided Calvinists did remain among Congregationalists, however. Among these were Edward A. Lawrence, professor of church history at Hartford Seminary; Daniel Dana, an Andover Seminary trustee; Nathan Lord, the president of Dartmouth College; and prominent pastors such as Leonard Withington, Granville Abbott, and Richard Salter Storrs.[43] However, observers both inside and outside the communion agreed that after 1870 the views of these Calvinist Congregationalists became steadily less influential.[44]

Although Presbyterians were fond of emphasizing that the Thirty-nine Articles of Faith of the Protestant Episcopal Church were Calvinistic, few Episcopalians in the period from 1870 to 1915 seem to have been consistent Calvinists.[45] Many of those who were committed to Reformed orthodoxy broke with the denomination and organized the Reformed Episcopal Church in 1873. By 1876 the new denomination had 60 ministers, 50 congregations, and 7,000 members. Forty years later, however, it numbered only 11,600 communicants, of which 5,700 were in the Synod of New York and Philadelphia.[46]

Many German Reformed leaders insisted that their denomination was not Calvinistic at all, even though it belonged to the World Alliance of Reformed Churches and held as its doctrinal standard the Heidelberg Catechism, which almost everyone judged to be Calvinistic. These leaders claimed that their theology was more scriptural, broader, and older than Calvinism because it went back to Swiss Reformer Ulrich Zwingli (1484 – 1531), a precursor of Calvin. They maintained, moreover, that never had their denomination, either in Europe or America, officially accepted the doctrine of predestination.[47] The Heidelberg Catechism did not limit the atonement to the elect and it taught that grace was free, equal, and sufficient for all.[48]

Some German Reformed leaders, however, considered themselves and their communion Calvinistic. James Good, a denominational historian, pointed out that in its meetings of 1748, 1752, 1755, and 1765 the early American "Coetus," analogous to a presbytery, had accepted the Calvinistic Canons of Dort. This action, Good said, "stamped our Reformed Church in America as Calvinistic in doctrine on the subject of the decrees."[49] Good and others maintained that many members of the communion were still Calvinists, which helped explain why leaders of the Reformed Church of America wanted the two denominations to merge.[50]

As Good claimed in 1896, there were two parties in the denomination. One clung to the old Calvinism; the second accepted modern German mediating theology. Judging from the control that the more theologically liberal German Reformed leaders held over denominational seminaries and periodicals, Calvinists in the communion were a minority.

Cumberland Presbyterians displayed even greater ambivalence toward Westminster theology. This group seceded from the main Presbyterian body in 1810, disagreeing with its educational requirements for ministers and its doctrine of predestination. As the century progressed, members of the denomination continued to reject Reformed tenets and attempted to develop a middle way between Calvinism and Arminianism.[51]

The debate that took place in 1884 over whether to admit Cumberland Presbyterians to the World Alliance of Reformed Churches exemplifies the actual situation. Almost all the delegates acknowledged that the Cumberland group did not hold to basic Reformed doctrines and were "antagonistic" to some of the West-

minster Confession's most "precious contents."[52] The revised
Cumberland Confession of Faith, adopted in 1883, was especially
offensive to Calvinists in other denominations. A. A. Hodge of
Princeton Seminary, for example, complained that it had so radically altered the doctrines of divine sovereignty, the Fall, and human freedom as to eliminate all distinctive Calvinistic elements.[53]

The Reformed army that sought to solidify and strengthen the
biblical underpinnings of American society, then, consisted of re-
cruits from various denominations who had varying degrees of
devotion to Genevan theology. In succeeding chapters we will see
how Calvinists distilled, declared, and defended their essential tenets against their detractors — agnostics, evangelical Wesleyans, liberal theologians, and proponents of the New Theology, as well as
Northern Presbyterians who wanted to amend radically the Westminster Confession. Even more significant, however, was the secularist attempt to shift the basis of American society and values
from its traditional biblical foundation to a religiously neutral one.

THE THEOLOGICAL CHALLENGE TO CALVINISM

THE ATTACK FROM WITHOUT

Despite its "many funerals," J. I. Vance told delegates to the World Alliance of Reformed Churches in 1909, John Calvin's theology had "a way of rising from the dead every generation. A doctrine that can . . . incite antagonism of the kind that confronts Calvinism," he concluded, "is feared, not as men fear a cause that is done for, but as they fear a force that threatens to undo them."[1] The many strong salvos fired against Reformed orthodoxy in the years between the Civil War and World War I, especially by four groups — agnostics, liberals moving toward modernism, proponents of the "New" or "Andover Theology," and evangelical Wesleyans — testifies to Calvinism's continuing vitality and influence during these years.

Noted lecturer and skeptic Robert Ingersoll set his heaviest artillery to shelling the Calvinist bulwarks. Edwards and Calvin, he proclaimed, "were infinitely cruel, their premises infinitely absurd, their God infinitely fiendish, their logic perfect."[2] In his oft-repeated address "What Must We Do to Be Saved?" Ingersoll denounced the Westminster creed as the worst in the world. "The Presbyterian god is the monster of monsters," he cried. "He will enjoy forever . . . the wails of the damned. Hell is the festival of the Presbyterian god."[3]

Other agnostics joined the assault. Skeptic Hugh Pentecost declared that no other religious system so shocked his moral sensibilities as Reformed dogma.[4] Sir Edwin Arnold announced that he preferred "the very darkest things of the Hindu faith to the brightest sunshine of Calvinism."[5] And James A. Bell, a wealthy New York book collector and liquor magnate, in his *John Calvin: His Errors, Ignorance, Misconceptions, and Absurdities and the Errors of Presbyterianism, Disclosed and Exposed* (1891), descried Calvin's system of religion as wickedly cruel.[6]

Liberal theologians moving toward modernist commitments also excoriated Calvinism. In 1880 Harvard professor Joseph Allen labeled Calvinism a dead issue. The important controversies of the age were over other matters, he wrote. While admitting that many people still affirmed Reformed theology, Allen insisted that their belief reflected only tradition, not advanced and aggressive thought. Systems of belief that once were strong and great, he said, retained their outward structure long after their inward vitality had disappeared. Like a tree that had been girdled at its base, Calvinism was slowly dying. Yet while Allen was convinced that the Westminster theology was incompatible with modern thought and culture, he praised its incessant battle against sin and its moral fervor.[7]

Another liberal critic, author Oliver Wendell Holmes, declared that the most significant dividing line among Protestants was the one that separated optimists from pessimists. Cheerful and progressive, optimists minimized theology while stressing the fatherhood of God, social harmony under a divine order, and the significance and comforts of this life. In contrast, pessimists were solemn, emphasized theology, taught human depravity, bemoaned America's immorality, and depreciated earthly life. As pessimists, Holmes continued, Calvinists misunderstood human nature, repressed the instincts of childhood, struggled against science, and resisted the advance of civilization.[8]

One of the most scathing attacks on Calvinism in the post–Civil War period was John Miller's *Fetish in Theology* (1875), a forthright critique of Charles Hodge's *Systematic Theology* (1872). Miller declared that Hodge's presentation of God's character discouraged people from worshiping him. Most grievously, according to Miller, Hodge totally neglected God's most significant attribute— his holiness.[9]

In 1890 Miller continued his argument in the Congregational theological journal *Bibliotheca Sacra*, insisting that the Calvinist system implied that God was unrighteous because it did not ascribe to him humans' highest ethical standards and it made his chief goal personal "display." Miller castigated the Princeton faculty for teaching that God's will, rather than the principle of righteousness, was "the ground of human moral obligation" and for suggesting that he sent persons to hell for his good pleasure.[10]

David Swing, a former Presbyterian minister, denounced Calvinism in his later years. Only Presbyterians, he argued, believed Christians could devise a perfect doctrinal expression that would never need to be modified. He chastised Presbyterians for refusing to revise the Westminster Standards to incorporate theological advances made since the Standards were formulated. If Presbyterians continued to espouse this outmoded creed, he warned, few would associate with their congregations.[11]

Proponents of the New Theology, which became popular among Congregationalists and Episcopalians after 1880, also found fault with many Reformed doctrines. Also called Progressive Orthodoxy, this New Theology was especially promoted at Andover Seminary, the most prestigious graduate school of theology among Congregationalists. Faculty there based their theology on the incarnation and person of Christ rather than on his atonement or God's decrees, as they believed the old orthodoxy did. They emphasized instead God's love, taught that Christ's death atoned for the sins of all people, and insisted that individuals had a second chance after death to accept the gospel.[12]

According to George A. Gordon, a leading advocate of the New Theology, popular Brooklyn pastor Henry Ward Beecher outdid all others in the crusade to "abolish the Calvinist Moloch."[13] While striving to adjust theology to the new findings of Darwinism, Beecher continually ridiculed the Calvinist concepts of sin, God, and election. He expected the new scientific understanding of human origins to make untenable the old "repulsive" and "demoralizing" theory of sin.[14] To Beecher, the idea that God placed two inexperienced people in a garden to be tempted by an arch-fiend and then transmitted their corruption through countless ages was "hideous."[15] If every person were totally depraved by virtue of Adam's fall, he protested, then the "business of God for 10,000 years has been to produce infinite sin and suffering."[16] Calvinism was, therefore, an "impious and malignant representation of God and His government."[17]

Beecher regarded the chapters in the Westminster Confession on predestination as "extraordinary specimens of spiritual barbarism."[18] Civilized people disowned these tenets "absolutely, unanimously, and with indignation."[19] Thus spoke the man who, according to one of his earlier biographers, sought to liberate from their Calvinist penitentiary "the vast, emotion-starved middle class of America" who were "haunted by their suppressions and driven by resulting fears into terrors of nonconformity."[20]

Similarly, George A. Gordon, pastor of Old South Congregational Church in Boston, denounced the Westminster theology as "immoral . . . unpreachable, and incredible."[21] Its portrayal of God as partial and vindictive had driven many to unbelief; indeed, he wrote, "consistent Calvinism" was "atheism."[22] Its champions improperly exegeted the Bible and misunderstood history and therefore set God "against humanity" and discredited his moral character. Their conception of God's sovereignty eliminated human freedom and destroyed personal responsibility.[23]

Gordon complained further that the old theology overstressed the corruptness of human beings and ignored the goodness that stemmed from divine influences upon them. Total depravity was simply "untrue to the facts," he wrote. Wickedness flourished only in exceptional cases; people were innately virtuous.[24] Rejecting Calvinism's "severely narrow" view of grace and its damnation of the "overwhelming majority of mankind," Gordon taught that the gospel promised salvation to all humanity. No educated, compassionate person could accept the Calvinist interpretation of God's relationship with human beings.[25]

The Western world, Gordon concluded, had rejected orthodoxy but had affirmed no new theology, a situation analogous to "having lost Ptolemy without having found Copernicus." God's sovereignty must be the foundation for the new orthodoxy as it was for the old, he declared, but the grievously wrong character that Calvinism ascribed to God must be rejected.[26]

Lyman Abbott, who succeeded Henry Ward Beecher at the Plymouth Congregational Church in Brooklyn and for years edited the *Outlook,* together with English cleric Charles Gore, the Canon of Westminster, showed a similar ambivalence in rejecting Calvinism. They censured its rigid limitation of God's love to the elect and insisted that this doctrine was a "heresy," inconsistent with Scripture and paralyzing to missions and moral reform. But they implored Christians to regain and strengthen the old orthodoxy's belief in God's eternal purpose and plan.[27]

Because Methodists considered Calvinists their allies in an evangelical front that sought to stem the tide of theological liberalism, their criticisms of Reformed doctrines were neither harsh nor cynical. New theological and ideological currents emanating primarily from Germany were profoundly altering contemporary assessments of the Bible, historical process, and the relations of science and religion. Under these circumstances, both Calvinists and Arminians believed they had to mute their traditional debate and unite forces to defend their common evangelical beliefs. In this spirit, a Methodist editor praised Presbyterians for their high regard for learning and for uncompromising adherence to their doctrinal standards. Every Protestant denomination, he said, had derived strength from their steadfastness.[28] Other Methodists added that Calvinist theology had sustained Christianity as thoroughly as had Wesleyan zeal.[29] Calvinists similarly extolled Methodists for their evangelistic efforts and their defense of fundamental biblical doctrines.[30]

Despite this growing solidarity, however, Wesleyans sometimes did criticize Calvinism. On one hand, they found fault with particular Reformed tenets, while on the other, they claimed that few Calvinists still believed their doctrines. Methodists protested that Calvinists often taught infant damnation; declared saving faith to be a direct gift of God, independent of any human action; inadvertently made God the author of sin; presented God as cold and uncaring; and proclaimed a narrow doctrine of election that had evoked a universalist reaction.[31] Wesleyans argued that Calvin's five points were not taught by Christ and contradicted Paul's doctrine of free grace and free will.[32] While challenging the scriptural and philosophical soundness of such Reformed beliefs, Arminians also claimed that very few people held them anymore. The editors of the *Christian Advocate* asserted in 1891 that a majority of Presbyterian ministers and laypeople rejected the doctrine of unconditional election.[33] Other Wesleyan leaders suggested that most Reformed Protestants in America embraced Arminian doctrines but "from sentimental or social considerations" remained in Calvinistic communions.[34]

Calvinists employed a similar defense against all these detractors, whether skeptics, advocates of liberal theology, proponents of the New Theology, or evangelical Wesleyans. They denied many of their critics' assertions, sought to show that their own doctrines were scriptural and that their opponents' were not, and praised the moral fervor their theology had generated.

The denials were straightforward. Calvinists insisted they did not teach, nor did their system logically necessitate, that God was the author of sin, that persons were not free moral agents, that the elect could do anything they pleased and still obtain salvation, that God for no reason foreordained the majority of the human race to eternal misery, or that those dying in infancy were damned.[35]

Calvinists also expounded in great detail what they believed were the scriptural foundations of their doctrines. They attempted to demonstrate that the Old Testament, Paul's epistles, and Jesus himself taught total depravity, unconditional election, definite atonement, irresistible grace, and final perseverance. Calvinism, they declared, comprised simply the doctrines of David, Isaiah, Jeremiah, Christ, and Paul formed into a logical system by comparing Scripture with Scripture.[36]

Calvinists' response to Progressive Orthodoxy illustrates their arguments that their opponents' positions were not biblically sound. Proponents of the New Theology, Calvinists declared, elevated the subjective "witness of the Spirit in the heart" and human reason over biblical authority.[37] This led them to improper understandings of God, humanity, sin, and the incarnation. Calvinists maintained that Andover Progressives depreciated God's righteousness and justice and overemphasized his love and mercy. By not recognizing that divine justice was rooted in both God's love for humanity and his wrath against sin, advocates of the New Theology made God seem lax toward evil.[38] They repudiated the scriptural doctrines of original sin and human depravity and insisted, instead, that humans were innately good.[39] This, Calvinists complained, encouraged them to treat sin as "an incidental misfortune" resulting from "unfavorable surroundings and circumstances" rather than as an offense against a holy God for which an individual was morally accountable.[40] Calvinists also believed that the New Theology depreciated the uniqueness of Christ by viewing him as the ideal man, a perfect example of what God wished human character to be, rather than as a union of divine and human natures. Calvinists feared that these doctrinal aberrations would inevitably lead those who had embraced them to Unitarianism and, ultimately, to Naturalism.[41]

Finally, Calvinists chronicled their theological, ethical, political, social, and educational contributions to church and society to answer their opponents. They emphasized that many of America's most influential theologians, educators, and preachers were Calvinists. Where, they asked, were the theological peers of Francis Patton, A. H. Strong, and B. B. Warfield; the missionary equals of Adoniram Judson; or pastors comparable to John Hall and Richard Storrs? More than any other theology, they maintained, Calvinism still inspired the intellectual and practical efforts necessary to solve the religious, social, and political problems of the age.[42]

THE ATTACK FROM WITHIN: ATTEMPTS TO REVISE THE WESTMINSTER CONFESSION

Conservative Calvinists meanwhile also faced strong challenges originating within their own denominations. In the late 1880s some

Northern Presbyterians began arguing against the requirement, dating back to the Adopting Act of 1729,[43] that ministers and elders affirm that the Westminster Standards substantially expressed the faith they held. While American Presbyterians had twice before divided over doctrinal matters (in the Old Side/New Side division of 1741–1758 and the Old School/New School split of 1837–1869), the Westminster Standards themselves had never been an object of contention. The reunion of 1869 took place on the basis of a strong reaffirmation of the denomination's commitment to them.[44] The widely publicized heresy trial of David Swing of Chicago in 1873 reveals that Northern Presbyterians disagreed at that time over how much latitude should be allowed in interpreting their Standards. The records of the trial, however, do not support William Hutchison's contention that Swing's acquittal demonstrates that by the 1870s many Northern Presbyterians accepted, or at least tolerated, liberal theological views.[45] A careful study of Northern Presbyterian sources for these years indicates that their commitment to Calvinism remained very strong prior to 1890.

This suggests that the movement in the late 1880s to revise the Westminster Confession was a new development, not simply the broadening of an old impulse. Thus, it seems dubious that the attempt to modify the Confession in the years following 1885 was, as historian Lefferts Loetscher argues, a continuation of earlier efforts to make the Northern denomination more inclusive of varying theological viewpoints and more attuned to the times. His argument implies that there were no fundamental theological differences between those involved in earlier ruptures and those advocating revision in the 1890s.[46] Earlier disputes had centered on how the Standards should be interpreted and how rigidly subscribers must hold them. Debates during the 1890s, however, revolved around whether Calvinism, especially as expressed in the Confession, was scriptural. Philip Schaff, the outstanding German-American church historian who led the revisionist party until his death in 1895, in 1890 called for "a theology and a confession that is more human than Calvinism, more Divine than Arminianism, and more Christian and catholic than either."[47] Many revisionists protested that they could not affirm Calvinism to be *the* biblical system of doctrine.[48] Some of them agreed with Thomas Hall who declared in 1900 that Presbyterians were no more officially Calvinists than they were Platonists or Kantians. They were simply "Christians under a Presbyterian form of government."[49]

During the 1890s three parties within the denomination actually advocated revision. But one party demanded that Presbyterians either radically revise the Standards or adopt a new confessional statement. The leaders were Philip Schaff; Charles Briggs of Union Theological Seminary in New York; Henry Van Dyke, poet, author, university professor, and pastor of New York's influential Brick Church; and Howard Crosby, also a leading New York clergyman. They favored a new, shorter creed, "Christian and catholic rather than Calvinist and exclusive."[50] Although some of these radical revisionists called themselves Calvinists, judged by the earlier New Side and the later New School doctrinal positions, they were not. According to theologically conservative Francis Patton, president of Princeton College, radical revisionists were not Calvinists; and, "whether consciously or unconsciously," they demanded changes "which could impair the integrity of the Calvinist system."[51] At the other extreme was the party led by Patton, W. G. T. Shedd of Union Seminary in New York, and B. B. Warfield of Princeton Theological Seminary, who opposed all revision of the Standards.

Between the radicals and the conservatives were two other groups. One of these, represented by such men as Edward Morris of Lane Seminary, advocated only a few minor changes in the Confession, which they and conservatives believed would not undermine its fundamental Calvinism. Those in Morris's party wanted to soften the creed's language in order to make Presbyterian preaching and witness "more practical, . . . irenic and friendly to other evangelicals."[52] Radical revisionists considered such changes insufficient, and conservatives thought them unnecessary. Members of a second intermediate party wanted to reduce substantially the existing creed or even to replace it with a new, shorter creed in order to promote Presbyterian unity and ministry.[53]

Although the revisionist current flowed in two waves, the first cresting in 1890 and the second in 1903, their similar contours allow us to examine it as a whole. (As my fundamental interest is to define the parameters of Calvinist commitment rather than to analyze theological variation within the Reformed camp, this discussion will evaluate the debate between radical revisionists and conservatives.) In 1890 revisionist efforts were completely thwarted; in 1903 they produced changes in the Confession that even B. B. Warfield admitted were minor.[54] In the years before 1915 conservatives were largely successful in keeping the Northern Presbyterian Church officially tied to its traditional Reformed theological heritage. Yet debates over the Confession diverted the energies of many conservatives from moral leadership in social and political battles to opposing what they judged to be Arminianism, liberalism, and incipient secularism within their own communion.

The primary issues in this debate were two: 1) Was the Confession faithful to the teachings of Scripture, and 2) Was it in tune with the times? Radical revisionists declared that Calvinist theology, as expressed in the Confession, was "directly opposed" to many explicit statements in Scripture. Each of Calvinism's five points was merely an inference from some great biblical truth and not itself a clearly revealed doctrine.[55] Many argued that the Confession was too logical and polemical. "Logic only deals with finite categories and cannot grasp infinite truths," Philip Schaff stated.[56] He protested further that the Confession, as a product of the most contentious and intolerant age of Christendom, was not suited to the irenic mood of the late nineteenth century.[57] Revisionists also claimed that the Confession overemphasized predestination and minimized divine love; it overstated God's sovereignty at the expense of human responsibility; and it began with his decrees instead of the human need of a savior.[58]

Conservatives countered that the Confession was completely scriptural because Calvinism embodied the central truths of the gospel.[59] The Westminster Standards, they claimed, contained all the essentials of evangelical Christianity. Francis Patton succinctly summarized the conservatives' case: Presbyterians should not modify their creed because Calvinism accurately described God's relationship with humanity and the world.[60]

To conservatives, the creed's consistency and coherence were not weaknesses but strengths; they agreed with Warfield that the Confession was irenic and properly proportioned.[61] It was impossible to modify the basic teachings of the Confession, W. G. T. Shedd declared, because the gospel was a system of truth that logically could only be understood in one of two ways — Calvinist or Arminian.[62] Wrench one key doctrine such as election from the Calvinist system, the editors of the *Presbyterian* added, and the entire structure would crumble to pieces.[63]

Far from being narrow and divisive, Warfield argued, the Confession's Calvinism was broad enough to enable it to serve as a standard for Presbyterians, Baptists, and Congregationalists.[64] Another conservative emphasized that the Confession contained no polemic against Arminianism.[65] In fact, Edward Morris wrote, the Westminster Standards did not criticize the beliefs of any Protestant communion.[66]

The debate over how accurately the Confession reflected biblical teaching revolved primarily around two related issues: predestination and the love of God.

Schaff insisted that the movement to compose a new confession was inspired by belief in God's saving love for every person, a central biblical truth the Confession neglected. The duty of preaching God's love had deeply gripped the minds and hearts of churchmen, he said, and it "must overrule the particularism and exclusivism" of a system of theology that had minimized God's compassion and stimulated so few efforts to convert the heathen.[67] Conservatives protested that their opponents used election as a smoke screen to camouflage their true target: the authority of the Bible. The heart of revisionist objections against election, conservatives argued, was not that the doctrine was unbiblical, but that it offended the sensibilities of late-nineteenth-century Americans.[68]

Alongside this debate over whether the creed was scriptural raged another. This conflict arose over the revisionist charges that in practical terms, the Confession thwarted the ministry and destroyed the unity of the denomination because it did not adequately express the faith of most Presbyterians; it prevented the communion from keeping abreast with the times; and debate over it diverted attention from building the kingdom of God on earth.

Largely using impressionistic evidence, the parties disputed whether, as the revisionists alleged, the vast majority of Northern Presbyterians no longer believed the Calvinism of the Confession.[69] Philip Schaff observed in 1890 that he knew of no Presbyterian minister in the United States who preached that the benefits of the atonement were limited to "a small circle of elect" or that all non-Christians were damned.[70] The editors of the *Independent* asserted in 1901 that the actual beliefs of educated Northern Presbyterians differed from those of the Westminster fathers "as much as the creed of the Andover faculty differs from that of Cotton Mather."[71] Conservatives replied that the great majority of Northern Presbyterians still believed and advocated the Westminster Standards in their historical sense.[72] The limited modifications adopted in 1903 suggest that the conservatives' assessment was more correct than that of their opponents. Revisionists maintained, however, that traditions, prejudices, fears, and other psychological and social factors had operated to keep the members of the General Assembly from voting their true theological convictions.[73]

Throughout the debate revisionists asserted that allegiance to a confession communicants did not believe and the culture despised hindered Presbyterian ministry. Laypersons refused to serve as church officers because they could not affirm it. Young men resisted becoming ministerial candidates in a communion that bound them to archaic and unchanging dogmas. Pastors could not preach these doctrines because the laity considered them repulsive. Worst of all, they claimed, the determinism of the creed depreciated human effort and individual responsibility in both ethics and evangelism.[74] Presbyterians could not become aggressive, argued pastor Charles Parkhurst of New York City, until they unhitched their horses from "the Calvinist chariot."[75]

Radical revisionists repeatedly protested that the Westminster Standards clashed with the thinking and culture of the late nineteenth century. A creed expressed in seventeenth-century language and preoccupied with the theological debates of that period was inadequate for Christians who faced the challenges of biblical criticism, Darwinism, the industrial revolution, and international conflict.

Simply because the church once affirmed a doctrine, revisionists continued, did not mean that Christians were obliged to believe it forever.[76] "We are told we ought to be loyal to the faith of the fathers," one of them quipped, "but who knows what the fathers believe *now*?"[77] The best way to revere the Westminster Confession, revisionists contended, was to advance in the direction toward which it pointed. To believe that the Christianity of the New Testament "was a seed which once germinated and grew," but could grow no more after flowering in the seventeenth century, was contradictory.[78]

Radical revisionists strongly felt the pressures of changing cultural conditions. The development of scientific naturalism, philosophical materialism, and theological liberalism during the nineteenth century made it increasingly difficult for them to believe and defend a theology so intrinsically tied to the transcendent, the supernatural, and the spiritual elements in Christian faith. These new intellectual and cultural forces encouraged revisionists to reject orthodox Calvinism for a more mediating theology—one they thought would be more applicable to contemporary social realities and more appealing to educated persons in the twentieth century.

While agreeing with revisionists that controversy over the Confession absorbed Presbyterian energies better devoted to other concerns, conservatives refused to capitulate because they judged the old standards to be a bulwark for faith and practice. They too wanted to move beyond controversy to evangelism and Christian nurture.[79] In order to advance effectively, however, an army must be well trained and adequately equipped; unless Presbyterians marched forward with the proper spiritual and theological armor, they might do more harm than good.[80] Although Calvinism was a "hard system," it was scriptural and thus "the best defense of Christian orthodoxy."[81]

Conservatives insisted that Reformed theology provided a solid basis for moral order, intellectual development, and personal virtue and it most effectively stimulated evangelism and missions.[82] They insisted further that their opponents' efforts to adjust the Confession to the culture were built upon faulty reasoning. Warfield warned that revisionists tended to "make the wishes of man instead of the revelation of God the norm"[83] and "harmony with present Christian thought and scholarship" the test of religious truth. Current opinion, however, was a "sorry substitute for the revealed work of the omniscient God."[84] Only distinctive Calvinism, he declared, could stem the tide of German mediating theology that threatened to inundate America.[85] Although by 1900 conservatives admitted that belief in the sovereignty of God and unconditional election was receding, they predicted that the theological pendulum would soon swing back to their position.[86]

Members of other Calvinist denominations closely watched this Northern Presbyterian dispute over whether the Westminster Confession was scriptural and whether it thwarted the mission of the church, because they realized its outcome would deeply affect their own communions as well. Most of them supported the conservatives' position, fearing that revision would mar the unity that had characterized all Reformed bodies and, as a Southern Presbyterian editor put it, so "mutilate the . . . doctrines of grace as to leave them a mangled corpse."[87]

Even the editors of the Methodist *Christian Advocate* supported the conservatives' stand against revision. They argued that the whole history of the Presbyterian Church in America and the language of the Adopting Act of 1729 demonstrated an intention to require ruling and teaching elders to affirm the Westminster Confession. They feared that those who rejected Calvinism would eventually become Universalists. They considered it impossible to revise the substance of the Confession without introducing Arminian principles, thus paving the way, logically, for the overthrow of the Augustinian system and a division of the communion. The Methodist editors considered Presbyterian conservatives stronger and more certain allies than revisionists in the larger struggle to maintain basic evangelical doctrines amid the growth of skepticism and modernism.[88]

During the late nineteenth and early twentieth centuries the artilleries of Arminians, liberals, and skeptics continually bombarded the Calvinist fortress. Such shelling gradually eroded the orthodox bulwarks, leaving them substantially weaker in 1915 than they had been in 1870. Despite this long and exhausting battle, however, Calvinists, as we shall see in the following chapters, supplied leaders and troops to fight in an even more demanding war: the struggle over what ideals and values would direct American public life.

THE CLASH OF WORLDVIEWS:
SECULARISM VERSUS CALVINISM

American intellectuals, publicists, and scientists, along with those of other Western nations, experienced a radical shift in their understanding of God, humanity, and the world in the nineteenth and early twentieth centuries. This transformation, generally labeled "secularization," describes a process "whereby religious thinking, practices and institutions lose social significance."[1] No longer did the vast majority of American intellectual leaders see the world as created and sustained by God. Many believed instead that it was a product of chance—that over vast ages impersonal forces had managed fortuitously to combine and through natural processes to evolve into the present world. An influential elite repudiated the doctrine that humans were created by God, viewing them rather as the highest product of this evolutionary spiral. For these intellectuals, man's autonomous reason, following the scientific method and the rules of logic, replaced the infinite, personal God of the Hebrew-Christian tradition as the standard of authority and authenticator of ultimate reality.[2]

By the end of the nineteenth century many Americans were commenting on the growing impact of the emerging secular worldview. Educator John M. Bonham noted that the "fruits of modern science" were weakening the masses' faith in supernatural things and therefore lessening their "sense of reverence for the sacred character of the precepts of conduct."[3] Prominent philospher Arthur O. Lovejoy observed that Americans were boldly questioning long held "fundamental moral presuppositions" about the world, the origin and significance of humanity, and the course of human history. The traditional religious assumptions about these matters promised "to be almost unintelligible" to current high school and college students.[4] Frederick Woodbridge, a philosophy professor at Columbia University, insisted that naturalism had "become a controlling disposition" for all college-educated persons. He concluded that naturalists and humanists should join forces to promote the secular worldview because they agreed on human origins, man's inherent rationality, and nature's power and primary importance.[5] Princeton theologian B. B. Warfield complained that the "empirico-scientific world and life view" had "invaded . . . every form of thought and every activity of life." Its argument that all phenomena could be explained by physical laws and processes was encouraging many to view philosophy, science, politics, history, and religion in naturalistic terms.[6]

Martin Marty has shown that in the west the road to secularism took three different paths. On the European continent, many academicians, journalists, and socialist ideologues, and some in the professions of law, medicine, and teaching relentlessly attacked the Christian faith. In England only a small minority denounced God and the churches. Most English intellectuals choose to ignore religion rather than to try systematically to supplant it. In America, however, most people continued to adhere to the inherited religions. Yet secularists became leaders in many cultural areas and strongly influenced American society.[7]

Secularism is not a new philosophy in Western history. Its roots lie in ancient Greece and Rome, especially in the belief of Plato and Aristotle that humans could achieve self-actualization through their autonomous rational and moral powers. Rejuvenated by Renaissance humanism, it flourished among the Enlightened elites of the seventeenth and eighteenth centuries. The philosophers of that period affirmed with Protagoras, the Greek thinker of the fifth century B.C.E., that man was the measure of all things. The secularism of the late nineteenth century added few new principles to those inherited from previous times. Its contribution, rather, was to use perspectives drawn from geology, biology, anthropology, and psychology to develop a popular rationale for embracing naturalistic materialism. While the secularism of the Enlightenment was limited to an intellectual and social elite, that of the nineteenth and twentieth centuries affected a much broader spectrum of society, including many in the laboring classes.

Yet few Americans adopted a thoroughgoing secularism. Many countenanced it only as public philosophy, suitable to a pluralistic culture, assuming instead that the values of most individuals would be drawn from the private practice of religious faith, chiefly Jewish or Christian. Accepting this secular "public" philosophy did not require people to cease worshiping God in their churches and homes, but it did demand that they consider him irrelevant in public, academic, political, and economic life.[8] Such philosophers as John Dewey and Walter Lippmann, who wished to interpret and direct American culture, insisted that both the churches and Christian teaching about God hindered, not helped, modern efforts to build the good society.[9] Judeo-Christian faith, however, did not vanish; institutionally, in fact, it prospered. But many cultural leaders pressed American Christianity to surrender its influence over the public dimension of life—political, social, economic, and educational—and generally to limit its role to the private aspects of individual morality, familial custom, and leisure. And this trend gradually forced believers to accept a reduced role in politics, higher education, and science, as well as in mass entertainment and communication.[10] By the end of World War I, the champions of secular humanism claimed preeminence over public life (although a broad spectrum of Christian and Jewish institutions and ideologies sharply resisted these claims).

Martin Marty argues that secularization deeply affected American culture prior to 1870. Marty, however, exaggerates the extent to which social forces in the generation before the Civil War lessened Christianity's importance in determining the values, mores, and public philosophy of most Americans. As he himself mentions and others have demonstrated, almost all higher education in America before 1860 was controlled by religious denominations, and much of it after this date; and every scholarly discipline, including the natural sciences, was dominated by believers "whose researches reinforced their creed."[11] Moreover, during this period morality remained rooted in an absolute basis—the Judeo-Christian God—and American laws enforced many divine sanctions. Although industrialization and urbanization were starting to dissolve the agrarian order, and increasing numbers of Catholic and Jewish immigrants were beginning to threaten Protestant dominance over society, the effort to keep America resting on biblical values was still quite successful in 1870, as Robert Handy and others have demonstrated.[12] The challenge of cultural and ethnic pluralism, scientific and social Darwinism, the new biblical criticism, and growing urban and labor problems, as well as the need to resist an increasingly pervasive counterview of the world were thrust upon Christians with full force only after 1870.

Stow Persons shows that naturalistic patterns of thought, based upon physical and social evolution and reductionism, strongly affected American life between 1865 and 1930. Although those holding naturalistic views were always a numerical minority, this philosophy exerted a powerful influence because its chief advocates were scientists, professors, lawyers, business leaders, and journalists.[13] Edward L. Yeoman's *Popular Science Monthly* championed the views of British naturalists Tyndall and Huxley. Carl Snyder's *The World Machine* pictured the universe as a cosmic mechanism. In his widely read and respected articles, Jacob Loeb of the Rockefeller Institute for Medical Research argued that physical and chemical laws could explain all of life. J. B. Watson used similar reductionist notions to develop behavioristic psychology. Clarence Darrow and Oliver Wendell Holmes, Jr. applied naturalistic conceptions to the understanding of law, denouncing the belief of Supreme Court Chief Justices Marshall, Story, and Kent that God's character and law were the foundation for human law. Thorstein Veblen led many others in applying naturalistic ideas to economics. Historian James Harvey Robinson and sociologist William Graham Sumner sought to base the social sciences exclusively upon empirical considerations, thereby eliminating any supernatural influences. In the novels of Theodore Dreiser, Jack London, Stephen Crane, and Frank Norris, God was absent and nature was stark, indifferent, and even hostile to man. H. L. Mencken attacked the idea that morality was engraved on the heart and insisted that life had no ultimate meaning.[14]

Thus, in the years between the Civil War and World War I, a battle for cultural supremacy broke out on many fronts in America. Humanism, the claims of scientism, and intellectual disdain for the Bible wrestled with theism, both Christian and Jewish, for control of American public life. Commenting on this struggle, Harvard philosopher George Santayana wrote in 1913: "The civilization characteristic of Christendom has not yet disappeared, yet another civilization has begun to take its place."[15] Although it may seem to modern observers that the outcome of the conflict was apparent, to the participants the issue was in doubt. Moreover, the result was not inevitable; other courses of action might have produced different results. As we will see, if Calvinists and other Protestants had not attempted to keep secularism out of the public marketplace of ideas, if instead they had supported a pluralistic public order where various ideologies had the right to affect public policies, secularism might not today dominate American public life under the guise of religious neutrality.

Although in the late nineteenth century secular humanism had not fully crystalized into a systematic set of beliefs, its outline was apparent. The cosmology, anthropology, and epistemology it offered conflicted with that of Christianity. Its primary premise, taken from scientific naturalism, was that physical nature constituted the sum total of reality. Supernatural entities either simply did not exist or, as Herbert Spencer maintained, if they did, they were unknowable.[16] Humanity was a product of natural evolution. Its dignity and worth were rooted not in the created image of a personal, all-powerful, and loving God, but in its position at the pinnacle of the evolutionary process. Humans were capable of determining their own destiny in this world, the only one that existed. They could solve their own problems, unaided by any deity, through reliance upon reason and the scientific method. Human knowledge owed little to reasoned faith in God's revelation, but was rooted in what reason discovered by experimentation. Human rationality was the final judge not only of material facts, but of moral values as well — of what was true, good, and beautiful. Society should be organized to promote human rather than divine aims. Ethics and all human values were grounded not in God's character and revelation but in this earthly experience. Since there was no immortality, life on earth was of supreme importance.[17]

SOUNDING THE ALARM AGAINST SECULARISM

Although Calvinists felt compelled to spend much time and effort countering the claims of Arminians, Andover Progressives, and advocates of theological liberalism, as well as in defending the soundness of the Westminster Confession, they never lost sight of this ultimate challenge from a secular public philosophy, which sought, with the help of humanist ideals, to conquer "private" piety and conviction as well. At the First General Council of the World Alliance of Reformed Churches held in 1877 in Edinburgh, Scotland, A. A. Hodge, soon to succeed his father, Charles, as professor of systematic theology at Princeton Seminary, denounced the new secularism. This philosophy, he asserted, demanded that all religious influence be removed from civil government. Its proponents insisted that questions pertaining to marriage and divorce, the civil Sabbath, the punishment of crime, and the education of youth should be decided by the light of natural reason, informed only by experience. Secularism, Hodge claimed, thus offered an alternative source of knowledge and a way of validating it as well. Its goal was to replace biblical revelation with historical experience and human reason. In particular, Hodge detested the efforts to secularize education: to write new textbooks purged of biblical thought or sentiment; to eliminate all traces of Providence and faith from the study of history; and to reduce mental and moral philosophy to a department of molecular mechanics. He warned that secularism, which was already emerging as a distinct philosophy, promised to be "the consummate instrument of Satan for the propagation of atheism and practical irreligion."[18]

The only way to quell this rising tide, Hodge concluded, was to reassert the Reformed convictions that God was sovereign, humans were totally depraved, God alone was Lord of the conscience, Christ reigned as King of Kings over families, churches, and nations, and civil government was a divine institution. With their commitment to both the authority of the magistrate and civil liberty, he explained, Calvinists occupied the middle ground between an authoritarian and a licentious political system. Likewise, Calvinism's reasoned piety stood between the extremes of traditionalism and rationalism. Its doctrine of the separation of church and state resisted both the papal doctrine, which subordinated the state to the church, and its opposite, subjection of the church to the state. Finally, Calvinism's belief in Christian, nonsectarian public education stood opposed to sectarian education in a papal and a Jewish sense and secular education with its "absurd pretense" that religion could be ignored and yet not denied.[19]

Other Calvinists joined Hodge in building dikes against the flood of secular sensibility. T. D. Witherspoon told Presbyterians gathered to celebrate the centennial of the founding of the General Assembly in 1888 that modern thought in its various forms — "Positivism, Agnosticism, Materialism and Pantheism" — was "organizing its forces and preparing for a multiform . . . assault upon every point of Christianity that involves the idea of supernatural revelation." Witherspoon challenged Presbyterians to don their armor, sharpen their theological swords, and march forth to defeat this enemy. In this battle, Calvinism was like a chain of mountains: "rugged in outline, its five points standing apart like disconnected peaks, yet all embraced in a single logical chain, the whole unutterably sublime." Orthodoxy alone could preserve civil and religious institutions from the growing threat of socialism, anarchism, and nihilism in America's great cities. Only a revitalization of Calvinist principles could halt the current disregard for law in society, growing economic concentration, and exploitation of the poor, Witherspoon concluded.[20] Unless the Promethean spirit of defiance is "changed into the Christian spirit of obedience to God," another Presbyterian added, American culture would eventually crumble in "unutterable grief."[21] Many other Reformed leaders similarly castigated secularism while offering homage to Calvinism.

Undoubtedly, such Calvinist jeremiads against secularism were due in part to what Richard Hofstadter has termed "status anxiety." In the late nineteenth century, businessmen, university professors, scientists, and politicians were beginning to play a more important role than the clergy in determining public policies. Calvinists frequently complained that secular trends were undermining the cultural influence they had long enjoyed through their ecclesiastical, educational, political, and social leadership in the antebellum period.[22] At the same time, however, their numerous positions as educators, journalists, lawyers, and ministers of prominent urban congregations kept Reformed Christians in contact with the leading thinkers of the era and thus made them more aware of and outspoken against naturalistic trends than most other theists.

Although on some issues Calvinists wished to join hands with Catholics and Jews to advance biblical ideals, they, like most other evangelicals, often envisioned a Christian America that excluded not only secular elements but also distinctively Catholic and Jewish ones. What most Reformed Christians truly wanted was a Protestant, or even a Calvinist, America.

KUYPER COMES TO AMERICA

Abraham Kuyper's *Lectures on Calvinism,* presented at Princeton Theological Seminary in 1898 and published immediately afterward, offered the most significant and influential Reformed discussion of these themes. Soon to be elected Prime Minister of the Netherlands, Kuyper was a man of immense erudition, deep spirituality, and great political insight. He had pastored several churches, founded and taught theology at the Free University of Amsterdam, served in the Dutch parliament, and edited two newspapers. Preacher, theologian, statesman, and journalist, Kuyper had profoundly affected all aspects of Dutch political and religious life. In the Netherlands his goal was to reestablish God's law "in the home, in the school and in the state"; to carve into the nation's conscience "the ordinances of the Lord" until it paid "homage again to God."[23] Kuyper's reputation in America stemmed also from several published articles and from two of his books, which had been translated into English. His trip to America established him as the world's leading proponent of a revitalization of Calvinism.

Kuyper did not define Reformed doctrine in sectarian, confessional, or denominational terms but as a system of thought and life that held religion, ethics, social happiness, and human liberty to be derived from God. It had "developed first a peculiar theology, then a special church order," and finally a particular form for political and social life and for art and science. The Calvinist worldview defined "the relation between nature and grace, between Christianity and the world, between church and state."

In his lectures at Princeton, Kuyper compared the history and structure of certain other great religious formulations of social and cultural ideals — pagan, Islamic, and Roman Catholic — with Calvinism. In their revolt against Catholicism, Reformed Christians had sought to create not merely a new type of worship and polity but an "entirely different form of human life." They aimed to redirect human thought and attitudes and to establish society on biblical principles.[24] But as the twentieth century approached, Calvinism's primary struggle was no longer with these older religious systems. Its new foe was Modernism, a secular philosophy that developed its view of humanity and the world from natural data alone. In this struggle, whether in Europe or in America, Kuyper insisted, only a comprehensive and powerful complex of ideas such as Calvinism could counter Modernism's all-embracing life system.[25]

According to Kuyper, all worldviews displayed a peculiar insight into the relation of human beings to God, to each other, and to the world. Calvinism neither sought God in people as paganism did, nor isolated God from people as Islam did, nor placed intermediaries between God and people as Catholicism did. Rather, it proclaimed with other evangelical traditions that, although God transcended human beings, he entered into direct fellowship with them as God the Holy Spirit. Modernism, by contrast, considered God "a hostile power, yea even as dead, if not yet to the heart, at least to the state, to society, and to science."[26]

Calvinism's conception of human relationships also differed significantly from those of other worldviews. Pagans, who believed that God dwelled only in certain people, worshiped those with outstanding talents and enslaved those with limited abilities. Muslims oppressed women and Catholics devised a hierarchical system of relationships among persons. Modernists aimed to treat all individuals identically, an action that would eliminate diversity and thus impoverish life. Calvinists and evangelical Christians generally, however, considered males and females, rich and poor, weak and strong, all to be fallen creatures of God. No group could properly dominate another because people stood as equals before God and thus as equals among themselves. Because the only distinctions among people that Calvinists recognized were those given by God in assigning talents and civil authority, they condemned all slave and caste systems as well as all covert enslavement of women and the poor; yet they encouraged variety and individuality.[27]

Kuyper insisted further that Reformed orthodoxy offered a very different understanding of human beings' relation to this world from that of other philosophies of life. Paganism valued the world too highly and thus both feared it and became absorbed in it. Islam undervalued the world and consequently promoted sensuality and debased morality. Rome set the church and the world against each other by teaching that the latter was still under God's curse, and by attempting to place all social life under the jurisdiction of the institutional church. "As a natural result the world corrupted the Church," Kuyper said; and by its dominion over the world the church obstructed its "free development." Calvinism, however, taught that "common grace" weakened the curse resting on the world and allowed humanity to pursue God's glory. Calvinism limited the institutional church's task to evangelism and Christian nurture but insisted that every aspect of human activity was under God's control and subject to his norms.[28] Modernism, on the other hand, insisted that the world was self-created and self-contained; humans were subject only to their own laws and guidelines.

Kuyper warned Christians that their principal foe in the twentieth century would not be these older systems but Modernism. By Modernism, Kuyper meant the secular worldview developed during the French Revolution, not the theological tendency growing in American Christianity. Secular Modernism offered an atheistic imitation of Christianity's central ideals: altruism, peace, and the dignity, brotherhood, and service of fellow human beings. In both Europe and America this philosophy was attempting to develop a new type of religious life, Kuyper observed; but so far it had succeeded only in lessening commitment to many valuable principles of earlier systems.[29]

The rising secular current was especially dangerous, Kuyper declared, because religion in the west had reached ebb tide. This was apparent in Schopenhauer's pessimism, Tolstoi's protest against the spiritual degeneracy of the race, Nietzsche's despair, the rise of socialism and nihilism, growing immorality, and increasing indifference to spiritual matters. During the two previous periods of spiritual decadence in the west — Greco-Roman culture and the age of the Reformation — people had responded enthusiastically to the gospel. In the present era this did not seem likely to happen, because Bismarck's maxim of the right of the stronger, rooted in Darwinism's struggle for survival, had largely displaced traditional

Christian morality in Europe. And modern theologians from Schleiermacher to Pfleiderer, Kuyper complained, retained the name "Christian" for their systems while basing them upon secular principles that were diametrically opposed to biblical religion.[30]

Despite his critique of Catholicism, Kuyper was eager to join forces with Catholics in the battle against Modernism. Rome, after all, did accept such biblical fundamentals as the Trinity, the deity of Christ, the atonement, and biblical infallibility. At the same time, however, Kuyper argued that Catholicism, as a worldview, represented an older and lower stage of development. Only Protestantism possessed ideological weapons that could successfully repel the Modernist onslaught.[31]

But Protestantism was "a purely negative conception without content"; it could not stem the tide of Modernism. And the two leading expressions of Protestantism in the late nineteenth century — the mystical and the practical — while representing important biblical emphases, were also insufficient to resist Modernism. Neither the Holiness movement, which stressed inward experience and personal piety, nor the Social Gospel, which sought to ameliorate society, was suitably armed to halt the Modernist advance. Kuyper insisted that only a unified worldview that consistently developed the Scriptures could successfully turn back this emerging secular philosophy. Calvinism alone provided such a holistic philosophy of life. Its principles of divine sovereignty, human depravity, and the triumphant advance of God's kingdom on earth had strongly affected the development of democratic government, capitalism, public education, and social life. Kuyper, however, did not argue that all Christians must accept Reformed doctrinal tenets or join Calvinistic denominations. Instead he challenged believers to rediscover Calvinism's fundamental principles and use them as a basis to understand and direct philosophy, aesthetics, jurisprudence, literature, and the social and natural sciences.[32]

THE CALVINIST APPROACH TO CULTURE

Kuyper's lectures elicited much response. The editors of the theologically liberal journal the *Outlook* concluded that these addresses demonstrated Calvinism's continuing vitality. They urged Christians, however, to distinguish that system's "worn-out form" from its essential principles, as they thought Kuyper had.[33] The *Methodist Review* praised the Dutch leader for ably describing the historic service that Reformed orthodoxy had rendered to the world.[34] William N. Clarke, a leading liberal Northern Baptist theologian, was fascinated to see Reformed doctrine described as something "far greater than most Calvinists ever imagined it was"—a comprehensive worldview instead of merely a system of dogma and doctrine consisting of five points concerning predestination.[35] Henry Beets, editor of the Christian Reformed Church's *Banner of Truth*, agreed that Reformed Christians for too long had treated their beliefs simply as a theological system.[36]

Many Reformed leaders, however, insisted that they had always thought that Calvinism presented a holistic vision of God, humanity, and nature. Francis Beattie, a Southern Presbyterian theologian, argued that since Calvinism was theologically true, normative ideas in contemporary history, philosophy, science, and sociology naturally supported it.[37] Northern Presbyterian Henry C. Minton declared that current religious developments that exalted "philantrophic altruism," repudiated systematic theology, and advocated mysticism were "utterly powerless" to reform individuals or society. Only the Reformed worldview provided a proper foundation for restructuring human culture.[38] Reformed Church theologian Nicholas Steffens spoke for many who considered Calvinism not merely a system of theology but "a Christian view of the universe and of life." He warned that the intellectual and cultural crisis of the early twentieth century was even "more acute" than that of the sixteenth century. "A new humanism knocks at our door," he wrote; "the spirit of our age has wide dominion."[39]

Across the Atlantic, Frederic Platt announced in the *London Quarterly Review*, a British Methodist periodical, that he fully expected a "Renaissance of Calvinism." This theology was not merely a dogmatic and ecclesiastical anachronism; it had a permanent place in the Christian view of God and the world. He insisted that belief in "the mother-principle of Calvinism, the absolute supremacy of God in human life and the affairs of the world," was the best weapon for fighting the rampant materialism underlying secularism. The difference between Calvinism and the evangelical system generally, he declared, was the former's "intense and jealous demand for the supremacy of the divine: *Deo soli gloria.*"[40]

Like Platt, Calvinists repeatedly emphasized that their theology exalted divine sovereignty. It taught that God was Lord over all, in complete control of every event, answerable to no one. Those who saw the doctrine of predestination as the essence of Reformed orthodoxy, argued Scot William Hastie in his widely influential *The Theology of the Reformed Church in its Fundamental Principles* (1904), misconstrued its true nature. Predestination was only a logical outworking of Calvinism's root principle—the total dominion of God. More than any other theology, Hastie and Holland's Herman Bavinck maintained, Reformed theology based religious faith in God. Belief in divine sovereignty made humans totally dependent on God's providence, foreordination, and election, and led them to recognize God as supreme in all aspects of life.[41]

Because God was sovereign, Calvinists reasoned, the creation existed for his sake, not for humanity's. While Lutherans emphasized the salvation of individuals, noted prominent German scholar Ernst Troeltsch, Calvinists made God's honor the central goal and his glorification the real test of genuine personal religion.[42] Since the world, including humankind, was created to reveal "the infinite and absolute God," added Hastie, God wanted human beings to manifest his glory in all of creation. Although individual salvation was integral to this goal, it must never be seen as God's sole or even primary object.[43] More so than most other Christians, Reformed believers insisted that God's kingdom was permeating this world.

Calvinists declared that because God was sovereign Christians must labor to bring all culture under his dominion. Believers should serve him in their vocations, families, churches, leisure — in whatever they did. Since God had appointed laws and ordinances for all of life, Calvinists explained, wherever people worked, whether in agriculture, commerce, industry, education, art, or science, they must labor to promote his glory.[44]

Reformed Christians were convinced that their cultural efforts were worthwhile because they believed that such work advanced the kingdom God was building on earth. This kingdom was manifested wherever the gospel was proclaimed, hearts were changed, sin and error overcome, and righteousness cultivated. The parable of the leaven plainly taught that God's lordship was intended, in the words of Geerhardus Vos of Princeton Seminary, to "pervade and control the whole of human life."[45]

Calvinists thought their emphasis on Christ's dominion over all public life made their approach to culture different from other theists.[46] While they acknowledged that all theists believed in God's sovereignty, Reformed Christians also claimed that they had most consistently and thoroughly developed the implications of God's absolute control over human history and culture.[47] Their heritage and their belief in the continuous growth of God's kingdom on earth made them more confident than most others that God's ideals for culture could be realized in America.[48] As discussed earlier, Calvinists considered Roman Catholicism deficient because it limited religion to the portion of life that the church had consecrated, thus drawing a boundary line between holy and profane activities. This led Catholics either to consider most of life outside the sphere of religion or to make the institutional church dominate all human activities.[49] Anabaptists, such as Moravians and Mennonities, on the other hand, tended to withdraw from worldly activity because they misunderstood the nature of God's kingdom and their responsibility to exercise dominion over the world as God's stewards. Such groups depreciated the significance of art, science, literature, and politics, B. B. Warfield argued, and, therefore, had little to do with these activities. Their scheme left the control of culture to unbelievers.[50] Calvinists also considered the Pietist and Jewish approaches to culture inadequate. Lutherans and other Pietists, as well as Jews, recognized the competition of public life and did not insist on formally dominating society but hoped rather that the leaven of a righteous remnant would eventually penetrate the whole. They failed to acknowledge, however, that nations, not just individuals, were commanded to follow biblical principles. Even some Wesleyans had given up trying to structure social institutions and practices upon biblical principles and sought only to restrain evil until the Lord returned. Similarly, dispensationalists believed that little social or political progress could be achieved in America.[51]

By contrast, Reformed conservatives admitted that theists may not be able to control public philosophy in all periods of history, but they believed the Scriptures commanded them to try.[52] Christians must realize that God was "saving the world and not merely an individual here and there out of this world," Warfield declared.[53] Since the kingdom of God on earth was "not confined to the mere ecclesiastical sphere," but aimed to extend "its supreme reign over every department of human life," A. A. Hodge wrote, it followed that believers must "endeavor to bring all human society . . . into obedience to its laws of righteousness."[54]

Considering God sovereign over all activity, Calvinists strongly opposed the contemporary tendency, which for one reason or another, they argued, Roman Catholics, Jews, Lutheran Pietists, and Baptists tended to share, to limit religion to spiritual experiences or practical action and to minimize its intellectual elements, particularly its ideological ones. If religion were confined only to human feelings and human will, the sphere of religious life would also assume the same partial character. Calvinists warned that a religion that abandoned the intellect, confined itself to spiritual experience and ethical enthusiasm, and regarded human consciousness as an adequate authority was insufficient and ultimately would degenerate into agnosticism. Such a view of religion supported secular humanist arguments that God's teachings were not relevant to public Life. Kuyper protested that religion was increasingly "excluded ... from the domain of public life; henceforth the inner chamber, the cell for prayer, and the secrecy of the heart should be its exclusive dwelling place." Once the central force of human life, religion was becoming a peripheral element, banished to the sphere of private concerns.[55]

Because Reformed theology exalted God's supremacy over both public and private life, Kuyper and Warfield declared it to be the most biblical expression of Christianity and therefore the best hope for advancing biblical civilization. Moreover, they insisted, in their heart of hearts all true Christians were Calvinists. Kneeling before the supreme, almighty God, almost all Christians acknowledged their absolute dependence upon him for salvation and sustenance.[56] "He who believes in God without reserve, and is determined that God shall be God to him in all his thinking, feeling, willing — in the entire compass of his life — activities, intellectual, moral, spiritual ... ," Warfield claimed, "is by the forces of the strictest logic ... a Calvinist."[57]

Believing that their doctrinal system provided a consistent worldview, many Reformed Christians joined Kuyper and Warfield in arguing that all Christians could use Calvinism's root principles to work out a biblical understanding of various cultural activities. They continually sought to explain how Calvinistic tenets could counter secular trends in politics, education, science, economics, business, and morality. They felt especially compelled to do this after 1890 as the secular challenge to their cultural ideals grew to alarming proportions, and other Christian strategies of dealing with it, whether liberal-humanist, evangelical Pietist, Wesleyan, Anabaptist, dispensationalist, or Roman Catholic, appeared to them more and more inadequate.

CHRISTIAN RESPONSES TO SECULARIZATION

The secular philosophy that Calvinists and other Christians opposed during the years from 1870 to 1915 was not unified; it was fragmented and multifaceted, incorporating many diverse ideologies.[58] Secularists sponsored only several small and rather uninfluential organizations such as the American Secular League. Before 1900 they had no leader with an audience any wider than that attracted by itinerant lecturer Robert Ingersoll. Skeptics, agnostics, and freethinkers all promoted secularism as a public philosophy, as did various groups of Unitarians, Jews, Catholics, Pietists, and liberal Protestants. Certainly many of those who supported secularization did so without fully realizing what they were doing. Most of them would not have condoned secularism as it was elaborated in 1929 by Walter Lippmann's *Preface to Morals* or in 1933 by the Humanist Manifesto I. Before the late twenties, however, this increasingly influential ideology had no articulated creed. Yet Americans increasingly came to believe that public life should be "secular" or "neutral" as their culture became more heterogeneous and as intellectual elites insisted that religion belonged only to private areas of life. Such belief about public life, however, rarely reflected a consistent commitment to non- or anti-Christian worldviews.[59]

Of course, many non-Calvinists also strongly opposed secularizing trends in the late nineteenth and early twentieth centuries. The revival meetings of Dwight L. Moody, R. A. Torrey, Billy Sunday, and others were one way they met the intensifying threat of skepticism and worldliness. The Student Volunteer Movement, the Laymen's Missionary Movement, the Salvation Army, the YMCA, the Volunteers of America, and the tremendous expansion of denominational programs for both home and foreign missions represented another. The rise of the Social Gospel within American Protestantism and growing Catholic and Jewish efforts to deal on a moral basis with social problems was a third response to secularism. Such cooperative agencies and movements as the Evangelical Alliance, the Federal Council of Churches, and the Men and Religion Forward Movement also sought to infuse Christian values into American culture. Many Protestants considered the ratification of a national prohibition law in 1919 to be the crowning achievement in their quest to rest American public morality upon biblical teachings. Religious convictions in fact underlay much of the Progressive impulse of the first fifteen years of the twentieth century.[60]

Despite these efforts to base American culture and life more firmly on biblical principles, secular ideals and values increasingly influenced American politics, education, morality, economics, and social life after 1890. Few Americans abandoned their belief in God or their institutional religious connections. The public life of the nation, however, became more and more divorced from its traditional religious undergirdings.

Exactly how this occurred is unclear. Many Christians and Jews apparently narrowed the sphere to which they thought their religious beliefs applied.[61] The revivalist tradition, with its emphasis on individual decision and personal piety, tended to minimize the importance of social structures and practices.[62] Others concluded that American culture was already largely based on biblical values and thus became apathetic about their mission to society. Losing sight of the fundamental distinction between Christ and culture, some Christians became unwilling or unable to criticize prophetically the society.[63]

American Christians increasingly rejected the traditional Calvinist view that politics could be used to advance God's kingdom on earth and accepted a more "pietistic view" of political action as simply a means to restrain evil.[64] By the late nineteenth century, many dispensationalists agreed with the historic Anabaptist position that believers had no responsibility to shape social arrangements.[65] By the early twentieth century some Calvinists were also accepting these views. Growing numbers of them subtly shifted their emphasis from shaping culture to maintaining sound doctrine. B. B. Warfield and J. Gresham Machen, both of whom taught at Princeton Seminary, argued that Christians could influence cultural life most effectively by fostering correct theological beliefs.[66] Thus, Christians contributed to the secularization of American culture in these ways, while the growing acceptance of secular humanism by intellectuals, scientists, journalists, and other cultural arbiters in the late nineteenth century played a major role, as did the quiet and subtle way secular ideas permeated society.

Although Calvinists' practice of their principles often did not measure up to their proclamation of them, they did strongly oppose secularism in the years between 1870 and 1915. Some Calvinists capitulated to cultural trends; some unwittingly accepted humanistic presuppositions. On the whole, however, they resisted secular principles as firmly as any other group of Americans. The remainder of this study will show how Calvinists waged ideological warfare against secularism across a broad spectrum of American society.

As we will see in subsequent chapters, though, Calvinists employed a faulty strategy in their battles against secularism. Their campaign would have been considerably more successful in the long run if they had not sought to squelch secular ideas wherever they appeared but rather had allowed their exponents to express these ideas freely in public life. If Calvinists had refrained from trying to make Protestant Christianity dominate government, schools, morality, and social practices, if they had not attempted to use law to coerce others into living by their views, if they had truly recognized the right of alternative perspectives to be heard in public life, contemporary society might be quite different. The public order, as in some European countries, could be pluralistic; that is, a variety of viewpoints could be expressed and supported by law. Pluralism recognizes the existence of contrasting faith communities with major philosophical differences and seeks to safeguard the rights of all groups within the common democratic order.[67] By insisting, however, that Protestant Christianity control public life, Calvinists and other Protestants encouraged Americans to develop a public order from which religion, narrowly defined, has almost been excluded and where one view of reality — secular humanism — has received a privileged position. To avoid religious controversy, American government and education today are supposedly conducted on a neutral basis. Yet, as we have seen, secular humanism offers a distinctive understanding of ultimate reality, humanity, and the world that rests as much on faith as do the worldviews of other religions. Nonetheless, those who disagree with the humanistic premises and values presently underlying much of our public order are forced either to submit to them or not to participate in the public system.

4

A CHRISTIAN AMERICA

How should Christians who live in a country with many religious traditions express their conviction that nations stand under the sovereigny and judgment of God? In what ways and on what foundation can they cooperate with citizens who belong to other religious faiths and with those who reject all traditional religions? How can Christians express their commitment to biblical ideals in the institutions, laws, and practices of society without infringing on the rights of citizens who do not share their religious convictions?[1] In the late nineteenth century many American Calvinists offered peculiar answers to these questions. This is evident in their conception of the state, their crusade to fortify the Christian basis of American government, and their differing attitudes toward political theory and participation.

An analysis of Calvinist political views and activities clearly demonstrates that their approach to culture was fundamentally flawed. Their efforts to force the values of the Christian majority upon all Americans produced both debate and division. Had Calvinists instead supported the concept of cultural pluralism they could have pursued more constructive political crusades and could have more effectively resisted the forces that sought to divorce religion from government.

CALVINISM AND GOVERNMENT

In the late nineteenth century all Calvinists, whether they belonged to Southern, Northern, United, or Reformed Presbyterian denominations, to the Christian Reformed Church or the Reformed Church of America, or to Northern or Southern Baptist, Congregationalist, or Episcopalian congregations, agreed on certain fundamental political principles. All of them insisted that church and state should be separate. Although John Calvin argued that the state should promote and enforce true religion, he maintained that each had its own distinct sphere. Each should support the other and neither should usurp the prerogatives and duties of the other.[2] His nineteenth-century followers no longer believed, as had most Reformers, that magistrates should compel people to attend Christian worship. They did, however, continue strongly to affirm Calvin's convictions that government was an ordinance of God and that political officials must, as God's servants, apply Christian principles to their administrations.[3]

In his Stone Lectures at Princeton Seminary in 1898, Abraham Kuyper expounded the principle of divine sovereignty over human government. Every political system in history, Kuyper argued, was rooted in either a religious or an antireligious conception.[4] Agreeing with Kuyper, many Calvinists rejected the increasingly popular view that national governments were religiously neutral. Governments, they believed, must either acknowledge the sovereignty of God over both their own operations and the whole cosmos, or root their power in the sovereignty of either the people or the state.[5] The Calvinist conviction that Christ was Lord over the political sphere, Kuyper explained, implied that God alone should control the political life of nations, for he created, sustained, and through his ordinances ruled them. Although sin had destroyed God's direct rule, the authority magistrates exercised was delegated to them by God.[6]

Governed by these assumptions, many Calvinists denounced the doctrines of both popular and state sovereignty. In doing so, Reformed Christians did not question that government should be based on a political compact between ruler and citizens, modeled on God's covenant with his people. Nor did they disagree that government should represent the collective will of the people. Rather, they rejected the secular concept of popular sovereignty, rooted in the French Revolution and the writings of Rousseau, which held that the state was "merely a human institution, a social contract, dissolvable at the will of the contracting parties" and in no sense a moral entity or a subject of divine government.[7] This conception dethroned God, Calvinists insisted, and crowned human will as lord over events. History condemned this theory, Kuyper asserted. In France, for example, it had shackled "liberty in the irons of state-omnipotence."[8] Southern Presbyterian theologian Robert Dabney repudiated Rousseau's social contract theory, which many argued provided the foundation for the doctrine of popular sovereignty. Rousseau's fundamental assumption, that humanity stood independent of God, Dabney argued, was simply untrue. Both the Bible and human nature showed convincingly that people were responsible to their Creator in all areas of life.[9]

Calvinists also denounced the concept of state sovereignty. Kuyper maintained that this doctrine stemmed from Hegel's philosophical pantheism, which taught that ideas were immanent in reality and that the concept of the state was the highest idea of the relationship among human beings. This doctrine, Kuyper complained, logically led to considering the laws of nations as right, not because they accorded with eternal principles but simply because they were the law. This based the good on the ever-changing will of the state, which, having no power above itself, usurped God's prerogative of determining the shape of social life.[10]

Kuyper's arguments summarized conclusions other Calvinists had reached earlier. Robert Thompson, a Northern Presbyterian who was professor of sociology at the University of Pennsylvania, declared that "those who see no God behind the state are driven by a kind of spiritual necessity to exalt the state into a god." Thompson warned that no appeal could be made against the actions and policies of a state that acknowledged no absolute right nor any transcendent standards of eternal justice. In the final analysis, he concluded, state sovereignty defined "right" to be what society judged to be advantageous.[11] Lyman Atwater, professor of moral philosophy at Princeton College, denounced state sovereignty for grounding punishment more on expediency than justice and for rooting all political obligation in desirability or self-interest, rather than on principles. This theory, he concluded, contradicted the biblical view of the origin, aims, and prerogatives of government.[12] If there were no fixed standard of right, added J. M. Foster, a Reformed Presbyterian pastor in Boston, all laws of morality could be resolved into one — the will of the legislature; might determined right and a bare majority could tyrannize the rest of the citizens.[13] In short, Calvinists charged that both of the two competing political philosophies of popular and state sovereignty repudiated the Hebrew and Christian conviction that people must constantly test existing laws by standards of eternal righteousness stemming from the nature and revelation of God.[14] Though they supported the separation of church and state, Calvinists and many other evangelicals living in the late nineteenth century proclaimed that religion should not and could not be divorced from politics. Underlying all governments were central presuppositions that either supported or undermined Christianity; there was no intermediate option.[15] Christians, therefore, as Abraham Lincoln reminded them, were to attempt to base politics on eternal ethical principles.[16] Separating politics from the biblical ideals that should govern all human activity, a Southern Presbyterian warned, would rob the political order of "the only salt" that could keep it from "utter corruption."[17] Because God created and ruled the world, Robert Thompson asserted, national life should emulate his divine kingdom.[18] Governments, others declared, were instituted by God to promote justice and morality.[19]

Leading Calvinists argued further that states were moral entities, just as individuals were. More so than most other Christians, Calvinists saw Old Testament Israel, a nation governed by scriptural principles, as a proper model for political life. They insisted that nations could not be neutral toward God any more than persons could; both were under moral obligation to serve him.[20] In a republican state, therefore, Christian legislators must strive to enact biblical laws.[21] In every capacity — private, public, official, or political — proclaimed Lyman Atwater, Scripture must guide human consciences. No officer of government could eliminate the first table of the decalogue without defying God. "Does a man acquire a right to deny or insult God," asked Atwater, "when acting as a ruler or magistrate, which would be impious if done by him as a private citizen?"[22] Speaking for most Calvinists, Atwater maintained that the second table of the Ten Commandments (which deals with interpersonal relationships) should underlie and control all legislation. Thus, he called on the state to punish adultery, prohibit obscene publications and divorces not based on the scriptural grounds of adultery or abandonment, restrain vagrancy and idleness, punish slander, and enforce contracts.[23] Atwater and Princeton Seminary professor William B. Greene, Jr. disagreed with those in the late nineteenth century who argued that morality could rest on natural law alone. Because God's moral law written on human hearts is distorted by sin, it must be supplemented by written revelation.[24] Only by explicitly following biblical laws and norms in all areas of their life, Calvinists concluded, could nations please God.

CALVINISM, CITIZENSHIP, AND CORRUPTION

Guided by these political principles and driven by their strong desire to make America a more Christian nation, many Calvinists engaged in political activities. Although they disagreed over the extent to which local congregations, denominations, and ministers should participate in politics, Calvinists in all denominations stressed the responsibilities of citizens, denounced corruption, and advocated civil service and municipal reform.

Calvinists labored diligently to promote the moral ends of government. Lyman Atwater insisted that the Bible prohibited furthering unrighteous measures by any means or the best policies by unjust means. Reformed leaders taught their members to cast their ballots intelligently and honestly in order to elect upright officials who would work to make government serve Christ. And they urged Christians to pray continually for their government and its leaders.[25]

Calvinists instructed members to evaluate political platforms carefully and to support the party that, on the whole, most promoted righteousness and the public good. Christians were expected to work to secure the nomination of good candidates at all party primaries. Atwater encouraged Christians, as many Christian Reformed leaders did later, to form an independent bloc at the polls, which, when no major party issues were at stake, could defeat unworthy nominees.[26] A United Presbyterian cautioned against devotion to political parties, warning that they often silenced conscience and compelled members to trample principle underfoot.[27] Seeking truth and righteousness was always to transcend party loyalty. W. G .T. Shedd of Union Seminary in New York City scorned the slogan "my party right or wrong" and reminded Christians that the claims of political parties were inferior to those of God.[28]

Calvinists demanded the same standard of honesty in political contests as in private life. They strongly censured bribery, intimidation, and fraud. Elections were to be waged on principles, not personalities, they declared; devices such as mass meetings and torchlight processions, which did not educate voters but aimed solely to arouse emotions, were not to be used.[29]

Reformed conservatives urged citizens to elect honest, independent representatives controlled neither by party bosses nor by desire for political and financial gain.[30] Doing so could help abolish America's widespread political corruption. The moral character of many prominent officeholders, a Southern Presbyterian complained in 1881, was no better than that of "any score of convicts taken at random from any penitentiary." He argued that many elected officials poured contempt on the law of God by encouraging lying, covetousness, and theft.[31] Only those with strong moral convictions, Shedd declared, could resist the temptations to injustice, deceit, and self-aggrandizement that beset office holding in the late nineteenth century.[32] Only belief in the Bible, others added, could produce the high moral character necessary to sustain good government.[33]

Abolishing corrupt and incompetent government, many Calvinists argued, required civil service reform. The patronage system, widely used in the late nineteenth century, was capricious and inefficient. They protested that no private business could survive that changed all its personnel every four years. Jobs should go to the best person in the community rather than to the most loyal party member. Moreover, the spoils system abetted political machines and produced a wild scramble for position and profit.[34] The assassination of President James A. Garfield in 1881, Atwater declared, demonstrated the debauchery of this system. For fifty years the power of appointment had been used to "dispense all public offices solely to friends, partisans, or the winning party."[35] Only civil service reform could guarantee that the competent, faithful, and energetic were not removed at the whim of a politician.

Calvinists also supported the early-twentieth-century campaign to improve municipal governments. Christians could not be satisfied, one declared, with "filling the churches with worshippers, while allowing the devil's side to hold all the offices and to make and execute all the laws."[36] Mark Matthews, moderator of the Northern Presbyterian General Assembly of 1912 and pastor of the world's largest Presbyterian congregation during the early twentieth century, First Presbyterian in Seattle, led Calvinist efforts to improve municipal governments. From pulpit and platform Matthews urged Christians to elect city officials dedicated to eradicating political corruption and to procuring better housing and more sanitary conditions. Moreover, he earned a law degree and used his part-time legal practice to promote good government in Seattle.[37]

In short, Calvinists insisted that biblical faith must purify American politics. Only commitment to God could produce the moral citizens a democracy needed to function effectively. Such faith alone could enable Americans to transcend regional, ethnic, social, and ideological differences and live and work together harmoniously.[38]

THE CRUSADE FOR CHRISTIAN GOVERNMENT

After the Civil War many warned that America's achievements and advancement as a Christian nation were in jeopardy. One of the strongest admonitions came from Josiah Strong, who claimed in *Our Country* in 1886 that seven "perils," including Catholicism, drunkenness, and socialism, threatened to undermine traditional American values. Calvinists reacted to these challenges by seeking to deepen the national government's commitment to biblical principles, especially by working with the National Reform Association.

The primary goal of NRA supporters was to amend the preamble of the United States Constitution so as to acknowledge the authority of Jesus Christ over the government. They wished the preamble to read as follows:

> We the people of the United States, humbly acknowledging Almighty God as the source of all authority and power in civil government, the Lord Jesus Christ as the Governor among the nations, and His revealed will as of supreme authority, in order to constitute a Christian government . . . do ordain and establish this Constitution for the United States of America.[39]

Although the NRA, which was founded in 1864, was interdenominational, its chief supporters were Calvinists scattered in various denominations. Among its leading proponents were Northern Presbyterians Charles and A. A. Hodge of Princeton Seminary, Herrick Johnson of McCormick Seminary in Chicago, Sylvester Scovel, president of the College of Wooster, and Associate Supreme Court Justice William Strong; Episcopalians Stephen Tyng, Sr. and Frederick Dan Huntington; Congregationalists J. H. Seelye, president of Amherst College, and well-known lecturer Joseph Cook; Reformed Church of America pastor Taylor Lewis; and Methodist bishops Gilbert Haven and Matthew Simpson. By the early 1870s the honorary vice presidents of the organization included one United States senator, two governors, three Federal judges, three state school superintendents, twenty-five college and university presidents, and eleven Methodist and Episcopal bishops.[40] Reformed Presbyterians, however, did much of the everyday work of the association. They edited the NRA's journal, *The Christian Statesman*, wrote most of the organization's promotional literature, and spoke frequently at NRA annual conventions.[41]

Although anti-Catholic and anti-Jewish sentiment contributed to establishing the NRA, the organization's primary goal quickly became to combat the alleged secular drift of American politics. In the 1870s and 1880s its adherents continued to fear the growing political participation of the large influx of Jewish and Catholic immigrants, but they were even more alarmed by the increasingly stated argument that government must be "neutral" and divorced from God's concern. David McAllister, a professor at the Reformed Presbyterian's Geneva College, northwest of Pittsburgh, denounced secularism as an "assailant" that sought to eradicate Christian influence from the American government.[42] Its proponents had already banished the Bible from the schools of some large American cities and had repealed the Sabbath laws of one state.[43] Secularists agreed with Robert Ingersoll who wrote that the government of the United States "derives its power from the consent of man. It is government with which God has nothing whatever to do. . . . The people [alone] must determine what is politically right and what is wrong."[44] Secularists contended that because the Constitution did not explicitly recognize God, all Christian influence in American government should be abolished. This argument prompted NRA supporters' efforts to amend the Constitution to acknowledge Christ's supreme authority over the nation.

NRA leaders advanced three sets of considerations—scriptural, philosophical, and historical—in their attempt to have the American government officially recognize Christ's lordship. Most important was the scriptural consideration. According to the Old Testament, God created, sustains, and controls the destiny of nations. Civil rulers are God's ministers and derive all just authority ultimately from him. The New Testament explicitly commands both rulers and subjects to obey Jesus Christ as King and to follow biblical principles and norms in their national life. Christ rules as King of nations by punishing those which violate his law and by rewarding those which obey it.[45]

McAllister used the testimony of such philosophers as Francis Lieber, Edmund Burke, G. W. F. Hegel, and William Gladstone to buttress his contention that the state was a moral agent, possessing both moral character and accountability. As a power with no earthly superior, the state had to be responsible directly to God and, therefore, it could not properly attempt to be neutral toward the Christian faith. In its legislation, its jurisprudence, its general political action, and, above all, its claim to be an educating power, the state was required to follow God's norms. McAllister also showed that many legal experts agreed that constitutional law could only have developed from or been sanctioned by an unwritten, preexisting right.

In America this underlying standard was Christianity. McAllister thought this was evident from the beliefs of the nation's first settlers, the founding of civil institutions upon scriptural principles, and the universal American acknowledgment of the Bible as the measure of political morality. Thus, McAllister concluded, the United States had an unwritten Christian constitution and a non-Christian written constitution; it must amend the latter to conform with the former.[46]

McAllister's historical argument was similar. He summarized the historical evidence that scores of Calvinistic supporters of the NRA had presented. They saw a basis for national Christianity in colonial charters, compacts, and laws; in the Declaration of Independence; in the proclamation of days of humiliation, fasting and prayer, and Thanksgiving; and in presidential addresses and state constitutions. Even in 1890, thirty-seven of the forty-two state constitutions acknowledged God's authority in either the preamble or the main body. Numerous Calvinists also pointed to America's Sabbath observance, Christian common schools, chaplains in the military services, and prayers in legislative assemblies as proof of the nation's commitment to Christianity in its public life.[47] In short, as Lyman Atwater put it, America was not as Christian as it should have been, but its responsibility to be Christian was evident in its "origin, history, traditions, institutions, in the whole drift ... of our social and national life," and in the fact that the vast majority of Americans who professed any religion confessed Christianity.[48]

Because secularists constantly maintained that the Constitution's lack of a specific acknowledgment of God was grounds for abolishing all Christian practices in American civil life, NRA leaders concentrated on remedying this "defect."[49] Since Christians were a majority in America, they argued, it was proper and fair for the government to be Christian. Yet because God's law recognized and protected individual rights, such a government would provide the most freedom of conscience and worship for people of differing religious faiths.[50] They believed further that only this proposed amendment could provide a secure basis for moral legislation on the Sabbath, the saloon, the family, or any other ethical issue.[51] Because it ignored God, one NRA leader emphasized, the Constitution offered no adequate basis for honesty and fidelity. Shifting his argument from theism to Christianity, as Calvinists often did, he declared that this omission obscured the fact that Christianity was the secret of American success — and this omission was a standing insult to God, the Source of America's existence and prosperity.[52]

In addition to campaigning for a constitutional amendment, NRA leaders worked to pass national laws forbidding postal service and interstate commerce on Sundays, standardizing divorce, requiring civil service reform, and instituting prohibition. They also fought to keep Bible reading and prayer in the public schools.[53]

To accomplish their purposes, NRA leaders used a wide variety of methods. Secular and religious newspapers thoroughly covered yearly NRA conventions. Copies of major addresses were widely circulated. District secretaries wrote hundreds of newspaper articles each year and spoke frequently to congregations, conferences, and conventions. The NRA sponsored numerous conferences at summer resorts to educate the public, and its leaders often lectured at colleges. NRA supporters cooperated with such related societies as the American Sabbath Union, the Women's Christian Temperance Union, and the Divorce Reform League. Through numerous petitions they called attention to the nation's obligations to God. NRA advocates also attempted to secure acknowledgments of God's authority from politicians convened to enact or amend state constitutions.

Despite NRA efforts, however, the United States House of Representatives twice rejected its proposed federal amendment. The first rejection came in 1874. At this time A. A. Hodge explained that the debate over the amendment involved three parties: the band of evangelicals working for national reform, secularists and skeptics, and the great mass of American Christians. Hodge was confident that members of this third group agreed with NRA principles and would support the organization when they better understood its aim and the feasibility of its enterprise.[54] These Christians, however, either never understood or never accepted the NRA's convictions. Some of them thought that government was a neutral enterprise that must exclude all religious principles. But most of them believed that national life could continue to be based upon biblical values without official constitutional recognition of Jesus Christ. The House rejected the NRA's request for a second time in 1896. At this hearing, a diverse group — including the president of the American Secular League, the secretary of the National Spiritualist's Association, a Seventh Day Baptist pastor, a Unitarian clergyman, and a Washington attorney — spoke against the NRA proposal.[55]

During the years that NRA supporters worked for this amendment, they encountered numerous objections to their position. Some opponents contended that it was not right for citizens to express their religious convictions in political documents. Samuel Putnam, president of the American Secular League, argued before the House Judiciary Committee in 1896 that the Constitution was "not for metaphysics or philosophy" but "for practical affairs of business." Disregarding much historical evidence to the contrary, Putnam claimed that this proposed amendment was "revolutionary" because the Founding Fathers had established a purely secular government.[56] Members of the House Judiciary Committee concurred with his views, declaring that the American government had neither a moral purpose nor an obligation to God. At the same hearing, William Birney, attorney, former Civil War general, and author of

"Functions of Church and State Distinguished" (1897), spoke for those who were committed to spreading religious values through voluntary organizations but thought the state must be completely neutral toward religion.[57] NRA supporter Judge John Alexander of Philadelphia complained that many Christians accepted this "secular theory" of government and thus constituted a great obstacle to the movement.[58]

Many evangelical Christians opposed the NRA proposal because they believed it was futile to use the law in an attempt to make people religious. Only conversion could accomplish that. Converts would naturally follow biblical principles in all areas of life and therefore infuse Christian values into the culture. Moreover, Southern Presbyterians and others insisted that the institutional church had no responsibility for political affairs; congregations should confine their work exclusively to spiritual matters.[59]

Other evangelicals added that Christianity could not be legislated. Although the state could pass laws to accomplish some of the same ends sought by Christians, Southern Presbyterian Robert Kerr declared, church and state were "separate and independent institutions and their methods, as well as their ultimate designs" were totally different. If the state publicly endorsed Christianity, he continued, it would logically have to punish those who disobeyed any of the Bible's fundamental requirements. Thus, he concluded, the NRA "should confine its efforts to securing moral legislation for the safety of the state and not religious legislation for the sake of the Church."[60]

Calvinist NRA leaders insisted that their opponents misunderstood the relationship between the gospel and civil law. They agreed that people could be regenerated only by a personal encounter with the resurrected Christ; but they insisted — as did many Methodists, Southern Baptists, and Lutherans — that the more that political, educational, social, economic, and familial arrangements were based on biblical principles, the easier it would be to lead persons to Christ. An environment modeled on biblical ideals would help to educate and to sensitize people to the Christian faith. "Putting one or a dozen mentions of Christ into the Constitution," one Calvinist wrote, would not "convert an infidel or save a soul," but it would "place all Christian laws, institutions, and usages on an undeniable legal basis in the fundamental law of the nation."[61] Moreover, NRA leaders contended, God commanded them to do this. And only by explicitly recognizing God's lordship could a state maintain order and liberty and promote prosperity.[62]

The argument that America was already a Christian nation, repeatedly affirmed by Supreme Court declarations throughout the nineteenth century, also thwarted the NRA's cause.[63] Many Northern Presbyterians and large numbers of non-Calvinist evangelicals held this view. A nation, like a person, insisted William B. Greene, Jr. of Princeton Seminary, may be Christian, although it was far from being as Christian as it should be.[64] Reasoning that other institutions in the United States were more significant than the Constitution, Lyman Atwater counseled Christians to devote their energies to maintaining the civil Sabbath and supporting temperance movements rather than to campaigning for a constitutional amendment.[65] NRA leaders repeatedly responded to this argument by insisting that these evidences of allegiance to Christianity were good but insufficient; America must also formally commit itself to God. Such a commitment would honor God, provide a solid basis for Christian legislation, and remove a potent weapon from the secularist arsenal.[66]

NRA leaders also repudiated the frequent claim that their proposed amendment would unite church and state. They argued that they did not wish to merge civil and ecclesiastical offices and functions, that church and state must be kept separate and independent.[67] Their convention in 1867 had stated that the union of church and state would not be "profitable, useful, or even endurable."[68] Yet NRA advocates maintained throughout the late nineteenth century that the Bible was the supreme law of both spheres. People's temporal and eternal interests were "so inseparably joined," R. W. Sloane declared, that they could not be severed. Since social and civic relations were vitally important to individuals' spiritual lives, he continued, God had not left their guidance to "erring reason and natural religion." Rather, he had given them the Scriptures to direct their civil affairs.[69] NRA leaders did not want the church or state to usurp each other's functions; nor did they want an established church — they simply wanted to make the political and moral principles of Christianity the basis of American legislation and administration.[70]

Secularists — and many Christians — protested, however, that the proposed amendment would tie the church and state too closely together and would abridge individuals' liberty of conscience. In the most scathing denunciation of the NRA's position, W. F. Jamieson in *The Clergy — A Source of Danger to the American Republic* (1872) insisted that ministers were "more dangerous to civil and religious liberty" than "slave-holders ever were." The proposed religious amendment would make the Bible the new Constitution and a jealous, cruel, devious "Jewish divinity" the source of all authority in the government.[71] A clerical empire would permit only Christians to hold political office and would stifle free inquiry. Jamieson warned that, if the proposed constitutional amendment were framed in terms of "Christianity versus Infidelity," hundreds of thousands of Christians would raise the banner of the NRA.[72]

NRA leader David McAllister responded to this argument by maintaining that the state had rights just as individuals did. The state could best promote its own welfare by practicing Christian principles. And, he insisted, such a government could best protect the rights of all citizens because only Christianity properly balanced liberty and law.[73] Like many other evangelicals, McAllister believed that American freedom and Protestantism were so closely linked together that there was no incompatibility between religious liberty and First Amendment rights and America's being a Christian nation.[74]

Jamieson's fears were never realized. The debate never became one of Christianity versus atheism because many Christians opposed the NRA's position. Rather, the battle was waged on other fronts. The amendment was defeated primarily because many Americans did not believe it was necessary, fair, or biblically justified to recognize officially the lordship of Jesus Christ over the nation.

The NRA position posed serious problems for a pluralistic culture. The effort to impose evangelical Christianity on others through the political process seemed to many, including Orthodox Jews, Catholic priests, and many evangelicals, to be in opposition to both the Constitution and New Testament teachings about the proper pattern of government in nations that were religiously, ethnically, and culturally heterogeneous. NRA leaders maintained — incorrectly — that the general biblical principle of divine sovereignty had only one possible application — the explicitly Christian one. While their campaign to amend the Constitution did not seek to unite church and state, it did attempt to force Jews, Unitarians, and Deists to submit to the civil authority of one whom they did not consider divine: Jesus.

This misdirected zeal tended to drive a wedge between Reformed Protestants and other theists. Protestants, Catholics, Jews, Deists, and Unitarians all acknowledged God's sovereignty over nations and events and all agreed that the Decalogue should be the foundation for law and political life. (Although Catholics historically rejected the complete separation of church and state, holding rather that ecclesiastical leaders should have civil powers, most

American Catholics recognized that their church would never be able to control this nation's government.) But the NRA leaders' campaign to amend the Constitution prevented theists from working together on the basis of their mutually held principles to shape governmental policies and practices.

Most Christians living in the late nineteenth century repudiated both the contention that the state must be religiously neutral and the claim that government should be directly under Christ's lordship. They believed that it was neither scripturally valid nor realistic to suppose that Americans could transform their society into a consistently Christian nation with laws that conformed completely to God's expressed will. They argued that the Bible taught Christians in the New Testament era not to expect to spread the gospel by aid of the civil government. Despite the thousands of immigrants who were streaming into American cities in the late nineteenth century, rejecting traditional evangelical values and making consensus on religious issues increasingly hard to achieve, most Christians still believed that political officials, citizens, and their laws could promote biblical principles without explicitly recognizing God and Jesus Christ in their official documents. Many of them worked individually and through voluntary organizations to persuade people to accept biblical values, but they joined secularists, Jews, Unitarians, Deists, and others to defeat the proposed NRA amendment.[75] Like many Christians today, some evangelicals living in the late nineteenth century confused civil religion — the mutually agreed upon religious sentiments, concepts, and symbols used by the state for its own political purposes — with biblical Christianity. Others thought American culture to be sufficiently Christian because of its historic development and its many continuing biblical influences. Still others supported efforts to divorce religion totally from political life. Some Christians even became preoccupied in the pursuits of profit and pleasure. Many Christians, however, worked in the streets of Chicago, the slums of New York, the back hills of Texas, the plains of Nebraska, and hundreds of other places to reverse trends toward secularization and to preserve Christian values in American culture.[76]

Despite their failure to achieve their central objective, leaders of the NRA claimed that their campaign had accomplished much. They had witnessed steadily to Christ's lordship over nations and all societal affairs. Through promoting civil service reform and encouraging the study of political science, they had helped raise popular expectations for public servants. And they had significantly aided such other reform efforts as Sabbath observance, prohibition,

Bible reading in the public schools, and stricter divorce laws.[77] As one NRA advocate put it, "the ordinary methods of evangelists, compared with the design of national reformers," were like "snatching a few valuables out of a burning dwelling, rather than putting out the fire and saving all."[78] By working to remove those public evils that corrupted morals, blunted social awareness, and hindered the ministry of the churches, NRA supporters believed they had helped make America a more Christian nation.

Although proponents of the NRA did promote several good causes, in the final analysis they may have done more to undermine than to aid the attempt to build a Christian America. By calling attention to a political issue that seemed even to many Christians to violate the separation of church and state, their proposal probably strengthened secular arguments against grounding American society upon Christian values.

In addition, their proposed amendment hindered Jews, Deists, and Unitarians from joining Christians to support programs and laws based upon fundamental biblical ideals. Their crusade also divided Christians, many of whom were having more and more difficulty harmonizing biblical principles with an increasingly pluralistic society, thus reducing their effectiveness in their fight for Sabbath observance, temperance, and other laws. Most greviously, the NRA's campaign tended to divert theists' attention from redressing many serious social injustices. Discrimination against racial, ethnic, and impoverished minorities was widespread in the late nineteenth century. In addition, the government did little during these years to curb economic exploitation or to diminish growing imperialism.

Despite all their protestations to the contrary, the root problem of NRA advocates was that they confused the Old Testament theocracy with the pluralistic pattern of civil government taught by the New Testament. They failed to see that states could not be explicitly Christian because political entities existed to govern mixed populations of believers and nonbelievers. While biblical values can still undergird a nation's political life, non-Christians should receive every opportunity and benefit in the political arena that Christians receive.[79]

In one sense Calvinists were overly alarmed about the political changes they thought were taking place in the years between 1865 and 1915. The period ended the way it began: with a president guiding American affairs who believed wholeheartedly in the sovereignty of God over nations and history. Woodrow Wilson, no less than Abraham Lincoln, had a deep confidence that God was directing the course of events and that he, as America's leader, must seek divine direction for his policies and strive to base both his domestic and his foreign programs upon eternal principles rather than pragmatic considerations. Moreover, between Lincoln and Wilson two others from a Reformed heritage — Grover Cleveland and Theodore Roosevelt — also occupied the White House.[80]

THE CHURCH AND POLITICS

While many Calvinists supported the efforts of the National Reform Association, Reformed communions displayed widely divergent attitudes toward politics. This is especially evident in their views of the role that denominations and congregations should play in the political arena. A good example of this is seen by comparing the radical positions of Reformed Presbyterians (the "Covenanters" of Scottish origin) and Southern Presbyterians with the more typical evangelical posture of other Calvinists.

Reformed Presbyterians were the chief supporters of the NRA. In the late nineteenth century their 10,000 members believed that Christians should not vote or serve as political officials until America's fundamental law explicitly recognized God's authority.[81] They maintained that only this position freed them from responsibility for such national sins as intemperance, Sabbath breaking, and the destruction of families by unscriptural divorces that the law permitted. "Because of the false principles of morality upon which the Constitution is based," wrote a Reformed Presbyterian in 1892, "many crimes against God and humanity are legalized, sustained, defended and practiced by the United States in its organized capacity."[82]

Most Calvinists, of course, disagreed with this refusal to vote and to hold political office. United Presbyterians, whose theology and worship were very similar to the Covenanters, argued that if all Christians followed the Reformed Presbyterian model, the leaven of the gospel would disappear from politics, and non-Christians would control the government.[83] Covenanters responded that their political dissent had done a thousand times more to arrest America's attention, mold public opinion, and bring God's kingdom on earth than all their votes in the elections of the previous one hundred years could possibly have done.[84]

Northern Presbyterians objected that even if the United States were not the Christian nation that they believed it in fact to be, nonparticipation would still not be the scriptural position. Christians were obligated to obey "the powers that be" — and casting ballots was the first civil duty.[85] Reformed Presbyterians countered that they obeyed all the nation's laws and were loyal to their country. Nowhere, however, did the Bible command Christians to vote or hold office. Dissent from doing so complied with the scriptural command to separate from the evil ways of nations that rejected Christ's authority.[86] Although they did not vote, Covenanters argued, they worked for social reforms in other ways.[87]

Southern Presbyterians also had an unusual view of politics. In the late nineteenth century most of them believed that the church was a spiritual body that should not interfere with or be involved in the civil relations of society. This belief made most of them passive toward the secession of the Southern states from the Union, the events of Reconstruction, and the continued exploitation of blacks.

Historians have debated whether James Thornwell, a renowned Southern Presbyterian theologian who died in 1862, developed this doctrine or whether his followers — B. M. Palmer, James Girardeau, and Robert Dabney — created it as an expedient policy for Reconstruction.[88] At any rate, by 1880 most Southern Presbyterians argued that the Westminster Confession and the history of the Presbyterian Church in America affirmed this doctrine. They also insisted that their denomination had severed connections with the Presbyterian Church, U. S. A. in 1861 because their Northern brothers had abandoned this position by siding with the Union.[89] Undoubtedly, the events of the Civil War and those of Reconstruction helped to create and reinforce this doctrine.

In 1883 William Boggs, a Southern Presbyterian professor of church history, explained the denomination's oft-repeated argument that the church should cofine its ministry to spiritual matters. By asserting that his kingdom was not of this world, by rejecting titles, by refusing to act as a civil judge, and by declining to decide the dispute about paying taxes to Caesar, Jesus clearly taught this position. Moreover, Jesus distinguished sharply between a secular and a spiritual kingdom. While the former was ordained to protect temporal life, property, and personal rights in this world, the latter sought to promote humans' moral and spiritual well-being and to prepare them for another world.[90]

Their belief that the mission of the church was exclusively spiritual made Southern Presbyterian political views very different from those of other Calvinists. It profoundly affected their attitudes toward segregation and disfranchisement of blacks, economic exploitation, political corruption, and even temperance.[91] Eventually,

Southern Presbyterians came to believe that one of their primary purposes was to defend this concept.[92]

Many of their leaders strongly opposed all attempts to make the American government a "Christian" one. Before the conversion of the Roman Emperor Constantine in the fourth century, Boggs asserted, Christianity had been a kingdom that was "not of this world." From Constantine until the seventeenth century, however, Christians had fostered one of two errors — church control over the state or state control over the church. According to the Westminster Confession, Boggs argued, the church should not interfere in the affairs of the state except to petition the government when it infringed on the church's right of worship. Northern Presbyterians, he continued, had affirmed or assumed certain principles in declaring their constituents' loyalty to the Union in 1861, which, if carried into action, would have entirely destroyed individual religious liberties. By doing so Northern Presbyterians required their members to support one political position and repudiate another.[93] Taking sides on political questions, Southern Presbyterian historian Thomas C. Johnson added, either would divide a denomination, as did the Presbyterian Church's 1861 loyalty resolution, or it would abridge the free thought of its members.[94]

Southern Presbyterians' commitment to the spirituality of the church led them to criticize the political activities of other Calvinists and to assert that congregations should only teach general moral duties. Pastors should not dictate how church members were to perform political duties; only individuals acting within the sphere itself could decide such matters.[95] They labeled as naive the Northern Presbyterian claims that they preached only on those political questions having moral elements, insisting rather that every political issue had ethical aspects. The Northern Presbyterian approach logically should lead to "Gold Presbyterians and Silver Presbyterians, High Tariff Presbyterians and Free Trade Presbyterians, Imperialistic Presbyterians and Anti-Imperialistic Presbyterians." This approach divided members over political issues instead of uniting them to promote spiritual concerns.[96] Southern Presbyterians also maintained that denominations or congregations, as organizations, should not support such reform agencies as temperance societies or antigambling associations. The management and education of children, the choosing of business associates, and the formation of political party affiliation were all part of the civil sphere and thus not properly subject to the church's control or influence. Denominational officials and local pastors should not even tell their members how to vote on such matters as incorporating God's name into the Constitution, adopting the Ten Commandments as a part of civil law, or reading the Bible in public schools, because these were political questions, no matter how deeply they involved moral issues.[97]

While insisting that the institutional church should not engage in political activity, Southern Presbyterians did urge Christians to influence civil laws and corporate life through their actions as individual citizens, workers, and homemakers. Church members should support every moral and religious reform advanced by the state. If congregations faithfully preached individual salvation and personal holiness, Southern Presbyterians maintained, society would be renovated and government purified much more certainly and quickly than if they participated in politics. Reforming social institutions, like purging a river downstream, would purify human life only temporarily; converting individuals, like cleansing the stream at its source, was the only way to bring lasting improvement.[98]

Other Calvinists rejected this position, insisting that both individual regeneration and structural reforms were necessary. While basing government, education, business, and social life upon biblical principles could not regenerate souls, declared many Northern Presbyterians and members of the Reformed Church of America and Christian Reformed Church, it could provide a wholesome living environment and encourage morality. Had not Christ commanded Christians to be the light and salt of the earth? Did not the Bible teach that Christians had a cultural as well as an evangelical mission? Thus in politics as in all other aspects of life, Christians should follow biblical norms in order to glorify God. These Calvinists believed that Christianity could direct society both by molding its institutions and its laws and by winning the commitment of free persons to Christian principles.[99]

AN EVALUATION

Calvinists, as we have seen, disagreed over how and to what extent denominations, congregations, and individual Christians should participate in the political process. Reformed and United Presbyterians participated deeply in politics, Northern Presbyterians and members of the Reformed Church of America and Christian Reformed Church moderately, and Southern Presbyterians and Southern Baptist Calvinists very little. All Calvinists agreed, however, that government was instituted by God and therefore subject to his ultimate control. Like John Calvin, they refused to equate the state with the kingdom of God or to believe that the two were totally unrelated. Rather, they constantly proclaimed that God was sovereign over nations and politics and repudiated the notion that government was a neutral enterprise, divorced from religious convictions and God's authority. This, along with their hegemony in the National Reform Association, demonstrated their opposition to secular trends in American politics and government.

At the same time, however, Calvinist arguments that Christian individuals and beliefs should directly control American government divided theists and inadvertently encouraged many of them to support the idea, advocated earlier by John Locke and numerous Enlightenment philosophers, that religion should be relegated to the private dimensions of life. Growing numbers of Americans came to believe that religion should no longer integrate cultural life as it had for centuries. Rather, religion should be assigned to the periphery of life and government should be completely secular.

During the years from 1870 to 1915 most Calvinists insisted that the views of the majority should dominate politics and government; since Christians were a majority, their values and principles ought to control political decisions and practices. This approach made Calvinists (and other Christians as well) vulnerable to charges that they were trying to exclude non-Christians from participating in government and that they were using government to compel people to believe, or at least to behave by, their worldview.

Had Calvinists living during these years supported the alternative of cultural pluralism, they could have avoided these criticisms. And perhaps they could have prevented the political outcome of the twentieth century, whereby a new ideology, which has attempted to exclude religion totally from government, has become dominant as it has achieved majority support. Cultural pluralism insists that the different groups which make up a society should be free to develop their own versions of public life. This position opposes the idea that a single, agreed upon set of attitudes and values must control the public order. Its advocates argue that people should not be forced to consent to civil religion and to majoritarian politics, which defines and limits the public rights of individuals, groups, and institutions. Proponents of cultural pluralism call instead for consociational democracies in which the "public legal order . . . takes seriously the rights of individuals, groups, and institutions representing different world and life views."[100]

Models of consociational democracy were available to Calvinists living in the late nineteenth century in two countries from which many of them had migrated to the United States: Switzerland

and the Netherlands. In these countries proportional representation and government based upon coalitions that shifted according to various issues replaced majoritarian, "winner-takes-all" politics. If America were to adopt a pluralistic system of government, religious ideologies of various kinds (such as Calvinism, Catholicism, or the secular religions of liberalism or socialism) could be recognized as such, the false dichotomy between the religious and secular could be abolished, and Americans could more easily discuss the fundamental principles which affect their political decisions.[101]

Understanding where Calvinists went wrong in their efforts to make the United States an official Christian nation is especially important today. New groups have emerged which have conceptions of government and political intentions that are quite similar to those of late-nineteenth-century Calvinists. Although some of the goals of the Moral Majority, Religious Roundtable, and Christian Voice are laudable, many of their tactics, like those of the Calvinists in our study, are misguided. These groups fail to recognize the pluralistic character of American society. They think it is biblically correct and politically possible to make the United States a distinctively Christian nation. Such a strategy is as divisive in our time as it was in the late nineteenth century. These groups display the same inflexibility, the same lack of tolerance of opposing views, and the same misunderstanding of biblical teaching on the nature of the state as did Calvinists one hundred years ago.[102]

THE CLASH OVER EDUCATIONAL IDEALS

At the center of Calvinists' attempts to keep American culture anchored to biblical bedrock was their campaign to preserve the traditional biblical foundation of the public school system. Honest government, upright morality, and healthy social relationships, they insisted, could flourish only where children received an education grounded in biblical truth. In the years following 1870, Calvinist leaders began to detect educational trends that threatened their ideals. A. A. Hodge of Princeton Seminary sounded the alarm in 1887:

> I am sure as I am of Christ's reign that a comprehensive and centralized system of national education, separated from religion, as is now commonly proposed, will prove the most appalling enginery for the propagation of anti-Christian and atheistic unbelief, and of anti-social nihilistic ethics, individual, social and political, which this sin-rent world has ever seen.[1]

The same ideological, cultural, religious, and ethnic differences produced debate over the nature of American government and the character and function of the public school system.[2]

How could people of differing religious traditions and beliefs express their convictions in their educational system? Upon what principles could they unite to teach their children? Should they even attempt to construct a unified system or should each group with a distinctive worldview provide its own education? Out of the century-long debate over these questions four distinct answers emerged, each gaining, in the years following 1870, its own adherents. The first group consisted of Protestants who believed that the state was a moral agent under God's control and that it could not teach properly without basing its training on a biblical, and, indeed, thoroughly Christian foundation. Catholics, who sometimes argued that common schools were too Protestant and at other times complained that they were godless, comprised a second party, which desired sectarian schools supported by the public treasury. Members of a third group believed that both the state and its schools should be neutral toward all specific forms or expressions of faith, but that the schools should be based upon general theistic principles common to Protestants, Catholics, and Jews. Proponents of this third view insisted that the state's power should not be used to impose religious beliefs. Some of them thought that mandatory Bible reading and prayer violated the rights of dissenting taxpayers, while others considered these practices so watered-down that they were of little value and perhaps even detrimental.[3] Although some Calvinists advocated the second and third positions, most of them supported the first party. A small but growing band of secularists comprised a fourth party, which sought to base the public schools upon humanistic rather than Judeo-Christian principles.

CALVINISTIC CONSERVATIVES: THE CALL FOR CHRISTIAN PUBLIC SCHOOLS

Calvinists have always been strongly committed to education. Their theology, church life, and history all encouraged them to value and promote education. Their theological system fostered intellectual discipline by teaching that Christians must love God with their whole minds and be able to vindicate their faith in the court of reason.[4] The laity's important role in congregational and denominational affairs required that they be well educated. Reformed worship appealed to the mind as well as to tastes or emotions; ideas and convictions were primary in it. Worship centered around the sermon, which was to be reasoned and thought provoking.[5]

Calvinist history also stimulated their educational concern. Always requiring an educated ministry, they had founded and maintained many colleges and theological seminaries; the schools and colleges of Switzerland, France, Holland, England, Scotland, Canada, and America bore their imprint.[6]

These educational convictions and achievements led many Calvinists to labor diligently to maintain the biblical undergirding of America's public schools. Although they used the terms "Christian," "biblical," "religious," and "theistic" interchangeably in their arguments over public education, they considered inadequate any training based only upon general theistic principles. They insisted that Christianity must be explicitly taught both through the devotional reading of the Scriptures and by directly showing the relationship of scriptural truth to the understanding of the various disciplines. Such Calvinists usually pictured the educational debate as three rather than four-cornered. Often they completely ignored the view, widely held in the nineteenth century, that supported nonsectarian schools that did not teach specific Protestant views explicitly but, rather, provided a basic moral training rooted in biblical values. Many Calvinists narrowed the real options to two: a thoroughly Christian school system or a completely secular one.

Their leaders insisted that America would remain strong spiritually and its Christians would effectively evangelize the world only if its public schools remain rooted upon biblical teachings.[7] The secularization of the schools was so dangerous to American society, A. A. Hodge declared in 1887, that in comparison "the issues of slavery and intemperance sink into insignificance."[8] "Secularism will deChristianize the world," argued Sylvester Scovel, president of the Northern Presbyterians' College of Wooster, "if it deChristianizes the schools of the world."[9] Such Calvinists believed the nation could no more remain half secular and half Christian than it could have endured being half slave and half free; "in education one system must prevail."[10]

Calvinists used many arguments in their attempt to show that education must be directly based on biblical (i.e., Christian) principles and values. They insisted that God required parents *and* the state to provide this type of education. While some Southern Presbyterians and many Christian Reformed leaders maintained that education was the prerogative of parents,[11] most Calvinists accepted an alternative view, dominant by 1870, that the state was responsible for elementary schooling.[12] Yet they all agreed with Charles Hodge that Christians were bound by the "express command of God, as well as by a regard to the salvation of their children and the best interests of society to see that their children are brought up 'in the nurture and admonition of the Lord.'" Christians, Hodge concluded, were required to do this "through the state if they can; without it, if they must."[13] Others buttressed this argument by contending that the state itself was subject to God's law and on that account responsible to provide moral and religious education.[14]

These Calvinists insisted further that a nation's schools should represent the convictions of its citizens. In the United States, Charles

Hodge said, church and state were as distinct as a church and a bank. Yet, if Christians controlled a bank, they must conduct its business according to biblical principles, so far as those tenets applied to banking operations. Likewise, Hodge declared, a nation where 90 percent of the citizens were Christians should be governed by Christianity, so far as its spirit and precepts applied to matters of civil government. If the state did not base its schools on the Bible, it trampled upon the rights of the majority.[15] While the state must respect the religious freedom of minorities, it could not justly ignore or disown its people's moral and religious natures or its own dependence upon the sovereign Lord.[16] Robert Dabney, a Southern Presbyterian theologian, added that the attempt to expunge religion from the schools was without historical precedent. "No people of any age, religion or civilization, before ours," he asserted, "has ever thought that a really secularized education was either possible or admissable."[17]

Calvinists and other Protestants also presented many historical considerations that they believed justified basing American public schools on biblical principles. The history of American common schools[18] as well as such customs as oaths, Sabbath observance, annual calls for Thanskgiving, tax-supported chaplains, and the opening of legislatures with prayer all testified that this nation was a Christian one. Eliminating theistic elements from school curriculums, A. A. Hodge declared, was directly opposed to the spirit and declared conviction of the founders of the nation's educational institutions. For two hundred years after the Puritans arrived at Plymouth, every college and almost every academy and high school, he claimed, had been erected to promote Christian goals.[19] Civic virtue would continue in America, Reformed Christians insisted, only if public schools provided moral training.[20] And only when moral instruction was based upon the Bible, God's authoritative standard, could it inspire proper conduct.[21] As schools became increasingly secular after 1870, Calvinists charged, they were producing less loyalty to truth, less reverence for law, and less personal integrity among their graduates.[22] In 1890 the Northern Presbyterian General Assembly summarized the common Reformed position:

> We affirm the importance of our public schools to the welfare of the people; that with intellectual cultivation must go moral training or the schools may prove a curse instead of a blessing; but this moral training must be based on religion, otherwise its conviction will not be strong enough to grasp the conscience of the people, or its utterances obligatory enough to

shape their character; that as the Bible is the source of the highest moral teaching, we regard its exclusion from our public schools as a menace to the national welfare.[23]

When America's public schools rested their education on biblical principles, Calvinists maintained, the nation received not only moral benefits but economic and political ones. Only such instruction could instill a proper understanding of vocation, stimulate diligence and thrift, and produce the concerned, unselfish citizens necessary in a democracy.[24]

Even more important to Calvinists was the argument that religious substance could not simply be tacked on to a neutral curriculum by Bible reading and prayer; rather, a biblical world and life view must undergird and inform the study of all subjects in the public schools. Although the facts of the various disciplines were the same to theists and secularists, they said, in textbooks and classroom instruction these were always selected, arranged, and reported according to one's underlying assumptions.[25] Instruction thus always reflected teachers' convictions about life. Only an education that began with biblical presuppositions about God, humanity, and the universe and that chose, classified, and proclaimed all facts from that perspective was satisfactory to most Calvinists. Reading the Bible, having devotional exercises, and even including special Bible courses in the curriculum were not sufficient to teach a Christian understanding of life.[26] Ignoring God's relationship to the world, Robert Dabney contended, was "like teaching *Hamlet* with the main characters omitted. Every line of true knowledge must find its completeness in its convergency to God," he concluded, "even as every beam of daylight leads the eye to the sun."[27]

Such Calvinists agreed with Charles Hodge that "education without religion is irreligion."[28] Failure to ground instruction upon biblical principles, a Southern Presbyterian warned in 1892, would make schools "nurseries of atheism and strengthen every downward tendency of our fallen nature."[29] "Even if overt assaults on Christianity" were not made, Dabney wrote, "studied avoidance" would produce "a hostile effect."[30] Ignoring God's relationship to history, mathematics, literature, and other subjects, Calvinists argued, promoted a false understanding: it suggested that God was irrelevant to the realities with which these disciplines dealt. Robert Thompson, a professor at the University of Pennsylvania, declared that if the schools totally ignored religion they would provide a "lesson in practical atheism that shuts God out of all but certain selected parts of life."[31]

Some added to this contention the conviction that every society had a theology that shaped and modified its culture, institutions, and laws; its schools would always teach its general view of humanity and nature.[32] Many Protestant Americans disagreed with this view. They thought that the state did not have a particular theology, but rather flourished out of the faithfulness of each religious community to its own convictions and out of the free interchange in the "marketplace of ideas."[33] Some Calvinists, however, believed that differences among Americans were becoming so significant that compromise in school instruction was impossible. Christians discerned God's hand in everything that happened while agnostics and atheists saw only natural causes and sequences, or mere accident.[34] Such subjects as ethics, law, and social science, A. A. Hodge said, could only be understood and presented either from a biblical or from a naturalistic point of view. Proposals to treat them from a neutral perspective were "absurd," for not to affirm God's relation to the universe was equivalent to its opposite — there was no middle ground, no third option.[35]

In an article written shortly before his sudden death in 1886, A. A. Hodge demonstrated his contention by analyzing several disciplines. Because the English language was the product of the thought, character, and life of an intensely religious people, a nontheistic treatment of vocabulary presented a false perspective.[36] Likewise, instruction that did not show how God's providence directed history was superficial and inaccurate.[37] And, if science classes did not recognize God as the foundation of order and rationality, Hodge continued, then they would promote materialism; for the universe could only be interpreted in terms of absolute mind or molecular mechanics.[38]

Because they believed that human beings were religious creatures and that God controlled nature and history, many Calvinists were convinced that education could not be impartial. They insisted that human beings were not born morally neutral, but rather totally depraved — inclined toward evil and at enmity with God.[39] This radically sinful bent was in conflict, however, with their religious nature. Because people were created to enjoy fellowship with God, they would always worship and give their allegiance to something or someone, whether that be God, money, self, or another human being. And as spiritual beings, their ethical natures would unfold, whether they wanted them to or not.[40] Educators, then, must seek to develop in biblically moral ways all aspects of their students — physical, mental, emotional, and spiritual.[41] The pioneers of the progressive movement in education in the late nineteenth century made the same point, though not always from a biblical perspective.

Some Calvinists supported these general arguments by insisting that secularism was itself a religion, a conclusion most American Christians living during these years rejected. Secularism, pure and simple, a Northern Presbyterian insisted in 1890, was the worst possible form of sectarianism, for it was "intolerant, zealous for its rights, bitterly opposed to anything that savors of Christianity."[42] A few secularists conceded that their philosophy functioned as a religion. Writing in the *Educational Review* in 1909, Daniel W. LaRue argued that the current instruction in the public schools reflected three major components of a religious system: a conception of the universe and its operations, a moral code that regulated conduct, and fervent devotion to a specific set of values. Restricted to the facts of science, American common schools taught a naturalistic scheme where creation, miracles, salvation, and divine providence were impossible. But they encouraged devotion to humanity and to righteous causes out of a belief in human dignity and in an orderly and beneficent nature. Finally, while rejecting faith in the supernatural and in all absolute ethical standards, the schools attempted experimentally to develop a moral code grounded upon rationalistic and humanitarian values.[43]

Calvinists repeatedly proclaimed a final argument against divorcing Christianity from public education: congregations and parents could not compensate for the loss of Christian influence in the schools. A Southern Presbyterian declared that since 60 percent of American children did not attend Sunday Schools or worship services, or read the Bible, education in biblical principles and morals could not be committed exclusively to the denominations. Moreover, even if all the children of America attended church services and Sunday School, their Christian training would be imperiled if the system of public education became "purely secular and wholly atheistic."[44] The schooling of children, Edward Morris of Lane Theological Seminary declared, "penetrates human experience at a hundred different points, influencing thought, feeling, purpose, labors, relations, [and] destinies, both earthly and everlasting."[45] Robert Dabney warned that the church could not repair the "mischief which her more powerful, rich and ubiquitous rival, the secular state," could do in "giving under the guise of a non-Christian, an anti-Christian training."[46] No court would permit a poison to be diffused, A. A. Hodge satirized, "simply because another agent actively employed an antidote."[47] Such polemics show the depth of Calvinists' fears that a school system not based upon explicitly Christian principles would eventually teach only secular values.

Thus did a substantial party of Calvinists, in conjunction with some other Protestants, seek to stem what they considered to be trends toward secularism in education and to keep American public education rooted as firmly as possible upon a biblical understanding of life. They argued that God commanded both parents and the state to give children an education founded upon biblical values. They insisted that the schools should base their teaching on the underlying convictions of the majority of their citizens. They demonstrated that Americans had originally established schools to propagate the gospel and that these schools had produced industrious, responsible, honest citizens. Secular instruction, they believed, was incomplete and morally harmful; it could not be neutral because secularism also advocated a distinct worldview. And the schools' failure to teach biblical values could not be remedied by any other means.[48]

CATHOLICS: PAROCHIAL SCHOOLS AND PLURALISM

Catholics fought what they perceived as a two-pronged battle against secularists on the left and Protestants on the right. Their frequent complaints that American public schools were too Protestant gave way after 1880 to protests that infidels and atheists were beginning to control American public education.[49]

Catholic spokesmen insisted that each denomination be given its fair proportion of the public tax fund to educate its children according to its convictions. About 1870, many Catholics in the Northeast and Midwest began a campaign to secure public monies for their parochial schools. The Third Plenary Council, held in 1884, inspired the rapid expansion of these schools and placed increased pressure on Catholic parents to send their children to them.[50] Protestants and secularists, Catholics contended, were absolutely irreconcilable; one or the other must eventually dominate the public schools. A simple and feasible plan, which would provide equal justice for Protestants, Catholics, Jews, and secularists, was to allow parents rather than the state to design and control education and to let each group have its separate system, supported impartially by a public fund. The state's role could be confined to examining and certifying teachers in all schools wishing tax support, and to apportioning funds according to the actual proficiency of a school's students in state tests. This system, Catholics argued, would correct the injustice of permitting the state to spend huge sums of money to teach an understanding of life peculiar to only one section of the community, whether it be Protestant, as they believed was the case before 1870, or secular, as it increasingly seemed to them after that date. Catholics wanted America's educational system to reflect the nation's ideological pluralism.[51]

It is ironic that Catholics and Calvinists were never able to agree on a solution to the educational problem, for they advanced almost identical arguments for basing schools on biblical values. Catholics agreed with Calvinists that God required parents to educate their children to serve and love him, and that this could hardly be done in public schools that ignored God's relationship to the world.[52] Like Calvinists, Catholics contended that reverence and worship of God were indispensable to promoting upright conduct, and they argued that American schools had been founded by Christians to promote a biblical worldview and way of life.[53] And they concurred with Calvinists that attempts to teach a few commonly agreed upon biblical doctrines and a few truths of natural religion were not enough. They wanted the entire curriculum and all instruction to be based upon Catholic principles so that their children would learn to see God in all of life.[54]

Catholic writers devoted much effort to counter arguments that their proposals would produce inferior schools in comparison with what the state's resources, centralization, and wide support could provide. State inspection and standardization were sufficient to produce good schools, Catholics replied; their parochial schools demonstrated that the denominations could provide high-quality education.[55] Catholics also denied that state schools were necessary to assimilate children into the American way of life.[56] The state's function was not to produce cultural uniformity but to secure for each individual the greatest good compatible with society's welfare.[57]

While a few Calvinists realized they agreed in substance with these arguments, most of them firmly opposed the Catholic approach because they believed it stemmed from a fundamentally different kind of Christianity whose schools would not teach freedom of conscience, civil liberty, or patriotism.[58] Many of them suspected that Romanists hoped to destroy the common school system in order to gain civil and religious power. Like many other Protestants, Calvinists were often so blinded by nativist fears of Catholic civil conspiracies that they could not see the issues clearly.[59] The two groups, therefore, were never able jointly to combat their common opponents—secularists on the one hand, and the combined Protestant and Jewish advocates of broadly theistic public schools on the other. In fact, Calvinist antagonism toward Catholics, one priest complained, was enabling a small band of secularists to take advantage of American's "dread of religious controversies" and gain influence in the schools.[60]

THE CONSENSUS VIEW:
NONSECTARIAN THEISTIC SCHOOLS

The third party in the educational dispute drew together Protestants, Unitarians, and Jews who believed that the separation of church and state and America's cultural and ethnic pluralism demanded a public school system that rested its teaching upon broadly humanitarian and theistic principles.[61]

The editors of the *Independent* and the *Outlook,* two organs of theologically liberal Protestantism, typify many who supported this view. Like Methodists, Baptists, and evangelical Congregationalists, the editors espoused this position primarily because they thought the separation of church and state mandated it, and that it best advanced Christian faith. They insisted that nations whose citizens supported and taught religion by their free gifts and not by taxation were those in which religion was most honored and most influenced peoples' lives. Thus they advocated a system where government had "absolutely nothing to do with religion" and made the public schools "entirely secular."[62] America had citizens of many faiths, they pointed out, and it was unconstitutional and unjust for civil authorities to use public education to try to promote religion. They applauded the New York City School Board for banning all "sectarian or religious" celebrations of Christmas. And they praised the Supreme Court of Nebraska for prohibiting Bible reading in the schools of that state. Using the schools to teach specific aspects of any faith, the editors argued, was both unnecessary and detrimental; by its innate superiority, Christianity would naturally win in the free competition of ideas.[63] Temperate and righteous teachers in the public schools could do much to help their students practice honesty, self-control, and goodwill.[64]

These editors uncompromisingly expressed the idea, well established before 1840 and accepted by many American Protestants after that date, that the state was a secular institution which should provide an education grounded upon general biblical and humanitarian truths. In the 1780s, when debates raged over the United States Constitution, most Christians, including Calvinists, had agreed that the federal government was to be neutral toward differences among denominations and was to mediate between conflicting groups. After the Civil War many conservative Calvinists protested that others were trying to reinterpret the concept of "religious neutrality" to mean that the government and its schools should be impartial toward the differences between theism and atheism. Accepting this reinterpretation, they complained, would sacrifice Christians' distinctive views of life and reality on the altar of cultural conformity and uniformity, while opening the way for secularists to use the government and the schools to propagate alternative views.[65] As early as 1878, Presbyterian Samuel Spear predicted this would occur. Since the government was "exclusively secular," it must prohibit all use of the Bible in the public schools. He pointed out, however, that the morality of the Scriptures could not be taught "separately from and independent of their doctrines." Because biblical ethics were based upon divine authority, they could only be taught in conjunction with the nature and character of God. This dilemma, he concluded, would eventually exclude all religious values from school instruction.[66] Others added that the Bible could not even be taught as history or literature in the common schools without "provoking controversy" or "ending inevitably in sectarian interpretations."[67]

SECULARISTS: HUMANISTIC SCHOOLS

The fourth party in the argument over the place of religion in American public education consisted of secularists who believed that frankly humanistic and naturalistic rather than biblical values should prevail. In 1909, secularist Daniel LaRue from Augusta, Maine, rejected an alliance between church and state in education as "undesirable" and "impossible." While the church assumed that through revelation it had final, absolute truth, he declared (inaccurately), the state had always affirmed that truth was relative. Rejecting experimentation, which he said the state favored, the churches encouraged "stagnation and fossilization." Because they possessed an inadequate basis for morality — God — the churches had developed a faulty educational code. They regarded humans as innately perverse and evil, whereas, he believed, the state considered them good, an opinion that finds little support in the constitutional debates of the *Federalist Papers*. He concluded by attacking one of the linchpins of both the conservative Calvinist and Catholic argument — that there was a necessary connection between religion and morality. Ethics could stand on a rationalistic, humanistic foundation, he claimed; it did not need to be based on religion.[68] Wilbur Jackson, professor of education at the University of Chicago, agreed that humanistic principles provided a better basis for morality than the Bible, which was "a bewildering confusion of myth and history."[69]

THE STRUGGLE TO CONTROL THE SCHOOLS

Until at least 1915 the theistic but nonsectarian view continued largely to control American public education, especially in small towns and rural areas. But after 1870 naturalistic and humanistic values slowly began to coexist with and in some cases replace biblical ones in common school instruction, a development bemoaned by many Calvinists and Catholics and applauded by some journalists and educators. Four factors contributed to this result: 1) By 1840, most Americans, including most Protestants, thought the state should provide education. Many of those who thereafter accepted the idea that the government — whether national, state, or local — should be functionally secular, also logically concluded that its education should be impartial, not simply toward the differences among denominations but toward distinctions between theism and atheism.[70] 2) Some Protestants underestimated or misunderstood secular challenges to American public schools and continued to believe that the schools were based more decisively on biblical values than they actually were. Thus, although Protestants held a numerical majority, their numbers and influence were reduced by the inactivity of those who saw little threat to their long-standing dominance of the public system. 3) Protestants were further fragmented by their widely differing understandings of what and how the schools should teach. Some of them thought the schools should not teach a distinctly Christian worldview. Others offered conflicting plans for incorporating the Bible into the curriculum. 4) Secular values were increasingly influencing American culture, especially its colleges and universities. As leading secularist thinkers gained teaching positions after 1890 at Harvard, Yale, Columbia, Cornell, Johns Hopkins, and other prestigious institutions, they were able to train many doctors, lawyers, teachers, politicians, engineers, and other professionals who were rapidly surpassing the clergy as cultural and moral arbiters.

Since in the previous chapter we discussed Americans' growing endorsement of a functionally secular government, in the remainder of this chapter we will explain the three other factors that enabled secular views more and more to challenge the traditional biblical foundation of American public schools.[71]

THE DEBATE OVER SECULARIZATION

After 1870 many Catholics and Protestants, especially conservative Calvinists, complained that American public schools were becoming increasingly secular; and secularists agreed. A Catholic bishop claimed in 1881 that New York had eliminated "every shade and semblance of religious instruction and usages from its common schools."[72] "Every theistic or Christian reference," A. A. Hodge lamented in 1887, was being "laboriously purged" from the public school curriculum.[73] Two years later a Southern Presbyterian study found that religious selections comprised 22 percent of the 1866 *McGuffey Reader* but only 2 percent of the 1884 *Barnes Reader*. And an investigation of textbooks used in Illinois public schools revealed that most of them ignored God's relationship to their subjects.[74]

These complaints greatly multiplied after 1900. On the basis of extensive research, William Faunce, president of Brown University, concluded in 1905 that many Northerners accepted "the extreme secularization of the schools."[75] That same year in a series of articles, Ethelbert Warfield, president of Lafayette College, protested that naturalistic evolution was widely taught in the elementary grades.[76] In 1909 Edward Goodwin of the New York State Education Department declared that even though some states allowed prayer and Bible reading in their schools, teachers could not "safely undertake to define the elemental principles that constitute the warp and woof of religious life." Growing secularization was evident, he continued, in the fact that ethical training was often based upon "the economic, utilitarian and ever-changing standard of individual and social expediency."[77] A British observer who spent a year studying conditions in American public schools reached a similar conclusion. Few teachers actually were secularists who wanted to banish all references to Christianity from the schools and their textbooks. Yet statutory and constitutional prohibitions increasingly made it difficult for them to bring their Christian convictions to bear upon their teaching.[78] Reformed Church minister David Burrell spoke for many Calvinists when he declared in 1910 that Catholics and infidels had conspired to drive the Bible from the schools.[79]

Despite these pessimistic judgments, some Calvinists who supported the National Reform Association argued that the American schools still strongly inculcated a theistic worldview. They noted that Bible reading and prayer remained widespread. The 1896-97 report of the United States Education Commissioner revealed that among the 808 schools in American cities having a population of over four thousand, 651 allowed Bible reading and 536 prayer.[80] In 1904 the Commissioner's report indicated that about three-fourths of the 1,008 schools in cities with more than four thousand inhabitants maintained one or both of these devotional exercises.

Only Wisconsin and Nebraska had decided that the United States Constitution prohibited the practice of Bible reading in the common schools.[81] Furthermore, Calvinists could have added that Protestants' numbers and social prominence gave them tacit control of the appointment of school superintendents, principals, and teachers, and that many of them labored diligently to teach biblical values. In addition, the progressive school reforms of such educators as Friedrich Froebel, Joseph Buchanan, and Francis Parker, which strongly affected American public schools after 1890, were inspired in large measure by religious conviction.[82]

Other Calvinists protested, however, that the schools retained a religious bias only in the incidentals. In their textbooks, classroom instruction, and even in their underlying worldview, public schools had largely departed from biblical convictions. The prayers that the public schools permitted were so formal and vague, A. A. Taylor, president of Wooster, objected in 1877, that they exerted only an "infinitesimal" religious influence.[83] Bible reading in American schools was made "as perfunctory and unimportant as possible," Robert Thompson complained in 1891.[84]

Leading conservatives protested that many Reformed Christians underrated the strength and influence of secularism in the schools, thus ignoring their warnings.[85] Some Calvinists did minimize the threat of secularism. Yet the exaggerated picture of secularization these outspoken conservatives presented encouraged them to do so. On the other hand, despite their many protests against secularists, Calvinists and others who wanted thoroughly Christian public schools frequently did not consider secularists their primary enemy. Often they were preoccupied with the perceived threat of Catholicism,[86] and marshalled historical reasons for considering it the more dangerous and powerful foe. Whereas Catholicism had a long history of dominating nations and still attempted to do so in Europe and Latin America, secularism was to Protestants a new philosophy, which most of them could hardly believe would ever gain political and cultural control.

CONFLICTING EDUCATIONAL STRATEGIES

While debating what values underlay American public schools, Calvinists and other evangelicals offered diverse plans for arresting trends toward and effects of secularization in education. Their inability to agree on one plan enabled secular views to gain ground.[87]

Many Calvinists who supported the National Reform Association insisted that America was a Christian country and should frame its school policy accordingly. "The only safe course" between secularism and ecclesiasticism, one NRA spokesman insisted, was "to recognize that the State had its . . . own relationship to God and the Divine Law" and thus had the right and duty to provide Christian education in its schools.[88] The majority ruled, proclaimed a Southern Presbyterian editor; it should be able to set up the kind of schools it wanted.[89] Some Christian Reformed leaders argued from this same premise that Christians should elect school boards pledged to insure that schools teach from a biblical perspective.[90] But Robert Dabney denounced this plan for "forcing the religion of the majority on the minority."[91] A Reformed Church spokesman added that it would "stir up a hornet's nest of ugly litigation."[92] Others maintained that since the public schools belonged to all citizens, including Jews, they could not be even generally Christian. Evangelical attempts to make them so violated the law and, by aiming to coerce the conscience of others, seriously hindered efforts to keep the schools on a broadly theistic foundation.[93]

Other Calvinists joined the numerous evangelicals who promoted schools that would continue to allow "simple reading of the Bible without note or comment" and prayers acceptable to Protestants, Catholics, and Jews. These schools could properly teach such religious essentials as the existence and sovereignty of God, the dependence of human beings upon him for the blessings of life, and human accountability for sinful conduct.[94]

Some Calvinists, however, protested that this solution was also unsatisfactory. A Christian Reformed editor argued that it had failed in Great Britain and would not satisfy all parties in America. Worse, it based education on a lowest common denominator of beliefs.[95] A. A. Hodge warned that if every party had the right of excluding from the public schools whatever its members believed not to be true, then obviously the ones who believed the least — agnostics and atheists — would ultimately prevail.[96]

Large numbers of Calvinists and other evangelicals wished to supplement public school education with religious instruction through such measures as Christian vacation schools, released time for students to go to classes in churches and synagogues, or voluntary religious instruction in schools before or after regular hours or during free periods. Although hundreds of school systems used one or another of these plans effectively, Calvinist critics insisted that all of them were impractical and inadequate to teach a biblical worldview.[97] Dabney added that even though these plans permitted dissent, they still amounted to the state's establishing a religion, for they used public monies to pay the costs.[98]

Still other Calvinists, like Catholics and Missouri Synod Lutherans, urged congregations to establish Christian day schools as alternatives to common schools. Some of them proposed that secularists, Protestants, Catholics, Jews, and others who desired it should have their own schools supported under what Catholics came to call a voucher system.[99] This plan advocated an educational pluralism based upon America's cultural diversity. For example, between 1846 and 1870 the Northern Presbyterians had founded 264 parochial schools, though the highest number operating in any one year was 100. After 1870, however, these efforts diminished — because of the expense involved and because many Presbyterians believed that common schools were effectively educating their children.[100] The Reformed Church of America and the Southern Presbyterians sponsored a modest number of Christian schools after 1870, and the Christian Reformed Church developed an extensive system of such schools after 1890, though of course without the help of local tax money.[101]

However, a substantial body of Calvinists, as we have seen, opposed parochial education. Some insisted that Christians should work to make their worldview dominate the public schools. Others thought public schools, as structured in the late nineteenth century, provided a satisfactory education, and many believed such schools were necessary to unify America's heterogeneous population. Some warned that efforts to secure support from public funds would produce unresolvable debates over tax monies, breed inferior schools, and undermine American consensus on values. And without such support Christian day schools would be very expensive and would divert resources from other important programs. Moreover, if Christians sent their children to these schools they would probably neglect the educational quality and worldview taught in public schools.[102]

Leaders of all parties eventually realized that their inability to agree on how to structure public education made it difficult for them to halt the secularization of the schools.[103] But their belief that public schools should be explicitly grounded upon their understanding of biblical values made it impossible for many Calvinists and numerous other Protestants to support plans that seemed to restrict Christian teachings.

COLLEGES CHART A NEW COURSE

After 1880 Calvinists increasingly complained that the growing proclamation of naturalistic and humanistic views in the nation's colleges also promoted the teaching of secular values in American public education. That year Edward Morris warned that the trend among professors and novelists to forget God's purpose and man's duty would undermine the religious commitment of those being trained in universities and colleges to direct elementary and secondary education.[104]

Some scholars have recently concluded that denominational control and guidance of collegiate education was reduced significantly in the late nineteenth and early twentieth centuries, which weakened the traditional biblical basis of the common schools.[105] As late as 1897, however, two-thirds of the nation's college students attended independent or church-related schools and two-thirds of America's more than four hundred colleges were denominational ones.[106] Secular trends, though, were apparent. State universities and colleges, especially large urban ones, which were rapidly increasing in number, were not actively hostile to Christianity, yet they did little in the classroom to promote it. Tax money spent on public colleges increased from $70 million in 1871 to $200 million in 1900, at which time it almost equalled funds given to private colleges.[107]

Several forces appear to have combined to transfer much of the influence denominations had in higher education to other hands. During the so-called Gilded Age many huge private fortunes went to support higher education, and industrialists and businessmen increasingly replaced denominations as the primary donors even for church colleges. As Christian colleges received this money, they gave businessmen more and more control over their management, curricula, faculty, and goals.[108] At the same time, rapid industrial and commerical development pressured colleges to teach more technical and vocational subjects. Students began flocking to state and urban universities that specialized in this type of training rather than to Christian colleges, which generally emphasized the traditional liberal arts curriculum aimed at producing well-rounded, cultured professionals.[109]

After 1880 increasing numbers of college and university professors rejected the Christian understanding of life and reality and taught positivist or humanist principles. Some in America's oldest private colleges and in major state universities began overtly to attack or subtly to undermine Christian orthodoxy.[110] This influence filtered down to other colleges in a variety of ways—through academic and literary journals, textbooks, scholarly monographs, and college professors trained in highly regarded universities.[111]

Like the presidents of other church-related colleges, A. A. Taylor of Wooster feared that the rise of state universities would drain students and money away from Christian colleges, thereby decreasing the church's ability to educate its youth, especially its future ministers. Because these new universities were under state control, he insisted, they would eventually become completely secular.[112] James McCosh lamented in 1880, perhaps in an attempt to gain support for Princeton where he served as president, that America's most prestigious colleges, notably Harvard and Cornell, merely bowed respectfully to the Christian faith. He insisted further that state and urban universities rarely taught orthodox Christian perspectives and principles; even if some professors were evangelicals, they did not wish to offend Catholic, Unitarian, or Jewish students and supporters.[113] Calvinists also complained that state colleges were producing very few candidates for the ministry.[114]

Other Reformed conservatives insisted, however, that much Christian influence remained in American higher education. In 1884 William Roberts reported that about half of America's 33,000 college students were members of Christian congregations, a substantial improvement over fifty years earlier. He attributed this largely to frequent revivals of religion at colleges.[115] By 1884 the "Christian Association in the Colleges," established seven years earlier, claimed to have 170 chapters and 11,000 student members.[116] Calvinists also applauded the teaching of Bible courses at Yale, Chicago, Wellesley, and other schools; and they praised the expanding ministries of chaplains, the YMCA, and the Student Volunteer Movement.[117]

Some observers insisted that most professors at state universities were earnest, reverent church members. These institutions produced many outstanding ministers, and their voluntary religious services were more effective than required chapel at Christian colleges.[118] Some even charged that Christian colleges falsely stereotyped state universities as "godless" to gain support for themselves.[119]

Meanwhile, Calvinists' protests that state colleges were increasingly attacking Christian faith and morality grew stronger. Certainly they were alarmed by the rapid increase in attendance at such institutions, and by the state schools' growing advantages in wealth and resources. By 1915 many Calvinists, while not wanting to disparage chairs of English Bible, chaplains, and the ministry of the YMCA at state colleges, believed that they were at best weak antidotes to the basically secular instruction given in classrooms.[120]

William Clebsch has argued that America benefitted as secular colleges became more influential than religiously sponsored ones after 1900 because the latter restrained free inquiry. Churchmen, he claimed, preferred indoctrination to education; their instruction was "inevitably dogmatic, domineering, and divisive," and they demanded conformity rather than encouraging the free response which intellectual progress requires. Because America needed an educational system that encouraged unrestrained inquiry into the foundations of humane, sociological, and scientific knowledge, Clebsch concluded, denominational colleges during the late nineteenth century became no longer able to serve both the nation and their sponsoring communions.[121]

In the late nineteenth and early twentieth centuries Calvinists and other Christian educators stoutly refuted similar claims that church-sponsored colleges stifled free inquiry;[122] and they argued that secularists were as bound to their naturalistic and humanistic presuppositions as Christians were to biblical ones. Christian and secular educational institutions, therefore, reflected different worldviews, rather than a commitment to reject or promote free inquiry. Those who believed God existed and directed all affairs were no less free to investigate phenomena honestly and openly than those who believed God was absent and the world operated by chance or fate. If God did exist and his providence did sustain the world, and if the Scriptures were his inspired word, then secular naturalists had a faulty view of reality; for they did not realize that an infinite, all-wise, and loving God was supreme over the universe and that human beings were responsible to him in all areas of life.[123]

In conclusion, then, the convergence in the period from 1870 to 1915 of these four factors—growing belief that the state should be religiously neutral, Protestants' misunderstanding of the nature and strength of secularism, their lethargy and their failure to agree on how to structure public education, and the impact secularism made on American society, especially through major universities—allowed secular views to gain increasing influence in public schools.[124] Arguments that basing state-supported schools on biblical convictions violated the liberty of conscience of nonbelievers, that schools which taught religious values were necessarily sectarian, that only religiously neutral schools could meet the needs of the whole community, and that humanistic education could still properly promote culture and inculcate morality were convincing to many Protestants.[125] In the years after 1870 all these factors challenged the traditional biblical foundation and direction of American education and helped prepare the way for the extensive secularization of public schools after 1930.

A MISGUIDED APPROACH

In contemporary America, busing, budget cuts, classroom discipline and violence, prayer in the public schools, declining test scores, teacher strikes, and conflicts over how to teach science, morality, and human sexuality are provoking considerable discussion about education. Those who pay tuition for private schools are placing increasing pressure on Congress for some kind of tax credit. Diverse groups of Americans are demanding greater freedom of choice and more educational opportunity in both elementary and secondary schools. Many want our school systems to recognize and reflect the spiritual, moral, and intellectual multiformity that exists among our citizens.[126] By arguing that the schools should be uniformly Christian, Calvinists unwittingly helped bring about the present public school system, which is uniformly humanistic. Their insistence that a common set of values should dominate public education has prevailed, but the values that underlie instruction have shifted from biblical to humanistic. Had Protestants in the late nineteenth century, when they were a majority, supported educational pluralism, our present system undoubtedly would be quite different and much more similar to the systems now used in Israel, Belgium, the Netherlands, Austria, and parts of Canada.

Our monolithic public school system forces those who disagree with the worldviews and values taught there to pay a second fee to send their children to schools that are consistent with their ideologies. An alternative arrangement, one suggested by Catholics in the nineteenth century, would be to establish a voucher system under which parents could direct their payment to whichever school or schools they chose. Or the state could simply apportion monies to schools on the basis of how many students they have, as some European countries do now. Under either proposal, the state could still make schooling compulsory, measure competence levels, certify teachers, establish health and safety standards, and guard nondiscriminatory regulations. Either of these systems would allow teachers to accept positions at schools consistent with their own philosophies of life. These proposals would also free schools from the tentacles of public bureaucracy, civil relgion, and federal, state, and local politics and enable them to concentrate on educational excellence. This type of system would introduce consumer choice, free enterprise, and competition into education, thereby driving inferior schools out of existence. Best of all, it would allow parents to send their children to schools that teach the worldview they want their children to learn.

6

THE CHALLENGE OF
SCIENTIFIC NATURALISM

At no time was concern about the relationship between science and Scripture any greater than during the late nineteenth century when Charles Darwin's developmental theories burst upon American culture like a deluge from a broken dam. Of all the challenges to orthodox Christianity in the years following Lincoln's death, none was more threatening than naturalistic explanations of cosmic and human origins. These new views questioned bedrock biblical assumptions upon which Christian faith and practice were based. As the most educated and informed guardians of late-nineteenth-century Christian culture, Calvinists were especially alarmed by this deluge of evolutionary theories.

In our own day, debates over how the physical world began and how to reconcile scientific and scriptural teachings have become as intense as they were one hundred years ago. Questions about the nature of evolution, the age of the earth, human, animal, and plant origins, and what to teach about all these matters in public schools are widely discussed today. Contemporary Christians are re-fighting many of the same battles waged in the late nineteenth century, but most combatants seem unaware of previous history. Examining the strategies, tactics, and results of earlier periods can perhaps help those addressing similar problems today.

In 1889 Edward Morris of Lane Theological Seminary in Cincinnati warned delegates to the Presbyterian Alliance, a worldwide association of Reformed Christians, that the scientific community could easily "become utterly oblivious of religion. The secularization of the scientific mind," he quickly added, "bodes greater evil to the cause of religion than all existing unbelief."[1] Southern Presbyterian Stuart Robinson voiced the fears of many Calvinists when he complained that the physical sciences threatened to usurp the crown long worn by theology and philosophy as "queen of the disciplines."[2]

Calvinists and other evangelicals vigorously opposed efforts during the late nineteenth century to remove scientific enterprise from its traditional religious foundation. They believed that divorcing science from its long-standing marriage with religion would seriously weaken the biblical underpinnings of American society. And it would diminish the status Christians enjoyed by virtue of their leadership in education and scientific investigation.

Historian Theodore Bozeman has recently argued that Calvinists' failure to come to terms with Darwinism in the late nineteenth century seriously damaged the credibility and cogency of their theological position, which in turn sharply reduced their cultural influence. Their commitment to a doctrine of static design in nature and their rigid understanding of objectivity, he insists, led Calvinists to cling to an increasingly repudiated concept of the universe and to drift gradually from significant interaction with the scientific community.[3] Although the Darwinian challenge to traditional orthodoxy was powerful, Calvinists responded much more effectively to it than Bozeman suggests. Their effort to reconcile new scientific discoveries with scriptural teachings was thoughtful, and their defense of theories of origins consistent with their worldviews was strong.

Calvinists in the antebellum period warned that if efforts to secularize scholarly inquiry were successful, social and spiritual chaos would result. They feared that science, conceived on naturalistic premises, would become a "snaring noose of unbelief." If science became autonomous, with no responsibility to, or dependence upon, God, a vision of reality would emerge in which both moral and spiritual values would no longer be important.[4]

In the half-century before 1870, most Calvinists remained firmly committed to the Scottish school of common sense realism, as mediated through Francis Bacon's method of induction. John Witherspoon, who arrived in 1768 to assume the presidency of Princeton College, brought this philosophy to America, where it remained the single most powerful current in general intellectual and academic circles until after the Civil War.[5] Their commitment to common sense realism led Calvinists to adopt a thorough-going empiricism, rooted in a confident trust in the senses and a belief that "abstract concepts not immediately forged from observed data" had no place in scientific explanation.[6] Devotion to induction prompted them to insist that reasoning must be founded on facts and that generalization (summarizing observed data) was the only legitimate type of explanation in science. Calvinists consistently used the inductive method of reasoning to evaluate scientific endeavors. They reminded scientists that they must base their theories solely on facts; they emphasized that hypotheses were "derivative and provisional"; and they argued that scientific explanations must incorporate all data, including that furnished by the Bible.[7]

After the Civil War, Calvinists continued to use Baconian principles for similar purposes; and this philosophy strongly influenced their response to the rise of Darwinism. James McCosh, president of Princeton College, and W. G. T. Shedd, a professor at Union Theological Seminary in New York City, were probably the two greatest American exponents of induction in the last quarter of the nineteenth century. Agnosticism was widespread among contemporary naturalists, Shedd concluded in 1893, because they followed deductive rather than inductive principles. Induction, moving from particular facts and phenomena to a general law that connected and explained them all, was favorable to the idea of a First Cause, according to Shedd, but deduction, moving from a general law to its innumerable applications, was not so favorable.[8]

Calvinists in the generation before the Civil War had to combat the assertion that mind and matter were not distinct and the claim that life was merely a chemical reaction, as well as new trends in phrenology, polygenism, and especially geology — all of which they deemed hostile to Christianity. These challenges to orthodoxy, however, were minor compared with Darwinism.

The theory of evolution did not, of course, originate entirely with Charles Darwin. His chief contribution was to supply abundant evidence that development occured in nature and, even more importantly, to devise the principle of natural selection to explain how evolution took place.[9] Because his scheme seemed totally naturalistic, it challenged orthodox beliefs in God, creation, the Fall, original sin, redemption, and life after death.[10] It questioned the long-held arguments from design as a proof of God's existence and sovereignty. And it offered a scientific basis for materialism, which previously had been lacking. Darwinism thus posed a much greater threat to Christian faith than had scientific trends of the years before 1860.[11]

STATIC AND PROGRESSIVE CREATIONISTS
ATTACK DARWINISM

For the first few years after 1859, when the *Origin of Species*
appeared, Protestant editors and ministers almost unanimously
condemned it as either atheistic or conducive to atheism and refused to make any concessions to it. Christians were not immediately troubled by Darwin's views because outstanding Harvard
geologist Louis Agassiz and other prominent naturalists assured
them that the scientific community would not generally accept Darwinism.[12] As years passed, however, more and more scientists embraced evolutionary theories and clergymen became increasingly
concerned. The appearance in 1871 of Darwin's *The Descent of
Man,* which detailed his view that humans had evolved from animals, deeply alarmed them. Along with many other theists, whether
Protestant, Catholic, or Jewish, Calvinists protested that Darwinism implied a distinct view of the universe and human life that
contradicted biblical views of God and man, sin and redemption,
society and culture, and the immortality of the soul.

Calvinists believed that scientific findings were confirming many
of their theological tenets;[13] at the same time, they considered naturalistic Darwinism an enemy. Leading Calvinists, conversant with
the major evolutionary theories, persistently labored to combat
naturalistic ones.[14] They closely followed the work of America's
most respected naturalists — Louis Agassiz and Asa Gray of Harvard, and their own Arnold Guyot of Princeton. Upon coming to
America from Scotland to assume the presidency of Princeton College in 1868, James McCosh announced that he favored theistic
evolution; and in 1871 in *Christianity and Positivism* he argued
that evolution was an organized process, guided by God, working
toward one final end. Yet he denounced naturalistic expositions of
evolution and urged Christians to separate the truth of Darwin's
theory from its error. The fact that no religious leaders attacked
his views convinced McCosh that their doubts about evolution
were due primarily to naturalistic interpretations and uses of the
doctrine. Following his illustrious instructor, Scottish theologian
Thomas Chalmers, McCosh sought to reconcile science and religion by accepting all the truths of both sanctioned by induction.
He believed he had demonstrated that the established facts refuted
the irreligious conclusions some had drawn from them; many scientific discoveries, in fact, confirmed the Bible.[15]

In the mid 1870s, Charles Hodge, who had taught systematic
theology at Princeton Seminary for five decades, joined McCosh in

challenging Darwin's theories. Hodge's *What is Darwinism?* (1874) and McCosh's *The Development Hypothesis: Is it Sufficient?* (1876), while both opposing Darwin's naturalism, elaborated two divergent Calvinistic positions on the origin of the universe: one represented the static creationist view and the other the progressive creationist. Although McCosh is usually called a theistic evolutionist, it seems more accurate to label his view progressive creation, as he differed with Hodge primarily over how God made the universe and everything in it and how long he took to do it.

An impressive group of Calvinist soldiers marched under McCosh's banner: leading New School Presbyterian theologian Henry B. Smith; Francis Patton, who succeeded McCosh as president of Princeton University and later served as president of Princeton Seminary; B. B. Warfield, Princeton Seminary's renowned systematic theologian; George Macloskie, an outstanding botanist at Princeton University; Joseph Van Dyke, a Presbyterian pastor who wrote *Theism and Evolution* (1886); A. A. Hodge, son of Charles Hodge and himself an influential Christian apologist; Congregationalist editor and amateur geologist George F. Wright; W. G. T. Shedd, who taught systematic theology at Union Seminary in New York City; and A. H. Strong, president of Northern Baptists' Colgate-Rochester Seminary.

Hodge also had able allies: Reformed Church theologian Nicholas Steffans; John Duffield, a Presbyterian minister who taught math at Princeton College; geologist John William Dawson, the principal of McGill University in Montreal; and Southern Presbyterians Stuart Robinson, a pastor, John Girardeau, a theologian, and George Armstrong, a scientist.

Although they disagreed over whether development had occurred in nature and whether Darwinism was necessarily atheistic, both groups of Calvinists advanced similar scientific and biblical arguments against naturalistic evolution and vigorously sought to reconcile science and religion. Examining these two approaches is especially important because, as James R. Moore has shown, they exemplify thoughtful Protestant responses to Darwinism.[16]

A staunch belief in Baconianism led both static and progressive creationists to denounce naturalistic evolution as an unproven hypothesis about events impossible without divine initiative and intervention. Both Hodge and McCosh insisted that Darwinism was at best a theory. Hodge underscored its "prima facie incredibility": that any single higher species could develop from a mere cell, he proclaimed, was such a wonder, "that nothing but the daily observation of the fact could induce any man to believe it."[17] Even

Darwin did not claim that his theory could be proved, Hodge asserted, but only that it was possible. This admission alone was telling to devotees of induction. With Hodge, such persons believed that ultimate certainty could be attained through inductive inference and that the only acceptable theories were proven ones. To be proven, however, a theory must explain *all* the facts — and Darwinism clearly did not. Moreover, Darwin had admitted that if one species were derived by slow gradations from another, connecting links — intermediate species — should be found everywhere; but he acknowledged that they had not been discovered. Because the genera and species of fossil animals were just as distinct as those presently living, Darwin was forced to concede that the transitional forms must have passed away without leaving any traces.[18] McCosh, Armstrong, and Shedd all agreed with Hodge that if evolution were true, a multitude of undisputed facts should be available to confirm it, which clearly was not the case.[19]

Both static and progressive creationists claimed that Darwinism contradicted other widely accepted scientific views as well: that like produced like; that inorganic could not produce organic; that mechanical power could not originate chemical action; and that genera and species displayed a fixed order. They pointed out that hybrids were infertile, that changes produced in the laboratory could not occur by natural means alone, and that artificially developed varieties tended to return to their original state. All laboratory experiments to produce life by spontaneous generation, Princeton scientist Arnold Guyot told the Evangelical Alliance in 1874, had failed. Therefore, he argued, using a common nineteenth-century argument that has been undermined by twentieth-century biochemistry, that inorganic matter could never rise to organic without outside aid.[20] No naturalist, other Calvinists emphasized, had ever discovered an example of the transmutation of the species. Darwin had shown how different types of pigeons could be produced, but not how pigeons could evolve into meadowlarks, or birds into horses. Shedd concluded that the experimental and scientific evidence for the transmutation of substance was so deficient that only "enthusiasts like Haeckel and Huxley" ventured to maintain "the evolution of the organic from the inorganic."[21]

The Achilles' heel of naturalistic forms of the Darwinian hypothesis, Calvinists continued, was that they could not explain the origin of life, the emergence within life of consciousness and reason, the order of nature, or the beneficence evident in so much of that order. Evolutionary theories, Charles Hodge asserted, did not even profess to solve the first and ultimate mystery of the universe but simply placed the origin of life in "an indefinitely distant past."[22] A. A. Hodge added that naturalistic evolution could not account for the "origin, causes, and ends of all things."[23] Neither experience nor reason, McCosh declared, could prove that matter produced mind, that mechanical action gendered mental action, or that chemical action created consciousness. Darwin's theories could not explain how life, sensation, intelligence, and morality developed.[24]

How could nature, operating by chance, produce the same regularity and order as if it followed a plan, asked other Calvinists. Charles Hodge protested that evolution ascribed to blind, unintelligent causes the wonders of purpose and pattern the world everywhere exhibited.[25] Ridiculing the idea that nature was experimental or haphazard, prominent Southern Presbyterian theologian Robert Dabney asked, Where were nature's failures, the vast remains of her random, orderless results?[26] McCosh argued that the unity and beneficence of the order running through the whole vegetable and animal kingdom indicated the action of mind.[27] "I would as soon believe that all is chance in the collection of grand paintings in the Pitti Gallery," he declared, "as that these lovely forms and colors and structures of plants and animals are not the product of an infinite intelligence."[28]

DEBATES OVER DEVELOPMENTAL THEORIES

While they shared these basic scientific agreements, static and progressive creationists disagreed over whether other scientific evidence supported the concept of development as the mode of divine creation. McCosh concurred that even the general notion of evolution as an organized cooperation of causes working toward a common end was by no means conclusively proven, yet in 1876 he acknowledged that several findings supported it. Among these were the gradual advance in geological ages from lower to higher forms; the artificial changes that experimenters could produce in plants and animals; the apparent correspondence between stages of animal life and growth of the human embryo; and the similar body structures of animals and humans.[29]

Although there was strong scientific evidence for the fact of evolution, McCosh repeatedly declared, its nature and limits had not been settled and its process was still a mystery.[30] He agreed, however, with George Macloskie, that the person who believed in the "orderly outcome by natural continuity of the present world from its past" was "an evolutionist," whether he were a theist, deist, pantheist, materialist, agnostic, or spiritualist.[31] While rejecting all understandings of development that did not hold that God created the original elements and continued to direct their unfolding, significant numbers of Calvinists by the 1880s accepted some form of progressive creation. And they generally admitted what most static creationists were very reluctant to concede: that most members of the scientific community were accepting evolution.[32]

The two groups also disagreed about the effect Darwin's theories would have. Most static creationists opposed his position because they believed that it logically led to atheism. Darwin's views had been much more widely accepted than those of earlier evolutionary theorists, Hodge and others contended, precisely because his theory denied both design and divine intervention in natural processes, and so very nicely suited the emerging secularist culture. Hodge charged that Darwin, explaining how the world might have developed mechanically without any divine involvement, had provided a scientific rationale for an atheistic understanding of life and culture. This did not mean, Hodge insisted, that Darwin and all who adopted his views were in fact atheists, but only that his theory tended to support that conviction. Excluding design from nature was, he declared, "tantamount to atheism."[33]

Progressive creationists disagreed with this conclusion. They did repudiate the "narrow and exclusive form" of Darwinism that overlooked four grand truths: the presence of God in all his works, the appearance in the cosmos of such new powers as self-consciousness and sensation, the pervasiveness of typical forms in nature, and the intuitive but irresistible notion of a "first cause" in the universe.[34]

However, McCosh and his supporters insisted that a doctrine of progressive development did not have to be interpreted atheistically but could be understood in a manner consistent with Scripture. Such Calvinists also rejected the deistic view of evolution, which asserted that God created the original germs and left them to develop solely by natural laws. "May not the God who created matter at first," McCosh asked, "interpose to introduce new powers and new agents?"[35] He believed that Darwin made a false distinction between natural selection and supernatural design, between natural law and special creation. To McCosh, the real question was not whether God existed or not, but whether he worked directly by divine decree or indirectly through natural laws. Although God could have acted immediately, he chose instead to arrange a physical cause for every physical event, except for biblical miracles. McCosh pointed out that just because God executed his purposes by agents he appointed, this did not mean that he had ceased to act. Though an event may have been decreed from all eternity, he emphasized, God was as much involved in it as if he had recently ordained it.[36] Thus, progressive creationists insisted that evolution could be construed as God's way of working out his purposes in the world. God could intervene to introduce new elements or could accomplish them through secondary agents, but either way, they maintained, he directed the developmental process.

Progressive creationists argued that rather than destroying the argument from final cause, the theory of evolution actually strengthened it.[37] While Darwin's scheme of natural selection was a plea for the reign of blind chance, Macloskie declared, the actual process of natural selection was not "a medley of accidents" but was "strictly limited and organized for a mission."[38] McCosh noted that even agnostics such as T. H. Huxley admitted that the concept of evolution did not undermine the doctrine of final cause or purpose in the universe. To McCosh, it had in fact furnished new illustrations of that doctrine and so displayed the wisdom of God. Nature perceived as evolutionary process revealed that subordinate ends were always planned and executed to promote the highest goal — the glory of God. Nature made adaptations to accomplish good results. The proof from design of God's existence and power was equally valid whether these adaptations were made in a moment of miraculous creation or in a process stretched out over millions of years. In this way, then, McCosh concluded, Darwin had unintentionally strengthened theological conviction.[39]

Progressive creationists also argued that atheism was not a necessary concomitant of evolutionary theories, but rather was fastened upon them by philosophers. It was not the ascertained facts of science that raised objections to the doctrines of creation and providence and to the practice of prayer, several insisted, but speculative theories built upon the facts.[40] Macloskie warned Calvinists that although scientific investigation itself would never result in atheism, if scientists began with atheistic premises, they would undoubtedly find them mixed with their conclusions.[41]

THE BIBLE AND ORIGINS

Although they disagreed over some issues, Hodge and McCosh and their respective allies held similar views of how to interpret the Bible, its divine authority, its agreement with recent scientific findings, and its incongruity with naturalistic evolution. They and their associates affirmed that the Bible's purpose was to teach spiritual or religious, not scientific, truth — to explain *why* not *how*. Furthermore, they insisted that since the lessons of Genesis were intended for people of all ages and all levels of culture, they were clothed in a simple, popular language that made them understandable both to the unlearned and the most learned.[42] What Genesis presented, McCosh suggested, was "not a scientific but an ocular description, such as might have been given by an intelligent observer as he witnessed the unfolding scenes."[43] Both groups believed, moreover, that the Bible was completely reliable and contained no scientific errors. Although it was not intended as a scientific textbook, the Bible was accurate in the material facts it described. It was impossible to consider the Bible's scientific teaching untrustworthy, John Duffield argued, without admitting a principle that vitiated its authority on all other subjects.[44] Of course, all Calvinists, like most Christians and believing Jews, thought the biblical story of creation was not simply a myth or an allegory to be interpreted figuratively. The first two chapters of Genesis were inseparably joined to the record of events and persons referred to throughout the Bible as real and historic.[45] "By its simplicity, its chaste, positive historical character," Arnold Guyot declared, the biblical narrative was "in perfect contrast with the fanciful, allegorical cosmogonies of all heathen religion." Its "sublime grandeur," "symmetrical plan" and philosophical orientation displayed its divine superintendence and argued for its truthfulness.[46]

Although they recognized that human interpretations of both Scripture and nature were fallible, both parties concurred that biblical and scientific evidence must, and when accurately understood, did agree. The book of Genesis, McCosh proclaimed, anticipated geology by three thousand years in describing the successive stages of the production of matter and life.[47] If the Genesis account of creation were discovered for the first time in the 1880s, he said, people would have denounced it "as a forgery," constructed by an expert in geological science.[48] McCosh believed that three North American scientists — Dana of Yale, Dawson of Montreal, and Guyot of Princeton — had clearly shown the correspondence between Genesis and geology.[49] Both Guyot and Southern Presbyterian George Armstrong spelled out the essential agreements between the findings of science and the biblical account on such matters as the earth's original creation, the separation of land and sea, and the appearance of animals and humans.[50]

Both parties of Calvinists also emphasized that the biblical account contradicted naturalistic interpretations of evolution. Materialistic evolution could not be accommodated to the Bible's assertion that humans had a spiritual nature.[51] Genesis 1:26-27 made it plain that humans were not merely one step above brutes. Members of both groups insisted that it was impossible to square the Bible's teaching that people were created perfect but fell, and thus are completely sinful, with naturalistic evolutionary conceptions that humans began in a low state and are working their way up to perfection. And both parties protested that agnostic forms of evolution rejected the necessity for, or the possibility of, the supernatural intervention upon which human atonement, spiritual life, and resurrection from the dead depended.[52]

Advocates of both positions believed that the Bible did not teach development by natural means alone; they insisted that evidence for the credibility of the Bible must be weighed against the probability of evolution without continuing divine direction. When evidence in favor of Darwin's theory became more conclusive than evidence that the Bible was not inspired by God, John Duffield asserted, "then and only then" would "candid seekers after truth" accept Darwinism.[53] Even though circumstantial evidence seemed to indicate that a defendant was guilty, Southern Presbyterian theologian Robert Dabney reasoned, he would not be convicted if an eyewitness came forward to vindicate his innocence and tell what actually occurred. The Bible was the divine eyewitness. If its literary, internal, moral, prophetic, and miraculous evidences sustained its testimony as credible, then, "even if the evolutionary hypothesis were scientifically probable, in the light of all known physical facts and laws, it must yield before this competent witness."[54]

McCosh insisted, however, that the Bible was not concerned with the question of the immutability of the species. He was convinced that Christians did not need to hold absolutely either that new species were "created immediately by God acting independent of all natural agents or that powers in nature, controlled by God gradually" raised species to higher forms "by aggregation and selection." The significant fact was that in the beginning God created the heavens and gave the original constituents their potencies, which began to act by his command.[55] As an effect could rise no higher than its cause, McCosh argued, it was necessary to postulate an outside force to explain the appearance of life, sensation, consciousness, rationality, and morality. God's progressive creating activities secured continuing order in the organic world, guaranteed the continuity of nature, and insured human progress.[56]

Other Calvinists agreed with McCosh that the method by which God shaped living things was to the student of Scripture an open question. Macloskie insisted that the term "create" did not exclude the use of the orderly processes of nature.[57] Like McCosh, Macloskie argued that God could work through natural causes (ordinary providence) just as easily as through miracles. Just because something could be explained in scientific terms did not mean that God was not working through these natural occurrences. The Christian evolutionist, Macloskie declared, could still believe in the virgin birth, divinity, miracles, resurrection, and ascension of Christ; for miracles were "extra-scientific." In short, Christians who believed that creation unfolded progressively could be completely orthodox.[58] After all, added Francis Patton, evolution did not pretend to account for the substance of anything, only its form. Even if evolution were the general pattern, miracles could still be exceptions to the norm.[59]

Static creationists, such as Southern Presbyterian George Armstrong, considered McCosh's view far superior to the common exposition of theistic evolution that pictured God as "a supreme, conscious Intelligence" and argued that "lower evolved into the higher by a whole series of successive grades and stages." What McCosh was actually talking about was the unfolding of a divine plan in harmony with the facts of science and the plain teaching of the Bible. Armstrong preferred to call this creation. Based on his understanding of Scripture, however, Armstrong raised two objections to McCosh's view of continuous creation. He asserted that Genesis 2:3 had always been understood to mean that God's work of creation ended on the sixth day. In addition, while McCosh claimed that he did not know how humans were created, Armstrong believed that Genesis 2:21-22 explicitly described how it happened.[60]

What is most striking in this extensive dialogue between static and progressive creationists was their mutual effort to combat naturalistic forms of the evolutionary theory. Although their disagreement — over whether scientific evidence supported the doctrine of development, whether all conceptions of evolution were inherently atheistic, and whether certain biblical passages should be interpreted literally or figuratively — led Calvinists to adopt different positions toward the origin of the universe and life, each group sought to protect the essentials of Christianity against naturalist challenges.

THE RECONCILIATION OF SCIENCE AND RELIGION

To counter the threat of scientific naturalism, Calvinists worked vigorously to reconcile science and religion. Unless they were reconciled, McCosh warned, intelligent youth who respected science would reject Christian faith. This reconciliation was imperative, he argued in 1888, because almost all naturalists younger than forty believed in some type of development. Continual, undiscriminating denunciation of Darwinian evolution by preachers, editors, and Christian educators could drive these scientists to a crisis of faith.[61] Thus McCosh spent his career in America trying to show how scientific and biblical truth agreed. In 1895 Macloskie credited McCosh's efforts with keeping Princeton free from religious-scientific conflict.[62]

Some static creationists, however, pronounced McCosh's approach a failure. A Reformed Church theologian protested that the "hybrid mixture of evolution and creation" was neither scientific nor biblical. Naturalists rejected progressive creation, and static creationists believed it could not be reconciled with certain biblical passages.[63] A Southern Presbyterian advised Calvinists that as a general rule attempts to "meet the skeptical scientists half-way and devise strained interpretations of Scripture," designed to make the gospel acceptable to the world's wisdom, would lead to "discreditable failure." Skeptics would give the effort little credit and Christians would lose confidence in ministers who compromised.[64]

Despite strong efforts by some scientists and skeptics to undermine the Bible's credibility and authority, both static and progressive creationists remained optimistic that religion and science could eventually be reconciled. Their belief that all truth was one, a concept many contemporary philosophers denied, led Calvinists to insist that true science could not contradict an infallible Bible. Before the First World War, few of them lost confidence that science and religion could be joined in a final holy alliance.[65]

Many Calvinists agreed with McCosh's explanation, presented to members of the Evangelical Alliance in 1873, of how science and religion would ultimately reach an accord. McCosh asked his audience to imagine that they had walked into a temple that displayed symbols and inscriptions to describe the character and history of the world. On one side of the temple was the religious explanation of reality; on the other, the scientific. To understand these figures and inscriptions, students must use their native powers and work by observation; they were not preserved from error by any special guidance. While the religious side ascribed everything to God, McCosh declared, the scientific side gave a different view, attributing all reality to the operation of natural law. Scholars did not yet see how the two views could be reconciled totally, but they saw enough harmony to satisfy them that the two corresponded. It was the same world, seen from different vantage points.[66] Macloskie, Armstrong, Charles Hodge, and most other Calvinists maintained that although faulty human interpretations of Scripture and nature prevented scientists and theologians from reaching total harmony at present, someday the conclusions of the groups would agree completely, for they were "tunneling at different sides of the [same] mountain."[67]

Dutch theologian and statesman Abraham Kuyper, however, insisted that discrepancies between religion and science would not eventually be resolved by more accurate scientific findings and more correct biblical interpretation. Such reconciliation was impossible because the human race consisted of two fundamentally different types of people—Normalists and Abnormalists—who would always develop two distinct scientific viewpoints. Declaring God unknowable and creation, sin, Christ's deity, and miracles impossible, Normalists accepted materialistic evolution. In contrast, Abnormalists assumed that God created the universe and that humans were distinct from all other species because they alone reflected the image of God. Sin had so corrupted human nature, they argued, that only divine intervention could restore humankind to its proper condition. Even though Normalists and Abnormalists agreed on many scientific facts, their root presuppositions caused the two groups to interpret and apply the facts in opposite ways. It was not science and religion that wrestled for cultural control, therefore, but two scientific or philosophical systems, each having its own faith. Disagreement over fundamental principles produced conflicts over particular issues.[68]

Progressive creationists W. G. T. Shedd and Francis Patton concurred with Kuyper that people's philosophical premises strongly affected how they weighed the facts of nature. Moreover, they maintained that the physical sciences could provide only relative knowledge because they depended upon the observations of the five senses, whose judgments were subjective and therefore unable to achieve a priori or absolute truth.[69]

Recent studies have underscored the problems of subjectivity in scientific investigation and analysis. They have shown that experimental verification is frequently of secondary importance in validating scientific theories compared to philosophical arguments and circumstantial and sociological considerations. Thomas Kuhn pictures scientific revolutions as changes from one paradigm to another by a process that is more like a "conversion experience" than a reasoned debate based on objective evidence. Moreover, Kuhn states, "since the paradigm includes not only a theory, but also a set of criteria for determining what problems are worth solving and how one recognizes a solution when he has it, there may not be any mutually agreed basis for determining whether the new paradigm is better than the old."[70] Kuhn and others point out that scientists do not habitually reject a theory if it fails to agree with all experimental facts. They repudiate scientists' claims to base their theories on nothing but logical arguments and evidence, and they demonstrate that in many cases the evidence demanded at the time a theory was introduced either was never found or else was discovered long after the theory had been widely accepted.[71] All of these considerations testify to how important one's presuppositions are in his or her scientific endeavors.

Like Kuhn, Kuyper believed that a scientist's foundational assumptions in large measure determined the conclusions he reached. Normalists and Abnormalists, he insisted, had incompatible starting-points, which led to different lines of development that would never intersect. People must choose one or the other.[72] If humans had not sinned they all would have come to the same scientific conclusions. Sin, however, distorts the understanding of unregenerate people and causes them to see the universe very differently from those who are regenerate.[73]

Kuyper urged Christians not to abandon science to Normalists, because biblical religion was based upon many facts drawn from nature. Only by presenting a comprehensive worldview built upon the Scriptures could Christians continue to win adherents. If science were severed from its traditional basis, many would lose faith in central biblical convictions.[74] Given people's different confessional stances, Kuyper declared, the only possible solution to scientific conflict was for Normalists and Adnormalists to establish separate universities.[75]

Princeton theologian B. B. Warfield, for one, strongly disagreed with Kuyper's view that theists and atheists inevitably produced two kinds of science. Although sin affected the operation of all human faculties, he argued, it did not destroy or essentially alter the nature of any of them. Thus unregenerate persons could still reach sound scientific conclusions. Moreover, Warfield asserted, conversion gave people no new faculties; instead, it substantially restored the old ones. Christians, therefore, could not produce a science different in kind from that of non-Christians. Rather, the two groups must work side by side to construct a common scientific edifice.[76]

While most Calvinists agreed with Warfield rather than Kuyper that science and religion could ultimately be harmonized, by the turn of the century almost all of them were convinced that the materialistic explanation of reality arising from science strongly threatened Christian orthodoxy. In 1916 Southern Presbyterian Robert Webb lamented that naturalistic evolution had swept across American culture like a tornado, wreaking havoc everywhere. "Every theological distress of the hour," he complained, was "traceable to its baleful influence."[77] By attributing everything that existed to matter and force, others added, naturalism excluded God, miracles, inspiration, providence, and prayer.[78] Calvinists recognized, then, that debates over Darwinism had profoundly affected many aspects of culture and society. Earlier naturalistic or atheistic schemes had never suggested that the hierarchy of the species was accidental. By asserting that the cause of all reality was not organized mind but blind force, that humans were not separated from animals by an impassable gap, and that moral law was not a revelation of God but only a statistical average, Darwinism strongly promoted trends toward secularism.

As John Dewey put it, Darwinism made possible new conceptions of the world and of man's role in it. "In laying hands upon the sacred ark of absolute permanency," he wrote in 1909, "in treating the forms that had been regarded as types of fixity . . . the *Origin of Species* introduced a new mode of thinking that in the end was bound to transform the logic of knowledge, and hence the treatment of morals, politics, and religion." The design argument, Dewey stated, had operated in two directions:

> Purposefulness accounted for the intelligibility of nature and the possibility of science, while the absolute or cosmic character of this purposefulness gave sanction and worth to the moral and religious endeavors of man. Science was underpinned and morals authorized by one and the same principle, and their mutual agreement was eternally guaranteed.

But, by demonstrating that all organic adaptations were due simply to constant variation, he argued, Darwin eliminated the necessity of a prior intelligent causal force to plan and preordain them. This, Dewey asserted, allowed philosophy to abandon the inquiry after absolute origins and finalities in order to investigate specific values and the conditions that produced them. It also encouraged concentration on the here and now and the experimentally true. Thus, Dewey contended, by redirecting human attention from transcendent absolutes to material and moral conditions on earth, Darwinism introduced new philosophical and scientific goals and confirmed naturalistic understandings of humanity and the cosmos.[79]

Realizing this, Calvinists joined with other Christians and Jews to try to prevent Americans from accepting naturalistic evolution by defending either the static creationist or progressive creationist positions. By World War I many scientists had rejected both of these views. Controversies over evolution and fundamentalism in the 1920s led many common people to reject the static creationist position. Yet Calvinists did defend an alternative that was intellectually viable for many Christians and provided a rationale for a consistent biblical worldview. They enabled Christians to maintain an island of absolute and ultimate truth while intensifying floods of pragmatism and naturalism threatened to sweep away all standards, leaving only relativity and flux in their place.

Popular perceptions and even some scholarly studies have tended to picture Charles Hodge's sharp opposition to evolutionary theories as representative of the views of the vast majority of Calvinists during the late nineteenth century.[80] As noted earlier, one major study has even suggested that Calvinists' failures to come to terms with Darwinism significantly weakened their ability to relate their principles to American culture and thought during these years.[81] However, as we have seen, Reformed Christians responded in quite diverse ways to the challenge of Darwinism.[82] While Hodge's party probably was most numerous, at least prior to 1900, during this period such leading Calvinists as James McCosh, Henry B. Smith, W. G .T. Shedd, Charles W. Shields, George Macloskie, A. A. Hodge, B. B. Warfield, George Wright, and A. H. Strong supported the progressive creationist (or theistic evolutionist) view. It is impossible to know how many Reformed laypersons agreed with them. Few ministers or lay leaders, however, criticized the citadels of Calvinist theology — Princeton College and Seminary — because of the developmental views taught there by McCosh, Shields, A. A. Hodge, Warfield, Macloskie, and others. A debate at the 1923 PCUSA General Assembly, in the midst of the Fundamentalist-Modernist controversy, indicates the position that many Calvinists eventually adopted toward developmental theories. Prominent Presbyterian layman and three time Democratic presidential candidate, William Jennings Bryan, asked delegates to pass legislation that would prohibit Presbyterian judicatories from giving money to any school that taught evolutionary theories. They refused, passing instead a substitute resolution by a two-to-one margin: a resolution declaring that the denomination would not approve schools that sought "to establish a materialistic evolutionary philosophy of life."[83] These considerations indicate that while all Calvinists opposed the naturalistic implications of Darwinism, many of them accepted or at least tolerated theistic evolution.

Their refusal to compromise with naturalistic Darwinism led Reformed Christians to debate vigorously with many scientists and philosophers during the years between 1870 and 1920. In doing so, however, they were able to defend their distinctive beliefs in a sovereign, all-sufficient God, the dignity but also the fallenness and depravity of humanity, and an inspired, authoritative Bible. And they offered to their generation and to us as well a conception of God, humanity, and knowledge not subject to the despair, relativism, and fragmentation of twentieth-century naturalism.

Contrary to the predictions of some Calvinists in the late nineteenth century, Darwinism has not been totally discredited. While scientists today continue to debate how evolution occurred, the vast majority of them agree that it has taken place. At the same time, Christians continue to argue about how the biblical account of creation can best be reconciled with scientific data. Some Christians, rejecting all concepts of evolution, insist that the world was created in 4004 B.C. and maintain that all signs of the earth's antiquity are a result of a cataclysmic flood. Other Christians believe that God originally created the world and the rules by which it operates but then allowed creation to unfold exclusively through natural processes. Still other Christians argue that God brought the universe into existence and has continued closely to guide its course. In this view, evolution has occurred, but God has carefully directed the process.[84] All groups can benefit from studying the way in which Christians in the late nineteenth century responded to similar challenges to their faith.

TRACING THE ROOTS OF MODERN MORALITY

Although church attendence and membership in America today are near an all-time high, and the number of those claiming to be born-again Christians has risen substantially in the past decade, our nation is experiencing a moral crisis. Abortions, child and spouse abuse, drug addiction, alcoholism, sexual aberrations, and crime have steadily increased in recent years. Fraud, economic exploitation, and racism continue to plague social relations. Underlying these manifestations and contributing significantly to them is a deep uncertainty about the nature of morality itself and the basis for law. Some have seriously questioned, challenged, and even rejected the traditional foundation for our ethical practices. Our present confusion over morality is in part a product of earlier historical developments. Tracing the rise of secular views of morality can help us understand the nature of many contemporary ethical problems. By teaching that all moral ideals and principles are socially produced and maintained and therefore relative, secular philosophies have weakened commitment to the Judeo-Christian foundation of ethics and law in America. During the most formative period in the development of these secular ethical systems, the years between 1870 and 1920, Reformed Christians repeatedly demonstrated what they believed were the fatal flaws of these systems.

By the first decade of the twentieth century, antagonism between two fundamentally different moral conceptions was clear. Traditional theistic moralities made divinely revealed truths the authority in ethics; such emerging secular moralities as pragmatism, naturalism, positivism, utilitarianism, and idealism did not. All these secular systems substituted various forms of situationalism or relativism for the long-standing belief in the Bible as the foundation for morality. Expressing this antagonism, such titles as "Are We Passing Through a Great Moral Crisis?", "Blasting at the Rocks of Ages," "The Modern Assault on the Christian Virtues," and "Can We Have Morality Without Religion?" adorned the pages of the popular American periodical *Current Literature.*[1] The clash between the traditional religious moral code and the one slowly evolving from naturalistic conceptions of the world, a British writer asserted, was producing conflicts between men and women, old and young, rich and poor, and nation and nation.[2] The editors of the *Outlook* warned that the moral practices during the early twentieth century threatened to sink lower than they had been in the days of Roman debauchery.[3] To the editors of *Nation* the central question of the new century was: Is secularism right? "It is right to take a purely human attitude towards life, to assume man is the measure of all things, and to believe that, even though the unseen may be there, still we can know our duty and our life without reference to it."[4]

By the 1920s it was apparent that secular ideas had significantly influenced American ethical standards and practices.[5] The impact of pragmatism and humanism in education, naturalism in the physical and social sciences, the application of Social Darwinism to business and social relationships, and even Christian antinomianism all promoted this effect.[6] Increasingly, in the years after 1890, American schools and universities taught their students to view ethics in a pragmatic way that identified the good, not with right, but with advantageous outcomes. Scientific naturalists attempted to undermine divine authority and insisted that ethics needed no absolute sanctions, but rather could be justified pragmatically. Naturalistic ideas had a strong impact not only in the physical sciences but also in such social sciences as psychology, anthropology, sociology, economics, and history. At the same time, business and social practices offered everyday confirmation of utilitarian ethics as Andrew Carnegie and scores of other businessmen applied Herbert Spencer's doctrine of the survival of the fittest to their operations. New directions in all these areas strongly encouraged Americans to base morality on flexible and practical guidelines rather than on fixed norms.[7]

While it was not until the first decade of the twentieth century that the debate between Judeo-Christian and secular moralities received widespread public attention, Calvinists had complained much earlier, as had many other Christians, that the moral implications of these secular systems were dangerous to traditional theistic views. In the first volume of his *Systematic Theology* (1872), Princeton Seminary professor Charles Hodge denounced the positivism of Auguste Comte (1798 – 1859) for teaching that the five senses were the sole source of knowledge and that therefore only matter existed for certain. Hodge and many other Reformed thinkers repudiated positivism's central premise that all morality was determined simply by physical laws and material changes.[8] James McCosh, president of Princeton College, complained in 1881 that Spencer's *Data of Ethics* and Sidgwick's *Method of Ethics* had seriously shaken the foundations of morality and had caused promising youths everywhere to question ethical sanctions. Many colleges were asleep on the edge of a volcano, McCosh warned, which was soon likely to erupt and spew ethical expediency across the land.[9]

In 1890 respected Southern Presbyterian theologian Robert Dabney joined the three major arguments — that all secular moralities had inadequate standards, improper goals, and insufficient power to inspire upright behavior — advanced by Calvinists against these systems in the years between 1870 and 1920. Speaking for many Calvinists, Dabney asserted that these systems would "never win a permanent victory over the human mind." For they provided "no moral distinction, no right, no wrong, no rational, obligatory motives, no rational end save immediate, selfish and animal good, and no restraint on human wickedness."[10]

By offering a materialistic explanation for all reality, Calvinists complained, the theory of naturalistic evolution had given strong support to such diverse philosophical systems as materialism, pragmatism, positivism, utilitarianism, and humanism. All of these systems, a Southern Presbyterian declared in 1891, denied "the existence of any eternal abstract principles of morality engraven upon the heart and read by intuitive consciousness. . . . In short, they all exalt subjectivity excessively."[11] While Kantians and pragmatists usually did not reject God's existence, Calvinists observed, they did not base ethical practices on his laws or authority. For Immanuel Kant, the great German metaphysician, the foundation of ethics was the autonomous human conscience — not divine standards. Pragmatists and naturalists agreed that the ultimate test of any human behavior was not whether it conformed to God-given rules, but whether it was socially advantageous and expedient. This meant, Calvinists argued, that they evaluated conduct not by norms, but by results.[12] Thus while they acknowledged that secular philosophies differed on some matters, Calvinists contended that none of them had a proper basis for authority, suitable ethical goals, or sufficient power to stimulate righteous conduct.

INADEQUATE MORAL FOUNDATIONS

Secular moralists could never construct a sound ethical system, Calvinists charged, because they built upon a deficient foundation. Reformed conservatives emphasized that Christian ethics were rooted in an unchanging, holy, and sovereign God who had revealed moral laws in the Bible. Because God was supremely powerful and entirely good, he provided both ultimate moral standards and the sanction to enforce them. Repudiating divine authority, secular moralities made human values the final standard for ethics. These systems provided neither a positive moral example like Jesus nor any threat of eternal punishment for disobedience.[13]

Calvinists protested especially that the ethical system of Immanuel Kant was built upon moral sand. Kant acknowledged that humans were obligated by conscience to perform their duty but declared conscience to be autonomous, independent of God. To Kant, reason legislated within the soul by its own right; the will of God had little to do with determining questions of duty.[14] Francis Patton contended that Kant failed to see that the most rational explanation for the intuitive idea of "oughtness" was that it resulted naturally from human subjection to God's moral government.[15] The conscience did not determine the good or make the law, James McCosh added; it was merely the faculty through which the good and the true were revealed. Standards of truth existed for morality just as they did for mathematics. Conscience played a vital role in ethical choices, he argued, but it could not be the final standard because it constantly erred; rather, God's infallible moral law must be the supreme authority.[16]

Agreeing with Patton and McCosh, William B. Greene, Jr. of Princeton Seminary contended that several considerations demonstrated that there was objective righteousness outside the conscience to which rational beings must conform, a view increasingly attacked by American scientists, professors, and journalists in the early twentieth century.[17] One consideration was that all peoples had a clear, distinct sense of right and wrong and, given human selfishness, the force and extent of agreement on morals among them was remarkable. Equally important was the pervasiveness of the concept of duty. Although individuals often desired emancipation from this idea, they could not silence its imperative. Moreover, Greene declared, human experience taught that the world was constituted and administered according to absolute standards.[18]

Despite Kant's belief that fundamental moral truths could be known intuitively, Francis Patton argued, in the final analysis he was a utilitarian. The German thinker declared that moral action was a response to an a priori dictate of the will without reference to the consequences; yet when asked for an example of a universal maxim, Kant gave one that promoted personal advantage or general well-being. To Patton, there were two ways to settle such a particular ethical question as "should laws be passed against theft?" Human beings must either have transcendent norms to guide their behavior, or they must pragmatically test the maxim by asking people whether they preferred to live in a thievish or honest community. "If I take the latter plan," Patton maintained,

> I surrender my a priori morality and am no better than Spencer, Mill, and the empiricists generally. This is exactly what Kant does. To Kant, if I seek for a norm of Right, I make a concession to heteronomy. I pay deference to an external will. This is exactly what, as a Theist, I am bound to do. And this only shows we must have a theistic basis for morality or accept some form of the happiness theory of ethics.

Kant's attempt to find a *via media* failed, Patton said, for morality must rest on a higher standard than the individual conscience. Ethical principles sanctioned only by the human will eventually come to rest on convenience and expedience.[19]

McCosh and others observed that subsequent thinkers had strongly assaulted Kant's view of conscience. John Stuart Mill explained human moral convictions by his theory of the "association of ideas." Herbert Spencer argued that conscience was merely the collective remembered experience of one's ancestors. Materialists explained moral beliefs as simply the product of the movement of molecules in the brain. All these alternative explanations had helped undermine Kant's view of intuitive morality.[20] In 1899 a writer in the *Presbyterian and Reformed Review* declared that

> Kant's categorical imperative used to be the final word in the ethical controversy, but today this is set aside for a doctrine which robs the inward law of its authority and sets the soul adrift on the shifting currents of human opinion. It doesn't matter what a man believes if he is sincere.[21]

Calvinists insisted that the naturalistic moralities rapidly displacing Kant's moral systems offered an even less suitable basis for ethical authority. Christians had always believed that morality was a law, written by a higher power on the tablet of the soul. Naturalists could neither account satisfactorily for the intuitive sense of duty nor show the intimate connection between the moral and religious natures.[22] History demonstrated, Calvinists and other theists repeatedly declared, that human beings could not abandon their religious beliefs and maintain righteous conduct, an indication that the moral and religious natures must have had a common origin.[23]

Naturalists, however, taught that the two natures arose from different sources — morality from the needs of sentient nature, religion from some "morbid imagination."[24] According to the chief architect of the new naturalistic ethics, Herbert Spencer, the theory of natural selection was destroying the sacred sanction of moral injunctions, causing them to lose their authority. Because so many were rejecting the conception of a supreme righteousness, whose codes defined what was good and directed conduct, it was imperative, he believed, to place morality on a secular foundation.[25] Behavior, Spencer concluded, should be considered good or bad to the extent that its total effects were pleasurable or painful. Moral standards were not given by the gods; rather, they had developed progressively through the interaction of social convention, education, and environment.[26]

Calvinists agreed with Spencer that epistemology and ethics were closely connected. If people abandoned belief in God, they would naturally reject the authority of the Bible and its moral system. Without a divine sanction, ethics logically would be subjective, based on each person's inclinations.[27] It was futile, McCosh maintained, to believe that people would love God with all their hearts if they thought that the argument for his existence had been demolished.[28] "If you take away from men the belief in the supernatural and the authority behind the categorical imperative," another Calvinist added, "you destroy all incentive to morality."[29] To materialists, Reformed conservatives argued, the concept of authority was, in fact, absurd. For will, conscience, and duty were not real entities or feelings but were merely the product of molecular movement in the brain.[30] Although most materialists would deny it, Francis Ferguson argued, their view logically implied that thought was "as mechanical as digestion"; conduct was as "purposeless as soda-water." Materialism, therefore, could not provide an authority sufficient to enforce the law.[31] Calvinists believed intensely, as Lyman Atwater put it in 1880, that "morality severed from the light and sanctions of religion" was "maimed and paralyzed." Thus they especially denounced naturalistic ethics, one of the systems arising out of Darwinism.[32]

Although appreciating their support against materialists, Calvinists believed that Idealists also had no adequate basis for moral authority. Idealists emphasized human moral freedom and the primacy of the mental or spiritual over the physical or material. Led by Josiah Royce, a Harvard philosopher, they attempted to show that naturalistic interpretations of Darwinism could not adequately explain the human predicament or inspire upright behavior. Francis Patton protested, however, that Royce attempted to do what "even Jesus could not do — find some self-supporting moral ideal." Royce discovered this absolute in Universal Will, a common consent underlying all thought. But, Patton argued, common consent was "not a proof of righteousness." By making human opinion the supreme arbiter in moral decisions, Royce had "founded the Lofty Ought on the Paltry Is."[33]

Calvinists strongly denounced materialism and idealism, yet paid little attention to Reform Darwinism, which was also a powerful current in the late nineteenth century.[34] Reform Darwinists, such as Henry George, believed that although human beings were the product of natural evolution, the emergence of consciousness and the capacity for care had added a new dimension to the evolutionary dynamic which made it possible for people to help and to love one another. Calvinists may have ignored the ethical views of Reform Darwinism because they were preoccupied with positivism, Social Darwinism, and materialism, all of which denied the existence of God, the authority of Scripture, the spiritual nature of human beings, and important biblical ethical teachings.

By the first decade of the twentieth century another ethical system, the pragmatism of Charles Pierce, William James, and John Dewey, was adding a further challenge to biblical ethical standards. While Pierce originated pragmatism as a philosophical system and Dewey spelled out its implications for education, politics, and social action, Harvard psychology professor William James was its primary popularizer. Although in some areas pragmatists had to battle against Social Darwinism and idealism, which were dominant in late-nineteenth-century America, their philosophy soon became more widely accepted than these others.[35]

Many factors made pragmatism appealing to Americans. The powerful impact of evolutionary theory, the alleged inadequacy of traditional logic, the extraordinary progress of modern science, the increasing emphasis on utility and effectiveness in industry, and the theological influence of Kant, especially as mediated through Ritschl, all contributed to its growing attractiveness.[36] Pragmatism's emphasis on the practical, its support of religion's claim that there was an area of human experience into whose fundamental meaning science could never penetrate, and its argument that the religious worldview was superior to a materialistic one from a functional and emotional standpoint made it attractive to many Americans.[37]

Despite pragmatism's differences with other current philosophies, Calvinists charged, the ethical views of pragmatists similarly repudiated divine authority as the basis for morality.[38] According to one Southern Presbyterian, pragmatists revived the ancient Greeks' and Romans' fundamental error of reducing every principle to a practical test.[39] For them, the postulate that was true would "work" the best in daily life. John Dewey claimed that ethical theory had been "hypnotized by the notion" that its goal was to "discover some final end or good or some ultimate and supreme law." Rather, he insisted, people must believe in a "plurality of changing, moving, individualized goods and ends."[40] This, Calvinists argued, was precisely pragmatism's central problem; it had no ultimate standard for judging what worked best. Granted, pragmatists were devoted to social expediency, not merely individual advantage; they insisted that the welfare of all humanity and not of any group or person was the governing goal.[41] But, Robert Dabney protested, utilitarian principles could lead people to use evil means to achieve good results. "If the consequences of the evil act, so far as foreseen, seemed beneficial, it would be right to do it."[42] Calvinists insisted that the chief weakness of all utilitarian systems was that expediency could never produce oughtness. In fact, without an absolute standard, they argued, the best would always be relative and in flux.[43]

All these philosophies — positivism, Kantian ethics, materialism, and pragmatism — a Southern Presbyterian concluded in 1891, had made "no authority" Satan's slogan in the present age. "In politics, business, science, morals, and religion he raises up anarchists, soulless corporations and impersonal stock companies, materialists, evolutionists, and rationalists to push the campaign, either by tearing down the flag of authority completely or by shifting the base on which it is planted."[44] Removing the divine sanction for moral conduct, Calvinists warned, left only human standards, which were temporal, whimsical, and insufficient. Without the protection of a transcendent lawgiver and a supernatural moral code, people could always be victimized by political, economic, or intellectual elites or subject to the tyranny of the majority.[45] To McCosh, doctrines of expediency and concern for the public good were inadequate to restrain selfishness and lust, and so keep humans from preying on one another.[46] Even naturalistic evolutionists, such as T. H. Huxley and Herbert Spencer, did not know by what sanctions the new morality would be enforced; they could only hope that the social instincts, hereditary conscience, and desire to serve others, characteristic of any "refined mind, conversant with history," would overrule passions and direct conduct. When Spencer banished religious sanctions to the region of the unknown and unknowable, Calvinists averred, he rested morality on political and social sanctions that depended on the general beliefs and sentiments of the community and the age. Spencer insisted that history was moving toward a millennium when all people would act morally, for all motives to sin would be eliminated.[47] But until this golden age was reached, he offered no ethical absolutes to inhibit and counteract people's natural depravity.[48] In short, Calvinists argued, all secular schemes of morality led to relativism and subjectivity, for lacking fixed and final commandments, the only basis they could offer for ethics was common human opinion, the will of the majority, or the arbitrary values of an elite.[49]

IMPOVERISHED ETHICAL GOALS

Not only did secular philosophies have no adequate basis of moral authority, they also seemed to Calvinists to offer insufficient goals for ethical behavior. They did so largely because they misconstrued human nature. Whereas Christian ethics declared that humans were dependent upon God and morally depraved because of sin, secular ethics falsely assumed that people were self-sufficient, able to be wise and good without any divine assistance.[50] How could secular moralists construct proper rules for either individual conduct or social life, Calvinists asked, when they so completely misunderstood human nature and destiny?[51]

Reformed leaders maintained that secular moralists' faulty ethical goals led them to devise inappropriate methods for promoting human development and achieving individual happiness. As utilitarians having no transcendent standards, secularists tended to consider collective humanity God, and serving humanity the supreme object of moral action.[52] Christians insisted, by contrast, that humanity's highest end was to glorify God.[53] But by serving God, Calvinists added, people would best help others and most enjoy life. Those who sought happiness as their chief goal would never obtain it; true felicity was a by-product of doing God's will. This was so, they continued, because God created human beings to have purpose and joy only as they realized their calling as his children and servants.[54] Nicely summing up this Calvinist contention, George Patton wrote in 1895:

The individual in order to realize his own best interests is, according to Christianity, bound also at the same time to manifest "brotherly love" (altruism) which is the life of the community and the condition of progress. ... And conversely in manifesting brotherly love which has its root in the love of God, the individual attains to perfect happiness. Only along these lines can the problems of social evolution be solved.[55]

While arguing that the ethical goals advanced by secular moralists would not promote good moral conduct, Calvinists also insisted that their goals were inconsistent with their naturalistic premises. Francis Patton objected that naturalistic evolutionists could not be consistent and defend ethical ideals, for their philosophy taught that whatever existed was right. On what basis, he asked, could materialists say that people should love each other and "struggle for the lives of others" to enhance survival?[56] If humans were merely accidents of nature, added Francis Ferguson, why were they significant? Strip evolution of its illogical presupposition that human life was intrinsically valuable, he declared, and it would seem pessimistic and nihilistic.[57]

INSUFFICIENT POWER

Calvinists further claimed that secular moralists could not inspire people to act righteously. While the example of Christ's sinless life and belief that God's kingdom was advancing on earth motivated most Christians to be loving, kind, and just, even under difficult circumstances, secular systems espoused no moral idea that would produce self-sacrifice and virtue in cases where such actions brought humans only suffering and danger.[58] Patton insisted that secularists' arguments would rarely convince those who considered virtue irksome to behave morally; secularists could merely plead with people to act uprightly.[59] The ultimate value of secular moralities, happiness, was not sufficient to regulate human conduct. Suppose, Ferguson said, that a Fijian told a positivist that he found his greatest happiness in murdering his fellowman. The positivist could only expound the beauties of altruism. But, Ferguson concluded, the single trait of beneficence would never be strong enough to counter the selfishness of humanity.[60] Only love for God, another Calvinist declared, not the quest for personal gratification, could inspire individuals to obey the moral law.[61]

Lack of potency, declared Scottish theologian James Orr, had been the fatal weakness of every ethical system divorced from Christianity. All purely prescriptive moralities had this defect.

Without the inner compulsion and incentive of Christian faith, he claimed, some individuals might live righteously but the masses would not. Only the example of Jesus and the empowering of the Holy Spirit, Orr concluded, could inspire people to obey the biblical commandments. For a personal relationship with God brought new light to one's mind, "new power to his will, new support in temptation, new elevation of his feelings and purification of his affections."[62]

The gospel, Francis Patton added, had the power to transform personality and a norm for character; naturalism had neither. Naturalists failed to recognize that the underlying principle of law was not "do this," but "be this."[63] Mere external conformity to right precepts was not enough, declared Baptist theologian A. H. Strong. All actions must be judged by the thoughts and motives from which they sprang.[64] Although some secular ethicists maintained that only those actions inspired by love were morally right, James McCosh wrote, they failed to recognize that by eliminating God, they had abolished the basis for and the source of love.[65]

While Christian morality affirmed humans' depravity and their inability, by their own strength, to keep the law, Strong said, it supplied reasons for obedience and the aid of the Holy Spirit to make this obedience possible.[66] By contrast, McCosh declared, secular moralities were powerless to prompt people who constantly sought to satisfy their own appetites to do noble actions or even to prevent them from doing evil.[67]

In fact, some Calvinists argued, the rigid materialistic determinism of naturalistic ethics made morality impossible because it obliterated human free agency. "If the mind of man," wrote a Southern Presbyterian, "is but a piece of organized, refined matter, subject to material laws, it is no more morally accountable than the falling tree which breaks your bone."[68] The logical conclusion of materialistic ethics, that one's behavior is completely determined by a chain of physical causes within him, others protested, absolved the individual of all responsibility and removed all motives for good conduct.[69] Although some made this same charge against the Reformed doctrine of predestination, Calvinists claimed that God's plan incorporated rather than eliminated free agency.[70]

SHIFTING MORAL STANDARDS

From the Pilgrims' landing at Plymouth to Lee's surrender at Appomattox, the public apologists for American morality had been Christians. Prior to the Civil War, American morality had, in the words of Stow Persons, a "distinctly religious cast." In the years after 1865, however, "the Christian view of life steadily gave ground to a more secular frame of mind," as secular moralities mounted a significant challenge to Judeo-Christian teachings that God created and imposed moral truths. Evolutionary doctrines, biblical criticism, and philosophical materialism, Person insists, joined to place religion on the defensive. Under these circumstances longstanding belief in fixed moral standards weakened as utilitarian, situational views were increasingly accepted. To Persons the most important factor in altering American views of morality was a newly emerging complex of naturalistic ideas propagated in literature, psychology, economics, and the physical sciences.[71]

During the years from 1870 to 1920 the biblical ethics espoused by Calvinists and other theists gradually became less and less practiced, for at least five interrelated reasons. One important factor, as we have seen, was the reduced influence of Christianity in the common schools. Before 1890 these schools had been a chief means for presenting biblical morality to the masses.[72] After that date they less forthrightly taught a morality based on a Judeo-Christian foundation.[73] Second, the increasing proclamation of secular principles in some state colleges and urban universities challenged traditional American ethical views. Their positions in these schools allowed secularists to teach their moral views to many educated Americans.[74] After attending classes, interviewing faculty, and examining professors' lectures from Connecticut to California, an author writing in *Cosmopolitan* during 1909 declared that much teaching in American colleges attempted to weaken allegiance to the Christian moral code. Many scholars repudiated "all solemn authority," he reported, and considered the decalog "no more sacred than a syllabus." The philosophies of William James and William Sumner, he concluded, had led many professors to regard moral laws not as finalities but as in flux.[75]

A third development that prompted increasing numbers of Americans to reject biblical ethical teachings was the rise of new viewpoints in the natural and social sciences. By advancing a naturalistic explanation for all reality, many scientists and professors helped erode belief in the authority of the Bible. Some of them strongly challenged traditional beliefs in fixed standards and eternal truth. In the years following 1870 many psychologists shifted the foundation of their discipline from metaphysics and theology to biology and the physical sciences. Anthropology and sociology, which emerged as new disciplines in the late nineteenth century, were also strongly influenced by mechanistic conceptions of evolution. In addition, history and political science increasingly employed relativistic and reductionistic methods during these years.[76] At the same time, for some Americans science replaced religion as an object of devotion and worship and a source of strength and certainty. It offered the most validated truth, provided the most venerated method, and guaranteed the most valuable achievements. Its amazing advances in knowledge and its marvelous technological improvements promised to bring a new age.[77] Both the natural and the social sciences then diminished confidence in the authority upon which Christian morality was based and sanctified the experimental methodology of the new morality.

Christians' neglect of biblical moral responsibilities and duties and their frequent failure to live by their own ethical standards during the early years of of the twentieth century was a fourth factor that promoted growing acceptance of secular moral principles.[78] During this period Calvinists and other evangelicals often protested that congregations were not providing sufficient instruction on moral issues. "One of the more notable defects" in contemporary preaching, the editors of a Southern Presbyterian periodical lamented in 1910, was "the absence of the ethical element, clear cut, outspoken, and bold."[79] Too many ministers, added William B. Greene, preached the gospel exclusively as a plan of salvation rather than as a way of life.[80] Christian attitudes and actions toward blacks, poor people, and immigrants, the crass materialism of some Christian industrialists and financiers, and the immorality of some confessed believers also encouraged Americans to reject biblical morality. Moreover, the growing polarity between Christians that erupted into the fundamentalist/modernist controversy of the 1920s further prompted some to question Christian doctrines and traditional ethical practices.[81]

A final factor that pressured Americans to abandon their longstanding moral beliefs was the industrial and social climate of the early twentieth century. During these years industrialization, urbanization, and massive immigration made human relationships more complicated and broke down traditional community and neighborhood restraints. For many the anonymity and impersonality of city life replaced the close ties and mutual accountability of small town and rural living. At the same time, countless Americans became preoccupied with business ventures, commercial achievements, and material gain. While some vigorously promoted industrial efficiency and productivity, others pursued pleasure and plenty, which were made increasingly possible by rising standards of living. All of these developments combined to diminish commitment to traditional ethical values.[82]

By the 1920s the conflict between secular and Christian moralists had become intense. Bertrand Russell complained in 1925 that current morality was a "curious blend of utilitarianism and superstition" (the latter word, to Russell, primarily meant theism) and that superstition still held the upper hand.[83] It was clear, however, to political philosopher Walter Lippmann in 1929 that the old morality could no longer inspire Americans to practice their traditional ethical values. Its authority has been radically undercut. Yet no new ethical system had clearly replaced it. Looking to the future, Lippmann called for a new humanist morality to replace the discredited biblical one and joined John Dewey, Harry Elmer Barnes, and others to bring this to fruition.[84]

Secular humanism differed fundamentally from many of the naturalistic schemes of the late nineteenth century. Its proponents found value in the teachings of the world's great religions and denied that the universe was totally mechanistic. With the advocates of biblical ethics they rebuked dishonesty, theft, slander, and greed and affirmed love and faithfulness. Yet they agreed with materialists that ethical standards were not given and sanctioned by God and that people must rely upon their own inward strength to act properly. And with pragmatists they affirmed that all norms must be tested by experience.

For the past fifty years American ethical practices have been based upon a curious amalgamation of secular and Judeo-Christian moralities, systems with fundamentally different views of ethical authority, goals, and motivation. Because biblical ideals have been so deeply imbedded in the fiber and flavor of American institutions and life, and because many individuals have remained firmly committed to biblical values, these convictions have continued to sustain the moral practices of many Americans. Yet since the 1920s secular philosophies, especially humanism, building upon foundations laid in the years between 1870 and 1920, have also powerfully influenced the validation and principles of ethics in American education, politics, economics, and society. Humanists' insistence that human beings are autonomous and that morality should be based upon common or shared human values rather than on divinely revealed teachings has contributed significantly to our contemporary confusion over moral principles and practices.

8

THE SPIRIT OF CAPITALISM REVISITED: WORK AND ITS REWARDS

After the Civil War the currents of Marxism, Social Darwinism, the Gospel of Wealth, and business pragmatism seemed to Calvinists to be pushing popular American economic philosophy and practice away from its traditional Christian moorings. Conceptions of the nature and meaning of work, emerging collectivist ideologies, intensifying conflict between management and labor, attitudes toward wealth and poverty, and standards of business ethics seemed to rest increasingly on secular assumptions. Calvinists responded to such developments by denouncing the "loveless competition of the business world, the unbrotherly relations of classes, the low level of business morals," the "ruthless and unfair" trusts and the "appalling" poverty and economic injustice of the large cities.[1]

Reformed leaders determined to advance what they considered a proper biblical understanding of economic tasks and relationships. Yielding to a secular vision in these matters would profoundly alter both churches and society. For people's jobs and standard of living helped shape their attitudes and their sense of self worth. And unrest, arising from changing industrial and economic conditions, was producing continual strikes and repeated violence.[2]

The Industrial Revolution, which had been gaining momentum in America since 1820, broke forth with full force after the Civil War and rapidly transformed the face and character of American society. While Christians could sometimes ignore or minimize new intellectual challenges to their traditional beliefs, they found it extremely difficult to neglect the immense social changes that industrialism produced — burgeoning cities, with their poverty, dilapidated housing, drunkenness, prostitution, and crime; massive immigration; and decreased agricultural opportunities that threatened long-established rural patterns and expectations.

Considering the economic realm vitally important and believing that the Bible commanded Christians to direct it, Calvinists strongly challenged the contention that economics was a "science of natural fact and law, from which all moral considerations" must be "rigorously excluded."[3] Christian Reformed professor Louis Berkhof repudiated the growing conviction that biblical teachings should have no influence upon economic activity.[4] Christianity was much more than a system of individual salvation that placed human beings in a new spiritual relationship to another world. It should also affect their status and conduct in the social and civil relations of earthly life. Indeed, the Bible supplied principles to structure all areas of individual and social life. Many Calvinists, therefore, urged Christians to labor to win individuals to Christ and to place social relationships on a biblical foundation.[5] They denounced the Gospel of Wealth for, as R. H. Tawney put it, trying to convert religion "from the keystone which holds together the social edifice into one department within it" and to make economic expediency "the arbiter of policy and the criterion of conduct."[6]

Reformed Christians refused to capitulate to increasing pressure to regard work primarily as a means of sustenance and material gain. In this they followed John Calvin who declared labor to be a divine service rather than a necessary evil as many in the Middle Ages conceived it to be. Christians should not renounce the world but master it for Christ's sake. Winthrop Hudson has demonstrated that Calvinists promoted economic development so strongly not primarily because they believed that material success indicated divine election, as Weber and Tawney maintained, but rather because they sought to glorify God in all areas of life and to practice Christian stewardship.[7] For most Calvinists, work was "part of the church's missionary faith," a "means of subduing the world to the purpose of God."[8] By teaching that Christians could serve God through business vocations as well as ecclesiastical ones, Calvin encouraged people in various occupations to dedicate their labor to God.[9] After the Civil War Calvinists continued to emphasize their traditional economic virtues — industry, frugality, thrift, and careful provision for the future.[10] Yet they also urged Christians to consider their vocations callings from God, means by which each one could help build culture on biblical principles.[11]

To Reformed Christians, God's sovereignty implied human

stewardship. The world and all its resources belonged to God; therefore, peoples' talents, treasures, and time were his, to be used wisely to advance his purposes.[12] The cultural mandate of Genesis chapter one, Calvinists maintained, instituted labor as a means of subduing the earth and creating a society pleasing to God. They therefore repudiated interpretations that work was a result of the curse placed on humanity after the Fall or that it was a purely secular activity devoid of spiritual and moral purposes. Rather, work should enable individuals to achieve material, intellectual, physical, and moral satisfaction.[13]

Calvinists also reacted sharply against the various forms of collectivism that were beginning to challenge Western capitalism in the late nineteenth century. Socialism, communism, rural co-operatives, and increasing governmental intervention into the life of society frequently prompted their protest. This is not surprising in light of the well-known historical connection between their doctrines and the rise of capitalism, through the idea of calling and the ethic of frugality and productivity.[14]

But Calvinism's affinity for capitalism is often overdrawn. The government of Reformation Geneva regulated prices, wages, and employer-employee relationships, prohibited monopolies, aided industry and commerce, and promoted social and economic stability through binding contracts. Calvin's early followers practiced a middle way between communal and individualistic economics. Private property belonged to individuals, but Christians were obligated to use their possessions for the common good. By preaching and personal example, Calvin hoped "to make the social and economic code conform more closely with the law of love."[15] Although his ideas promoted the development of commerce and industry, they neither produced nor sanctioned that form of *laissez-faire* capitalism which, as in Adam Smith's economics, made the law of nature supreme and taught each person to seek his or her own benefit. Calvinists believed, rather, that a sovereign God controlled all things and commanded his servants to bring him a bounteous harvest.

Although they disagreed with secular economic philosophies, almost all Calvinists strongly supported a free market, accenting the responsibilities of individuals more than those of communities. By and large, they believed, as did most evangelicals, that capitalism was the most biblical, practical, and just economic system, and they resisted all forms of collectivism.[16]

Calvinist combat with socialism illustrates these themes. While they realized that socialism could take several forms, they correctly judged that Marxism was and would remain its chief expression. And they considered Marxism a complex movement that challenged traditional religious, moral, economic, and political beliefs.

THE CRITIQUE OF MARXISM

Calvinists' primary objection to Marxism was philosophical rather than economic. They regarded it as an alternative worldview stemming from the application of materialistic notions of evolution to history. It seemed to them to be the economic wing of a naturalistic offensive that sought to alter conceptions of culture that Christianity had previously shaped.[17] Not only did Marxists reject the biblical God, but they replaced him with a false god — the state — and sought to empower it to override God's providence.[18] For thousands of workingmen, declared Northern Presbyterian social activist Charles Stelzle, socialism itself had become a substitute for the church.[19] Marxists sought to abolish all traditional religions because they considered them an opiate the bourgeoisie used to dull the discontent of workers.[20] Marxism, Calvinists warned, wanted not only to destroy religion but the social and moral underpinnings of American life, especially marriage and the family, as well. By rejecting God, Marxists had abandoned "the foundation of all morality and virtue" and consequently had embraced ethical relativism and expediency.[21] Only property and religion, Marxists argued, caused more social misery than marriage did. Because this institution encouraged selfishness, produced conflict, and hindered the collective interests of society, they sought to abolish it. In so doing, Marxists "disavowed the sacredness of family relations and marital vows" and ignored the role the home played in fostering affection, loyalty, care, and nuture.[22] By divine design, Calvinists contended, marriage and the family guaranteed individual and social welfare by propagating the race, regulating sexual activity, and socializing children. Destroying these institutions would therefore undermine God's pattern for social relationships and produce a decadent society.[23]

To Calvinists, the Marxist economic scheme was both visionary and unjust. It was quixotic because it assumed that changing economic relations would effectively transform society; it attempted to make the world better without making people better.[24] Calvinists considered Marxism economically impractical because they believed it was built on several economic fallacies and would not sufficiently motivate people to work hard. Marxists refused to acknowledge that land always produced more under private ownership than under common ownership. By decreasing personal involvement and stake in the economic success of a venture, they argued, Marxism reduced individual incentive.[25]

Furthermore, Marxism would not merely depress economic productivity; at its very core it was an unjust system that proposed using "robbery" to accomplish justice.[26] To take away savings from those who had foregone pleasures to build them was to Lyman Atwater of Princeton Seminary not only unfair to individuals but destructive to the best interests of society.[27] Marxism could not be instituted without stealing from some to give to others and, other Calvinists declared, it could not be perpetuated without additional unfairness. "Justice allows to each man," one of them argued, not an equal share in society's returns, but one "equivalent to the element which he contributes to those returns."[28]

Marxism also abolished the God-given right of private property. According to Charles Hodge, the privilege of owning property rested "on the will of God as revealed in the constitution of our nature and in our relations to persons and things around us." It was analogous to the rights of life, liberty, and the pursuit of happiness.[29] The socialist argument that property was theft conflicted with the eighth commandment, which protected individual ownership, and with biblical teaching that all possessions were a trust from God. It also nullified the tenth commandment, which prohibited coveting one's neighbor's property.[30] The desire to own property sprang from a God-given "primal instinct of acquisitiveness." Because socialism denied this instinct, argued William B. Greene, Jr. of Princeton Seminary, it was a "reform against nature."[31] God had so constituted human beings, Hodge declared, that they desired and needed the "right of the exclusive possession and use of certain things." Moreover, he added, God made the right of property essential to the health of society and implanted a sense of justice in human nature that condemned all violations of this right.[32]

Calvinists considered Marxism's root problem to be its belief, inherited from Greek and Renaissance philosophers, that humans were essentially good and self-perfectible. Its theorists ignored the evidence of revelation, reason, and history that humanity was fallen—morally and spiritually helpless without God's redeeming and restraining grace. To believe that merely destroying competition would eliminate human vices and produce an ideal society, Calvinists argued, was hopelessly naive.[33] Societal ills could only be corrected by chopping away their roots in human selfishness and materialism.[34] A Southern Presbyterian proclaimed that if legislation could solve social problems, the law of Moses would have

remedied them long ago.[35] While Christians should seek to develop
the best possible social and economic system, other Reformed conservatives added, true hope for a better society lay not in reforming
the environment but in regenerating persons.[36]

Their faulty understanding of human nature led Marxists to
what Calvinists argued were unrealistic views of work and economics. Because people were prone to selfishness and sloth, they
would not work as diligently under socialism as they had under
capitalism. "Who would work hard," asked Lyman Atwater, "just
to have the excess taken away?" Marxism would quickly demolish
all capital formation, he protested, by removing every inspiration
to abstinence, frugality, savings, and accumulation.[37] And if capital
were not recompensed properly it would not be invested, and therefore laborers would lose their jobs and societies built on industry
and trade would collapse. Offering a standard Reformed objection
to all forms of socialism, one Calvinist wrote in 1891 that the great
defect of social critic Edward Bellamy's *Looking Backward* (1889)
was not so much its lack of economic as of moral and social insight.
"Insure to man half a life of leisure and a large command of
wealth," he warned, "and the tragic element in life would soon
overwhelm society."[38]

Calvinists also charged that Marxism was built upon faulty
political principles. It rejected the biblical concept that each societal
institution — which in modern times meant home, church, factory,
school, and state — was supreme in its own area.[39] Denying biblical
teaching that the state should not control other societal institutions
but merely settle conflicts between them, Marxists sought to extend
the tentacles of government into all aspects of life. Making the state
all-powerful, Calvinists protested, would destroy the check and
balance among social organizations, make totalitarianism likely,
and greatly restrict human freedom.[40] Socialist efforts to establish
equality ignored the sacred right to individual liberty and thus
would hinder social development.[41]

These convictions also led some Calvinists to protest against
excessive government involvement in the economic sphere. Most
of them believed that government could significantly help the poor
and working classes by providing police, sanitation, pure food and
water, safe factory conditions, and good common schools, by in-
specting tenement houses, and by passing child labor laws. They
insisted, however, that governments could not change certain economic facts or human nature. The cost of food and the level of
wages varied with supply and demand. The state was powerless to
redeem people and remove their desire to exploit one another.

Moreover, Calvinists proclaimed, the Bible limited the functions of the state for sound reasons. If not restricted to its proper province, the state could dominate life, stifle other institutions, and crush individual freedom.[42]

While they denounced collectivist ideologies, Reformed Christians admitted that many of the abuses which Socialists deplored were serious and demanded immediate attention. Society's true foes, one of them declared in 1883, were not Karl Marx and Henry George but the callous rich. Christians should applaud Marx and George for so clearly exposing the social evils of the day.[43] A Southern Presbyterian agreed with Edward Bellamy that nearly half of the products of America were "seized by middlemen" and that the present tendencies of competition were anti-Christian.[44] Neglect of the law, mocking of justice, "oppressive inequality among men" and the mad rush of educated and influential classes for "the dollar, for prominent positions, for sport or leisure," others lamented, explained the growth of socialism.[45]

Although most Calvinists rejected Christian Socialism as an impossible hybrid, a tiny band supported it. Speaking for the majority, William Greene disagreed with Charles Stelzle, who said that a "Christian had a perfect right to be a Socialist," if he or she was convinced that the system was "morally and economically" sound. Socialism, Greene insisted to the contrary, was essentially irreligious and unjust.[46] Yet some Calvinists, like William Sloan of Helena, Montana, praised Christian Socialists because they stressed industrial cooperatives and educating the working classes, yet acknowledged that without changes in human hearts, bettering external conditions could not remedy social problems.[47]

The Calvinist answer to social problems, like that of most other evangelicals, was thus a blend of individual transformation and societal improvement with the accent placed much more strongly on the former. As Sloan put it in 1902: "social regeneration would only follow individual regeneration."[48] "Certainly," Greene added in 1911, "the civic corruption and the social evils in America demand radical reformation." He insisted, however, that churches, families, and governments could best bring God's kingdom on earth by attacking the causes of social ills rather than the results, by stressing what he called "preformation," the nurture of individuals in the Christian faith, more than reformation.[49]

THE LABOR QUESTION

Adding to the growing conflagration that threatened to engulf society in the late nineteenth century was the intensifying clash between management and labor. Charles Hopkins, Henry May, and others have extensively described this conflict and have pictured Calvinists either as aloof from it or as strong supporters of property rights and the status quo.[50] In the years between the Civil War and World War I, however, Reformed conservatives expressed great interest in industrial problems, tried to help both owners and workers, and after 1900 some of them endorsed labor unions.

Before 1900 most Calvinists supported only those unions which restricted their activities to resisting unfair practices of their employers and to supporting members in times of adversity through savings banks and life insurance policies.[51] Lyman Atwater, the most influential Reformed spokesman on industrial relations in the 1870s and 1880s, objected, however, to unions' demands of equal wages for all who did the same task, no matter how varied their skill, conscientiousness, or efficiency. This policy destroyed craftmanship, decreased productivity, and encouraged sloth. Atwater also denounced unions' practice of limiting the number of apprentices who could learn a trade, calling it a "conspiracy against the fundamental rights of men to choose the occupation for which God and nature have fitted them and of society to enjoy the most advantageous use of the faculties of its members." And he deplored union interference with the liberty of employers and employees to hire or accept employment by whomever they pleased and upon whatever terms. The success achieved by unions, he protested, was gained not at the expense of capital but of nonunion labor.[52]

Similar objections to union practices prompted Christian Reformed leaders to encourage Christians to organize their own unions. Spokesmen protested that the aims of existing unions were "unmitigated, selfish materialism" rather than the glory of God; their approach toward both employers and nonunion workers was hostile rather than constructive; and they used means that infringed on the rights of others—boycotts, strikes, closed shops, and, occasionally, violence.[53] Thus, following Abraham Kuyper's example in the Netherlands, members of the denomination organized the Christian Labor Association in 1910, the Christian Business Alliance in 1911, the Christian Carpenter's Union in 1913, and two other unions in 1914. None of these, however, was very successful or influential.[54]

Many Calvinists especially objected to unions' calling of strikes. In the long run, Atwater declared, the effectiveness of all other objectionable features of trade unions depended "upon the success of the strike," which usually involved "some lawlessness and violence."[55] Some Calvinists also complained that unions sought to prevent nonstrikers from taking the places of the strikers — a direct violation of the God-given right to work. And strikers attempted to force capitalists to stop production and to keep them from promptly fulfilling their contracts.[56]

Strikes, others added, brought no financial benefits to any party because they could not permanently alter the normal rate of wages determined by the relationship of supply and demand. The free competition of capital for labor would raise wages more quickly and permanently.[57] Any action that prevented labor or capital from being fully utilized, whether it were strikes, business timidity, or economic stagnation, decreased production and thus lowered the rewards of both capital and labor. Strikes especially hurt all parties, for when they occurred laborers received no wages, capitalists made no profits, and consumers were forced to pay higher prices.[58]

After 1900 some Calvinists began to take a more positive attitude toward unions. Alexander McKelway, a Southern Presbyterian editor and social activist, declared in 1902 that in spite of certain abuses, unions had significantly helped workers, especially by encouraging them to cooperate and by making their jobs more secure.[59] George Greene argued in the *Princeton Theological Review* in 1913 that unions had benefitted workers by raising their standard of living, shortening their work day, making working conditions safer and more sanitary, preventing the exploitation of women and children, providing safeguards against unemployment, supporting public education, assimilating immigrants, and promoting temperance and international peace.[60]

Most Calvinists insisted, however, that improved industrial relations could be best achieved not by pressure tactics on the part of either management or labor but by applying biblical principles to employer-employee relations and to labor legislation. They repeatedly maintained, as James McCosh did before the Evangelical Alliance in 1887, that just as Christ had refused to divide inheritances among heirs, the church could not take either side in the battle between capital and labor. Rather, the church must mediate between the two parties, supporting both of them in their common ends.[61] Industrial relations could be amicably adjusted, a Reformed Presbyterian argued, only "by writing the law of Christianity upon the minds of both employer and employed and infusing the spirit of Christianity into their hearts."[62] Others stressed that the Bible commanded employers to pay fair wages, guided by principles of love and brotherhood, rather than by the law of supply and demand. As God's stewards, accountable to him, employers should be just in their requirements and assignments, get to know workers personally, and provide job security and such practical benefits as evening classes, sick pay, and savings banks.[63] At the same time, however, Calvinists urged laborers to respect and support their employers, to work conscientiously and diligently, and to realize that in serving their companies, they were serving God.[64]

Although they continually declared that legislation alone could not abolish industrial strife, Reformed Christians did support laws they judged would help laborers or society. Through publications, sermons, the resolutions of their general assemblies, and sometimes through political action they backed legislation advocating reduced working hours, one day off in seven, a minimum wage, cleaner and safer factories, conciliation and arbitration in industrial disputes, protection of consumers, and restrictions to keep trusts from crushing smaller competitors.[65]

Many Calvinists considered arbitration a key that could open the door to better industrial relations. They endorsed conferences that brought management and labor together for discussion and mediation, and urged each side to cooperate and compromise for the common good in order to give laborers a decent wage and capitalists fair compensation.[66]

Profit-sharing plans also gained the support of some Calvinists. America could solve its industrial problems, Lyman Atwater maintained, if laborers were allowed to share "in the fortunes of the business." Pointing to a factory in Fall River, Massachusetts, where profit-sharing had resulted in "astonishing prosperity and unexampled development,"[67] he concluded that such plans made workers much more content and efficient. Atwater also praised a cooperative building and loan association in Philadelphia that had enabled laborers to own stores, homes, banks, and even small manufacturing companies.[68]

In the final analysis, Calvinists thought the effectiveness of proposed methods of dealing with the labor question — unions, legislation, arbitration, and profit-sharing — depended upon the faithful exercise of Christian principles in the industrial arena. The Fall had shattered individual and social life; both needed to be redirected. Most schemes to improve industrial relations, however, assumed that human problems stemmed from outward circumstances and thus exaggerated the importance of changing the environment.[69] Most Calvinists believed that regeneration would make employers just and generous, and workers honest and diligent.[70] "The Christian virtues rightly adjust all relations, parties, and duties," Lyman Atwater declared, "and the anointing of the Spirit so lubricates all the parts and movements of society, that friction and collision disappear."[71] Thus, while supporting education, legislation, negotiation, and economic principles they thought would better conditions for workers, owners, and consumers, Calvinists insisted that the regenerating power of the gospel was "the mightiest instrument in ameliorating and elevating" social conditions.[72]

BUSINESS ENTERPRISE AND THE GOSPEL OF WEALTH

After the Civil War America's growing glorification of the pursuit and possession of wealth also challenged Christian economic beliefs. Many historians have argued that after Lincoln's death Christians departed from their own historical ideals in developing the Gospel of Wealth. Rejecting their traditional beliefs, which had allowed for failure and poverty and had provided solace for the poor, Christians increasingly endorsed acquisitiveness, success, and riches.[73] Clergyman Russell Conwell and industrialist Andrew Carnegie both insisted that it was the duty of every person to get rich. Advocates of affluence declared wealth to be the just reward of talented entrepreneurs and organizers and argued that most poor people were indigent because they were lazy. Historians have often assumed that because most Calvinists belonged to the middle and upper middle classes they promoted, or at least tolerated, the Gospel of Wealth.[74] There seems, however, to be little evidence to support these assumptions.

By and large, Calvinists neither glorified wealth nor condemned poverty. While not critical of honestly acquired riches, they took very seriously Christ's teachings that people could not serve both God and money and that earthly treasure tended to keep individuals from heaven. Union Seminary professor W. G. T. Shedd protested in 1893 that most Christians sought too high a standard of living. "Any careful reader of the Bible" would see, he maintained, "that competency and not wealth" was the Christian's proper goal. He concluded that love of money was the root of many of the evils afflicting believers.[75] Making the pursuit of riches one's chief end, others added, destroyed spiritual life.[76] A Southern Presbyterian emphasized that Christ's warning about wealth aimed not only to foster spiritual growth but to prevent overindulgence, hoarding, and oppressing the poor.[77] In 1905 a Northern Presbyterian editor declared having riches to be a great responsibility that could be truly enjoyed only by those who use them for the good of others.[78] "The greed of Mammon," he protested later that year, was "the peril of the new century."[79] Others spelled out the nature of the peril: the misuse of wealth decoyed people into "worldliness, idleness, and frivolity" and nourished indifference toward both God and his creatures.[80]

Many Calvinists denounced fraud, speculation, and practices that crushed competitors, gave unfair advantages, and hurt the public. A Southern Presbyterian insisted that speculation in future values violated the Golden Rule. In legitimate trade both parties should benefit, he argued, but in speculation each tried to gain an advantage at the expense of the other.[81] Lyman Atwater maintained that such a "venture" was "simple gambling."[82] "If a rich man steals $5,000 from the poor by speculation," a Reformed Presbyterian pastor lamented, "he is pronounced a shrewd man of affairs."[83] The editor of the *Presbyterian* complained in 1880 that the recent business boom had been a false one caused by "a reckless and audacious spirit of speculation"; and he excoriated manufacturers who ceased production when their products were selling slowly in hopes of creating a boom by enforced scarcity.[84] Other Reformed leaders protested that corners, freezing out, and watering stock were counter to the Spirit of Christ. Although Calvinists believed that monopolies could prevent the problem of overproduction, they generally deplored their attempts to crush competition, control wages, and force the public to pay unreasonable prices.[85]

Calvinist spokesmen urged businessmen to be rigidly honest, unvaringly just, and unceasingly generous.[86] They denounced railroad rebates as dishonest and unfair and repudiated attempts of businessmen to transfer moral responsibility from themselves to an artificial person called a corporation, which could act by different ethical standards.[87] The leading theologians of both the Northern and the Southern Presbyterian churches, Charles Hodge and Robert Dabney, condemned such violations of the eighth commandment as representing an article for sale to be other or better than it was; adulterating food, medicine, and cloth; taking undue advantage of the ignorance or necessities of buyers; and depriving people of property on legal or technical flaws. "However we get our neighbors' goods without his intentional consent and without fair market value returned," Dabney argued, "is theft." If a buyer took advantage of the urgent need of his neighbor to force a sale at a lower price than would have prevailed under normal circumstances, Dabney reasoned, he robbed his neighbor of the difference.[88]

Calvinists especially opposed the growing inclination to consider productivity and profit rather than service and benevolence the primary goals of business. America's well-being should not be measured by the level of its production, some Reformed leaders maintained, but by its spiritual health, domestic peace, and social justice.[89] They deplored the increasing emphasis on self-reliance, cutthroat competition, efforts to sell to consumers products that brought them no benefits, and obsession with profits. Rather, Calvinists urged Americans to depend on God, cooperate in the marketplace, consider consumer needs in designing and selling products, and make serving God their chief aim.[90] Although secularists and Reformed Christians agreed that diligence and hard work were essential, they differed fundamentally over economic goals, motivations, and purposes. Calvinists argued that love not utility should guide all social ethics including economic practices.

While believing that poverty frequently was a result of character, some Calvinists insisted that environmental factors also strongly contributed to it. True, many poor people were lazy, shiftless, and wasteful.[91] But slums, saloons, crime, and soulless corporations also helped to produce poverty. Oppression, exploitation, and legalized vice, some declared, prevented the poor from making a decent living. A Northern Presbyterian pastor argued in 1874 that the densely populated cities fostered ignorance, indolence, and immorality, which soon became a "necessary inheritance," entailed "with all the force and regularity of law ... from one generation to another." The cities often created conditions that crushed or at least discouraged "every ennobling aspiration." This "tide of corruption" swept its victims along into thievery, drunkenness, and prostitution, often making people unable to help themselves.[92] The 1910 Northern Presbyterian General Assembly stated similarly that much poverty was "due to preventable disease, uncompensated accidents, lack of education, and other conditions for which society is responsible and which society ought to remove."[93]

Although Reformed conservatives often proclaimed that both great riches and dire privation were hinderances to spirituality, they believed both wealth and poverty had their uses.[94] Christians could seek wealth as long as they kept this goal secondary to promoting God's kingdom and righteousness. Although the Bible often associated divine blessing with the increase of worldly possessions, some said, the Christian's chief rewards for work were moral and spiritual rather than material.[95] Likewise, poverty was neither an accident nor a punishment. With divine help it could promote salvation because it kept one's attention riveted on God rather than on goods.[96] Economic losses, like other adversities, often brought blessings that were "richer, greater, stronger and more productive"; they encouraged perseverance, dependence upon God, and deeper companionship with family and friends.[97]

Leading Calvinists also underscored the obligation all Christians had to provide for the poor. Both the Old and New Testament instructed believers to assist those in need.[98] Only those willing to renounce all their belongings for Christ, some argued, were truly his disciples.[99] Others insisted that helping the poor required Christians not only to practice charity but also to stand strong against oppression and economic injustice.[100] "Any church which fails to bring the Gospel to bear upon the poor," Charles Hodge observed in 1871, "fails in its duty to Christ."[101]

Some Calvinists insisted upon a more equal distribution of wealth, even while resisting socialism. "The object of giving as set forth in the New Testament and observed in the apostolic church," a Northern Presbyterian proclaimed, was to diminish "those trying differences which appeared where there was both superfluity and want."[102] Many others shared his belief that laborers were not receiving their proper share of American wealth, and called on Christians to pray and work for a more just apportionment.[103] They generally argued, however, that redistribution be done voluntarily. Under proper Christian guidance, large portions of existing fortunes could be used to relieve poverty and suffering, to propagate the gospel, and to establish and endow educational and benevolent institutions that would primarily benefit the poor.[104]

Although Calvinists were pleased by the phenomenal growth of American wealth after 1870 and the social benefits it made possible, they warned that the pursuit of riches brought great temptations. They refused, therefore, to glorify a "gospel" of wealth, to sanctify "getting ahead," or to reject the poor as necessary victims of the struggle for survival. As Charles Hodge put it, "the monstrous doctrine . . . that the strong are always right; that those who succeed ought to succeed; that we must always take sides against the afflicted and downtrodden is simply diabolical."[105] Like the Social Gospelers, but in a different manner, many Calvinists insisted that biblical principles must reform society, control the use of wealth, and direct the care of the poor.

In the late nineteenth century the currents flowing from Adam Smith's *laissez-faire* economics and its "secular doctrine of calling," from the rationalist notion that God was unconcerned about earthly life, from Social Darwinism's glorification of competition and progress, and from the Gospel of Wealth's accent on acquisitiveness and material success, came together to provide a complex and powerful rationale for excluding biblical principles from economic policy. These developments influenced Americans living in the early twentieth century to restrict Christ's rule to the inner consciousness, the "spiritual life," of individuals.[106]

Most Reformed Christians refuted the assertion that economics and work were totally profane activities divorced from God's concern and direction. And many of them also denounced attempts to conduct business purely on pragmatic principles.[107] They repudiated the argument that industrialists, financiers, and merchants should do whatever was necessary to make the highest profit, regardless of the means or the principles involved. Biblical standards of justice, honesty, cooperation, and mutual love, they declared, applied in economics as much as in any other sphere of life. Calvinists insisted that the secular understandings of economics and work, of relationships between capital and labor, of wealth and poverty, and of business practices that arose in the late nineteenth century would be deleterious to individuals and society. Only by grounding economic life on biblical principles, they proclaimed, could people find enjoyment and fulfillment in their work and could society achieve harmony and justice.

Many of these same economic problems continue to plague contemporary America. Materialism is widespread, fraudulent advertising abounds, dishonest and unfair business practices are prevalent, many workers feel alienated, absenteeism, vandalism, and employee theft are common, and the debate between capitalists and socialists persists. Fortunately, increasing numbers of Christians are recognizing that the gospel applies to their business and financial practices. Many are again realizing that scriptural principles should guide how they spend their money, what type of investments they make, what kind of houses they buy or rent, what type of jobs they do, and a host of other economic questions. Some Christians are offering sound counsel on these matters and growing numbers of believers are attempting to organize businesses consistently on biblical principles.[108] All Christians today can benefit from studying the response of nineteenth-century Calvinists to similar economic issues.

9

THE CROSS AND THE SOCIAL ORDER: CALVINIST STRATEGIES FOR SOCIAL IMPROVEMENT

Massive immigration from Eastern Europe, industrial and technological innovations, the expansion of urban centers, racial tensions, and the rise of socialism and Social Darwinism combined to produce much social upheaval in the late nineteenth century. Industrial exploitation, financial manipulation, the unchecked growth of private fortunes at the expense of the poor, widespread political corruption, moral complacency, and intensifying nationalism made this period one "of unrest, of deep dissatisfaction, and perplexed questioning."[1] These and other social problems, Calvinists warned, threatened to undermine Christian standards in the state, marketplace, and society.[2]

As we have seen, Calvinists employed several different strategies in dealing with sociocultural issues. Southern Presbyterians and some Northern ones insisted that the institutional church should not "meddle" in civil and social affairs and were generally passive toward social questions. Reformed Presbyterians refused to vote or hold civil offices, but they, along with United Presbyterians, continually worked to improve social conditions through denominational, congregational, and individual efforts. Members of the Christian Reformed Church and the Reformed Church of America as well as most Northern Presbyterians displayed considerable diversity toward social questions. Some of these Calvinists ignored social problems; others diligently worked to ameliorate them; most expressed concern about them but did little to alleviate them directly.

Despite their differences, however, most Reformed Christians held several common assumptions about social issues. While sig-

nificant numbers of Calvinists enthusiastically promoted both individual regeneration and social reform, most of them labored more
strenuously to win souls to Christ than to remake society. Like
most other evangelicals in the late nineteenth century, Calvinists'
preferred strategy for abolishing political, economic, and social
evils was striving to redeem individuals. People themselves, not
their living and working conditions, caused most social problems,
Reformed Christians declared; as individuals committed their lives
to Christ, they would naturally begin to improve social conditions.
Yet, even though they gave priority to individual conversion, Calvinists made significant efforts to eradicate social ills directly and
accomplished more than most historians have credited to them. In
the final analysis, however, most Calvinists did overemphasize individual change; few of them recognized or worked to remedy
those structural and institutional patterns in American society which
perpetuated exploitation and injustice. An examination of Reformed strategies for social melioration, of their response to the
Social Gospel, their efforts to help the unfortunate, and their attempt to abolish the liquor trade verifies these contentions.

CONVERSION AND SOCIAL RECONSTRUCTION

Calvinists often argued that evangelism and social action were a
yoked team that must work in tandem to advance the kingdom
convoy. The two were not antagonistic, one said, but "bound together by the benediction of God in the holiest wedlock."[3] Individual and social change reinforced each other, James Howerton
added; "progress towards one is essential to progress towards the
other."[4] Princeton Seminary professors Charles Erdman and William B. Greene, Jr. taught students that social service and evangelism were "indivisible." And Calvinists in all denominations
supported the Men and Religion Forward Movement, which in
1911 – 12 successfully joined these two emphases in a continent-
wide crusade.[5]

Yet, even while they declared Christian progress hitched to this
yoked team, Reformed Christians tended to spur evangelism and
bridle social action. Working to convert individuals, many of them
insisted, was the most effective way to improve society. They repeatedly claimed that good schools, just social relations, honest
and wise economic practices, and righteous laws were collateral
benefits of Christianity; congregations best promoted such things

not by working directly to accomplish them but by faithfully carrying out their main duty — preaching the gospel.[6] This was so because Christ first changed individuals' hearts and *then* their new life-styles began to affect social conditions.[7] Philanthropy, unless it was tied to spiritual renewal, rarely did much to better the world, but conversion often inspired believers to reform society.[8]

Moreover, many Calvinists warned, engaging directly in politics or making social improvement their primary aim would divert congregations from their more important evangelistic and spiritual tasks.[9] The Bible directed congregations to make worshiping God, proclaiming salvation, and instructing converts in the Christian faith their chief priority. The careers of Social Gospelers, William Greene added, demonstrated that "the church was shorn of her strength" when it substituted "the programme of social reform for the gospel of [the] grace of God."[10] Yet many Calvinists urged Christians to work through voluntary organizations to improve social and political conditions.[11] Many insisted further that clergy held a prophetic office that required them to denounce political oppression, economic exploitation, and social injustice from their pulpits.[12]

While all Calvinists believed that society could be reformed only as individuals were converted, many also agreed with James Howerton that "individuals cannot be easily saved except as social evils are remedied."[13] Improving living conditions, making government more effective and factories safer, some argued, would not save souls. But as human hands had once rolled away the boulder allowing the resurrected Lazarus to walk out of his tomb, so Christians could remove the barriers of ignorance, drunkenness, divorce, poverty, and political corruption that hindered people from committing their lives to Jesus Christ.[14] Thus many Calvinists urged each pastor to engage energetically in social service "not as his chief work, but as an aid to making men hear his Gospel message."[15]

Most Reformed Christians sought to enact good laws, arguing that such statutes could both restrain human depravity and educate people about their moral and civic duties and so produce at least outward conformity to God's standards.[16] Many of them insisted with John Calvin that law could order and guide human life in such a way that God's grace became embodied in the social order.[17] By producing a higher level of morality and a more informed public conscience, Christianity could help develop a more humane and benevolent society.[18]

While laws served these good aims, Calvinists continued, they could not eradicate all social problems. Even the best ones could not make the poor rich, the criminal honest, or the drunkard sober.[19] "No party platform, act of Congress or decision of the Supreme Court," George Greene of Princeton Seminary wrote in 1912, could "enforce the supreme principle of Christianity — love of God and neighbor."[20] Even Woodrow Wilson wished to curb peoples' "appetite for laws as the remedy for all ills."[21] Legislation is truly effective, Reformed conservatives declared, only when individuals willingly choose to obey it.[22]

SOCIAL REFORM AND THE KINGDOM OF GOD

While holding these views about the relationship between evangelism and social action, most Reformed Christians were confident that Americans could construct a better society by building more firmly on a biblical foundation. Calvinism, they declared, had contributed significantly to the development of political liberty and industrial democracy and constantly promoted efforts to establish a more just social order.[23] Especially important in determining Reformed views of the means, nature, and pace of social melioration were their history and theology, particularly their understanding of Christ's kingship. William Greene emphasized that the doctrine of God's sovereignty in history and salvation stimulated Christians to serve God through their vocations, homes, and statecraft in order to bring the affairs of society under the rule of Christ.[24] Calvinists, who believed that biblical principles should guide all human activities, denounced efforts to confine the influence of Christianity to the church and family life. Most of them expected the city of God someday to be established on earth, but they contended that spiritual weapons alone would enable the gospel to triumph over the tremendous forces of evil that opposed it.[25]

While Christ was the supreme King, in the present age his empire was locked in a struggle to death with the kingdom of this world. A truce between these two foes was impossible, Reformed Presbyterian professor James Coleman declared, for they were diametrically opposed and irreconcilable; one must ultimately dominate the world and direct society.[26] Calvinists claimed that Christ's soldiers would triumph in the end; in fact, whenever the gospel was properly presented, it won the day.[27] "He who constantly fears that the Kingdom of God is going to ship-wreck," wrote a Reformed Church editor, misunderstood its nature and strength and was not equipped to serve God effectively.[28] Reformed Christians thought these convictions, which they usually expressed in postmillennial or amillennial terms, motivated believers more than alternative ideologies. They argued that those who thought the kingdom of God was an obtainable ideal "capable, if not of perfect consummation, of approximation on earth, not only in the redemption of individual men and women, but in the purification of all political, economic, and social relationships and institutions" were most likely to apply the gospel's social principles throughout the world.[29] These beliefs help explain why orthodox conservatives fought so fiercely to stem the advance of secular forces, which they often considered agents of the kingdom of this world.

CALVINISTS AND THE SOCIAL GOSPEL

These convictions led many Calvinists to criticize the preeminent effort to improve social conditions in the years between 1880 and 1915 — the Social Gospel, an interdenominational movement led by theological liberals.[30] Praising their passion for social justice and their labors to reform industrial and urban conditions and to help the downtrodden, Reformed Christians supported some of the programs of the Social Gospelers. Calvinists joined with them to form the Federal Council of Churches in 1908 and to sponsor the Men and Religion Forward Movement in 1911 – 12, and both groups helped create denominational agencies to combat social problems.[31] Yet Reformed evangelicals were skeptical from the start about the Social Gospel's roots in the New Theology, promulgated by Andover Seminary professors such as Newman Smyth, and its increasing connection with the theological liberalism of Washington Gladden, Walter Rauschenbusch, and Shailer Mathews. As the twentieth century progressed, Reformed conservatives protested more and more vigorously that the movement's leaders misunderstood biblical teaching about sin, redemption, and Christian hope.

Christian Reformed theologian Louis Berkhof chastised social activists in 1913 for forgetting that "the sad problem of sin" underlay "all social misery and injustice." Their attempt to reform individuals primarily by improving their income and living conditions ignored Christ's method of bettering society by remaking individuals.[32] Treating symptoms — the social environment — would not cure social disease, other Calvinists protested. Such efforts might even delay their cure by diverting attention from the true cause of the illness — individual sin and selfishness.[33]

Social Gospelers not only neglected human depravity, Calvinists charged, they also depreciated the divine remedy for social ills: the saving power of Jesus Christ. The forces Walter Rauschenbusch claimed would produce God's kingdom on earth were to Calvinists inadequate to effect this result.[34] Proponents of progressive Christianity especially tended to minimize the ministry of the Holy Spirit, William Greene and Charles Erdman complained, and often implied that fallen people could make themselves righteous.[35]

Calvinists argued further that Social Gospelers saw social conditions through the spectacles of naive optimism. Their theological presuppositions blinded social reformers to the negative and destructive forces at work in society. Walter Rauschenbusch was "woefully mistaken," a Southern Presbyterian declared, when he asserted that all the causes which historically had kept the gospel from directing sociocultural life—"hostile civil government, asceticism, . . . the union of church and state, and a lack of political rights and interests among the masses" had "strangely disappeared or weakened" in recent times.[36] Social Gospelers failed to recognize, others added, that only God's restraint of evil by common grace, his blessings in providence, and his direction of history, especially through the first and the promised second advent of Christ, assured either individual or social reformation.[37]

THE SOCIAL MINISTRY OF THE CHURCH

Although the Calvinist program for social betterment centered upon the regeneration of individuals, a few leaders urged Christians to apply biblical teachings to state, school, marketplace, and social relations just as fervently as did Social Gospelers. Southern Presbyterian James Howerton declared in 1913 that Christians were called not only to produce "the perfect man," but also to realize "on earth the Kingdom of Heaven, of which love, justice, and truth are both the constitutive and regulative principles."[38] The role of the church, Louis Berkhof wrote that same year, was not only to nurture individuals spiritually but to teach basic biblical principles, which should direct social institutions and relationships. While ministers should not attempt to provide detailed, authoritative solutions to social problems, they should "fearlessly and clearly proclaim the broad underlying principles" upon which solutions should be based. Berkhof urged congregations to study biblical social teachings, to aid the poor and the working classes, and to form Christian philanthropic organizations. By doing so, Berkhof promised, believers would be "the leaven permeating the lump, God's chosen agents to bring science and art, commerce and industry in subjection to Him."[39]

Many Reformed conservatives shared this view of social ministry. Among them were Northern Presbyterians David Waters of

Newark, New Jersey, Charles Aiken of Princeton Seminary, and William Sloane of Helena, Montana. Waters wrote in 1884 that because the gospel brought "a saving power not only in a spiritual sense but also in a social sense," Christians must seek to make all of life "Christ-like."[40] In 1892 Aiken challenged believers to redeem society by developing a more progressive court system, meliorating industrial conflicts, and improving education.[41] A decade later, Sloan urged Christians to ease the plight of the poor, abolish social distinctions, provide jobs for everyone who wanted to work, and make factories clean and safe.[42] Numerous Reformed Presbyterians and Reformed Church of America leaders also sought to stimulate their members to improve social conditions.[43] Even some Southern Presbyterians affirmed that "hundreds of examples from the Old Testament and the New" proved that the Christian pulpit must not ignore social questions.[44]

This understanding of Christian mission led many Calvinists to support numerous constructive crusades in the late nineteenth century. Thousands of them worked to achieve a more equal distribution of wealth, child labor laws, fairer treatment of immigrants, prison reform, temperance, more wholesome conditions for the insane, and better relations among nations. As is discussed in more detail elsewhere, many Calvinists also labored to improve industrial relations and working conditions and to reform municipal governments. Conferences led primarily by Calvinists, such as the National Reform Association Convention of 1900 and the Second World's Citizenship Conference of 1913, drafted resolutions on most of these topics.[45]

Although often accused of callously justifying the accumulation of great wealth, Reformed conservatives frequently denounced those who gained fortunes by fraud or exploitation. Some of them charged that the quest for riches caused many societal ills, and they labeled materialism the chief danger to American society.[46] Behind such social evils as prostitution, gambling, alcoholism, and political corruption, declared James Howerton in 1913, stood the love of money. Only when Christians cast mammon from its lofty throne could they abolish these evils.[47] The frantic pursuit of wealth and corrupt use of power by giant corporations, others warned, was adding much fuel to the growing social conflagration.[48]

Reformed conservatives also attacked other social evils. "Child labor," lamented a Southern Presbyterian editor in 1905, "is our modern slaughter of the innocents." Joining another leader of his denomination, Alexander McKelway, the principal American proponent of child labor reform, the editor deplored the exploitation of "helpless childhood" and its sad consequence, "an ignorant manhood."[49] In churches, clubs, magazines, newspapers, indeed, to any audience that would listen, McKelway urged Americans to improve working conditions of adolescents and to establish compulsory education laws forbidding children under fourteen to work in factories unless they could read and write.[50]

THE WAR AGAINST CRIME

During the late nineteenth century Calvinists were especially alarmed by the rapid growth in crime and in the number of those incarcerated. Although firmly believing that humans' moral depravity inclined them to be selfish and to violate laws, Reformed Christians also thought that physical surroundings could either encourage people to, or dissuade them from, committing crimes.[51] Gambling, prostitution, drunkenness, poverty, and parental neglect, they argued, promoted immorality and weakened individuals' incentives to keep the law.[52]

Indigence, idleness, ignorance, and child abuse, leading Calvinists declared, encouraged criminality. When society did not restrain the powerful and wealthy and ignored the needs of the workingclass, some charged, it contributed to certain crimes. Unless people had employment that was rewarding psychologically and financially, their physical needs and their frustration would tempt them to disobey the law.[53]

Some Reformed leaders complained that prisons were neither reducing crime nor reforming offenders. Instead, they developed a professional criminal class by allowing some inmates to teach others how to commit more serious crimes, permitted and even practiced brutalities, and fostered immorality by bartering prison jobs at the counter of partisan politics. Prisons would continue to fail, some added, as long as they were based upon the principle of punishment or retaliation. Experience taught that people could not be beaten into betterment; suffering and fear were destructive, not constructive.[54]

To reduce crime, Reformed conservatives urged families, congregations, and schools to give more attention to personality development, and they challenged Christians to minister to those in circumstances conducive to crime, to develop better programs to rehabilitate violators, and to help released convicts readjust to society. They considered proper socialization in homes and schools the most certain antidote to crime. If more money and time were spent on moral and civic training, then much less of each would be necessary later in punishment and correction.[55] By developing better schools, building more adequate housing, providing jobs, closing down saloons, brothels, and gambling operations, and especially by establishing mission congregations and working with the uneducated, unemployed, and impoverished, Christians could help arrest the spread of crime.[56]

Better treatment programs for offenders, some Calvinists added, could also do much to reduce lawlessness. McKenzie Cleland, a Municipal Court judge in Chicago and a United Presbyterian elder, championed probation as an alternative to imprisonment. He favored probation because it did not penalize the offender's family by removing his financial and emotional support, and it taught him that the law was not his enemy but his friend. While less than 2 percent of offenders in the first decade of the twentieth century received suspended sentences, the judge argued, it could benefit at least half of them. Thus he established a probation program in Illinois that helped reform almost 1,500 offenders in its first two years of operation and stimulated other states to initiate similar programs. In addition, he organized and served as president of the National Probation League.[57]

Since most serious offenders were placed in prison rather than on probation, Calvinists also worked to ameliorate conditions there, which Cleland termed "the tragedy of modern society."[58] In the first stages of imprisonment, they complained, offenders were thrown together irrespective of age, sex, or degree of criminality. Such a grouping taught them terrible traits and habits. Most incarceration suppressed desirable human qualities and fostered "terror" and "bestiality." Prison officers should not be guards but therapists, counselors who could rehabilitate, not just detain and punish; prisons should attempt to reform offenders and restore them to society.[59] Penal and degrading labor could not accomplish this. Rather, convicts needed to develop self-confidence and self-respect through learning new skills and experiencing rewarding jobs.[60]

The final step in reducing crime, concerned Calvinists declared, was helping ex-prisoners readjust to society. If society did not accept released offenders, Reformed conservatives warned, they would eventually return to prison because there was no middle ground in which they could live. If they were ostracized and refused employment, few would succeed. Christians must welcome these persons into their congregations, help them find work, and encourage others to accept them socially.[61] Judge Cleland also pioneered in this endeavor, establishing a halfway house in Chicago in 1909, which in its first five years of operation cared for 3,500 men.[62]

Although Calvinists insisted that individual salvation was the best antidote to crime, they refused to consider it a panacea.[63] A good living environment, a wholesome social life, and a satisfying job, they held, were also indispensable in preventing crime and reforming criminals.

THE PURPOSE OF PROHIBITION

Like many other nineteenth-century Christians, Calvinists believed that excessive drinking was just as threatening to American moral and social life as the rising crime rate. Thus many of them took up their swords and joined the Protestant crusade to destroy demon rum.

The legal prohibition movement is often castigated as a retrogressive campaign of Protestant pietists to force their middle-class standards of ethical behavior upon immigrants and the poor. It is commonly seen as incongruous with the early-twentieth-century Progressive movement, which chiefly sought to correct American political, economic, and social abuses.[64] Recently, some scholars have challenged this contention. They argue that prohibition was a logical plank in the Progressive platform because reformers saw drunkenness as contributing to such other social ills as ignorance, crime, prostitution, gambling, the decay of the home, political corruption, and industrial monopolies, which they sought to remedy.[65]

Although Methodists were the chief champions of prohibition, Calvinists, especially Northern, United, and Reformed Presbyterians, also strongly promoted it.[66] In the years between 1870 and 1915, most Calvinists insisted that the Bible did not explicitly prohibit all drinking. While some claimed that a pledge of total abstinence should be a qualification for belonging to a Reformed congregation, most of them refused to make this a requirement.[67] Only in the many social evils arising from the liquor traffic in the late nineteenth century did most Calvinists find justification for total abstinence and prohibition.

To attempt to convince Americans of the evils of intemperance, Calvinists, along with other evangelicals, advanced an interlocking set of scientific, educational, political, economic, moral, and religious arguments. These arguments reveal that Reformed Christians, like most other evangelicals, primarily sought to abate social ills associated with the liquor industry rather than to regulate individual moral behavior. To many of them, the combination of scriptural truth, medical science, and human experience taught that only total abstinence enforced by legal prohibition could eradicate the misuse of intoxicants that ruined so many individuals and significantly harmed America's political, economic, social, and religious life. Concern about social control of immigrants was rarely expressed in private or public Calvinist writings. Rather, their goal was to develop a more humane and materially better social life.

In an address to the World Alliance of Reformed Churches in 1909, D. Stuart Dodge of New York City summarized Calvinist arguments. Liquor was a poison, similar to opium or arsenic, he declared, which weakened the brain and heart, diminished alertness and energy, shortened life, made workers less effective, and lowered industrial output. Producing alcoholic beverages cost $2,000,000,000 annually while creating nothing of value. Drunkenness was a public nuisance that corrupted morals and promoted lawlessness. And most significantly, he asserted, excessive drinking hindered spiritual development. "Every interest of the family, of social well-being, of education, of trade, of righteous government, and of true national prosperity," Dodge concluded, demanded "the extinction of the liquor traffic."[68]

Other Calvinists joined Dodge in denouncing the liquor industry's interference in politics. By offering bribes, buying votes, helping to elect dishonest and unscrupulous candidates, and pressuring legislators, the liquor trust, in alliance with urban political machines, did much to corrupt politics and to make city governments unjust and inefficient. Without first abolishing the saloon or at least curbing its power, some leaders argued, municipal reform could not be achieved.[69]

Many Reformed conservatives found another justification for prohibition in the liquor industry's hinderance of national and individual prosperity through wasting money, increasing taxes, reducing production, and producing poverty. One leader complained in 1881 that Americans paid $6,000,000,000 per year for alcoholic beverages, six times as much as they spent on education and twelve times as much as they contributed to spread the gospel at home and abroad.[70] Each year, another declared, 6,000,000 people visited America's 250,000 saloons; 600,000 became drunkards, and 60,000 died. The 10,000,000 barrels of liquor sold yearly, he lamented, would fill a canal twenty-one feet deep and five feet wide, extending from New York to Philadelphia.[71] Excessive drinking often produced poverty by making workers less productive, squandering monies needed to support families adequately, and even causing some laborers to lose their jobs. Where legal prohibition had been enacted, some Calvinists claimed, millions of dollars used to pay for courts, judges, jails, and support of the poor had been saved. By making workers less efficient, others added, liquor slowed the wheels of commerce and industry, thereby thwarting economic progress.[72]

Moral and religious considerations were even more important to Reformed conservatives. Some of them charged that excessive drinking was a factor in at least three-fourths of all crimes committed in America and was integrally related to gambling, prostitution, and rioting. A Southern Presbyterian noted in 1905 that Texas counties which allowed drinking had one convict for every 500 people, while prohibition counties had only one convict for every 1,500 people.[73] Others complained that liquor damaged marriages, destroyed homes, and produced abandoned children.[74] Drink was a "cruel tyrant" that brought disease and suffering upon its subjects, one wrote; it bred "poverty, strife and contempt of God's works."[75] Calvinists also advised people to shun liquor because it thwarted the ministry of congregations and because drunkards would not go to heaven.[76]

To these arguments for legal prohibition, some Calvinists also added the contention they often used in arguing about political questions: nations must follow biblical principles in their corporate life. Only those countries which prohibited the liquor trade could properly glorify God, promote his justice and righteousness, and enhance the physical, mental, and moral good. Nations had no right to allow any practice that God declared to be harmful.[77]

Calvinists did not think legal prohibition would terminate all drunkenness any more than they expected "law to put an end to all arson, theft and murder." But they did believe that "it would greatly diminish the evil and all its attendant results."[78] Radical measures were necessary; moderate approaches had failed.[79] Americans must destroy the liquor industry, leading Calvinists concluded, because the wrongs arising out of it were not merely incidental — not a product of some occasional abuses of the system — they were inherent and inevitable.[80]

Although they believed that prohibition laws were necessary and useful, Calvinists insisted that only the preaching of the gospel could eradicate the depression and despair that led people to excessive drinking; God's grace alone could transform human nature and remove the desire to drink. Christians must, therefore, "labor diligently to secure a transfer" of God's commandments "from the book of law to hearts."[81] Proclaiming God's word faithfully, practicing church discipline, and teaching children that intoxication was not an infirmity or a disease but a sin would best promote abstinence.[82] Thus Calvinists attempted to provide both outer constraints and inner compulsions to motivate Americans to resist drink.[83]

In short, many Reformed Christians worked to abolish the liquor traffic primarily because they believed doing so would help solve other pressing social problems. They promoted prohibition chiefly as a moral crusade based on humane and social concern, though it also reflected their conviction that wherever possible biblical principles should be enshrined in law.[84]

MINISTRY TO THE URBAN POOR

In addition to supporting these campaigns, Calvinists also established many social agencies, institutional churches, mission chapels, and social settlements to minister to physical and spiritual needs of the poor. While Reformed Christians were not as active in such endeavors as Methodists, liberal Congregationalists, or Episcopalians, their contributions were substantial. In proportion to their numbers, United and Reformed Presbyterians led these efforts, working to meliorate factory conditions, give laborers higher wages, establish homes for the aged and abandoned, build schools for blacks and the poor, and improve the lives of Indians and immigrants.[85] Calvinists in other denominations supported similar programs as well.

Under the leadership of pastors Wilbur Chapman and A. T. Pierson, Bethany Presbyterian Church, a Northern Presbyterian congregation located in Philadelphia, reached 10,000 persons each week through its educational, economic, recreational, and evangelical ministries. The congregation maintained a home for women and children, an inn for men, a social club for the poor, a cooperative society that provided sick and death benefits, a day nursery, kindergartens, diet kitchens, an employment bureau, and a dispensary. Members established Bethany College, an institute for artistic, musical, business, and industrial training, and the First Penny Savings Bank to stimulate thrift.[86] Through similar institutional churches such as First Presbyterian in Seattle, pastored by Mark Matthews, and ministries to immigrants, blacks, and poor whites, other Reformed Christians also worked steadily for social improvement.[87] By 1898 Northern Presbyterians alone maintained over one hundred mission day and industrial training schools and by 1911 the denomination sponsored forty social centers in immigrant communities.[88]

Calvinist interest in institutional churches and urban missions testifies to their belief that the gospel must save the cities. In the decades following the Civil War, they became increasingly concerned with the poverty, corruption, and filth accumulating there. By 1880 many argued that rapid population growth, increasing strength of Romanism and atheism, and widening separation between rich and poor required Christians to develop more urban ministries.[89] "In the great cities lies the danger of our modern civilization," one asserted; they were "the hotbeds of vice and crime, the dens whence issue forth the vast criminal army which must be conquered or become the conqueror."[90]

Concerned Calvinists urged Christians to develop more institutional churches and mission congregations, encouraged ministers to preach on social problems, and challenged the laity to meet the physical and spiritual needs of the homeless, the jobless, and the poor. Churches must use their deacons and women leaders more effectively to evangelize the sinner, educate the ignorant, visit the sick and imprisoned, feed the hungry, and provide clothing and shelter for the destitute. Neither professional evangelists nor mission congregations could cover the ground; the efforts of all Christians were needed to help the urban masses spiritually, socially, and materially and to involve them in Christian fellowship and ministry.[91] Despite these varied ministries, critics, both outside and inside the Reformed camp, continually attacked the tradition's complacency about social conditions. Stephen Colwell's *New Themes for the Protestant Clergy*, published in 1851, uttered a complaint many subsequent historians accepted.[92] According to Colwell, Calvinists' belief in predestination and human depravity led them to argue that poverty stemmed almost exclusively from idleness and sloth and limited their compassion for victims of injustice.[93] In Chapter VIII, however, we saw that this attitude was more typical of popularizers of the Gospel of Wealth than of orthodox Christians. During the last decades of the nineteenth century, Reformed conservatives repeatedly stressed their efforts in foreign and home missions and especially in their ministries among immigrants and the poor in answering this charge.[94] For example, in 1893 a Northern Presbyterian pastor in Terre Haute, Indiana, claimed that in America and overseas Presbyterians were aggressively ministering to urban populations by maintaining schools and colleges, hospitals, kindergartens, orphanages, homes for the aged and abandoned women, and reformatories for drunkards.[95]

Other Calvinists, however, apologized for their limited efforts to reach the poor in America. Typical of their views was the plea of Southern Presbyterian professor Thomas C. Johnson in 1900 that his denomination "quit robbing the masses of the gospel." He chastised congregations for moving from areas of cities where the poor lived to more wealthy neighborhoods.[96] Nearly every article written between 1870 and 1915 on Calvinist attempts to reach the indigent and city dwellers explicitly or implicitly lamented, as one pastor did in 1888, that "Presbyterians have not made the progress expected of us in evangelizing the masses."[97] Such laments certainly challenged such self-righteousness and complacency as Reformed conservatives displayed. The volume of discussion devoted to this problem in the reports of the committees on missions to the General Assemblies of the several Calvinist denominations, and the recorded activities of mission efforts, institutional churches, urban congregations, and settlement houses indicate that an accurate appraisal lies somewhere between the few reports of glowing success and the many jeremiads of the concerned. Certainly, the latter were intended to goad Reformed Christians to greater efforts to do what almost all believed was their duty to the poor and oppressed.

A QUESTION OF PRIORITIES

Calvinists, as we have seen, considered the dramatic social unrest of the years between 1870 and 1915 alarming. Like the majority of their Christian contemporaries, however, they rejected the socialist solutions proposed by Karl Marx, Henry George, and George Herron. And most of them criticized the Social Gospelers' approach as unrealistic and unbiblical. Calvinist efforts to achieve slow, orderly reform by proven principles were consonant with desires and methods of American progressivism.[98]

The firm conviction that converting individuals was the key to solving social problems was both the strength and weakness of the · Reformed approach. Calvinists called upon those reformers preoccupied with external arrangements to remember that humans were innately sinful. They steadily proclaimed what recent history has repeatedly affirmed: human problems are rooted not only in our environment but in ourselves. At their best, Calvinists joined other evangelicals in arguing that spiritual development was more important than material advancement.

Yet this basic strength was also a major weakness. In emphasizing individual conversion so strongly, Calvinists sometimes depreciated social action, usually inadvertently but occasionally on purpose. Many Calvinists naively believed that redeeming individuals would automatically solve social problems. Thus, they did not spend enough time in training Christians how to analyze and improve social conditions. Moreover, they did not generally recognize the extent to which the sociocultural environment affected individual's attitudes and behavior.

While many Reformed leaders repeatedly called on Christians to build the kingdom of God on earth, few of them clearly delineated how that could be done. Rarely did they forthrightly declare that evils could be incorporated in social and economic institutions and structures as well as in individuals. Seldom did they attempt to change social arrangements that either promoted or permitted discrimination or ones that prevented people from responding positively to the gospel. When greed, prejudice, and selfishness are woven into the fabric of corporate patterns of human interaction, institutions then perpetuate and reinforce these qualities in people. When opposite principles are incorporated into public life, then institutions promote kindness and love. As one contemporary Calvinist argues, to change society Christians must do more than change individuals. "Constitutions must be rewritten, labor codes changed, jokes and stories debunked, self-images repaired, communities rebuilt."[99]

Calvinists' traditional emphasis on individualism helps explain why they adopted this approach to social problems. Advanced by most other evangelicals as well, this ethic taught that the combined effects of individual actions would refashion social relationships and conditions. Their growing commitment after 1700 to capitalism, the association of collectivism in the late nineteenth century with atheism, and new departures in theology which stressed social action all encouraged many Calvinists to overemphasize the role of individual initiative in bringing about social change. As the practices of early-twentieth-century economic and social orders became increasingly impersonal and complex, this individualistic ethic became more and more difficult to apply.

In light of their attempt to defend a comprehensive understanding of the universe and life against secularizing trends in politics, education, science, morality, and religion, it is surprising that Reformed Christians did not during these years develop a comprehensive strategy to restructure economic and social relations. Clearly, these Calvinists never worked out a biblical understanding of these areas comparable to that of John Calvin.[100]

10

CALVINISM AND SECULARISM: A FINAL EVALUATION

This study has shown that after 1870, Americans, especially intellectual and cultural leaders, increasingly accepted secular understandings of public life. During the years between 1870 and 1915 the "giant plates" of American culture were slowly shifting deep beneath the surface. While this shift was beginning to affect popular cultural patterns and practices during these years, major transformation in these areas occurred after 1920. After this date biblical teachings were increasingly regarded as relevant only to private life, and secular understandings of political, educational, moral, economic, and social life became widely accepted. Growing numbers of Americans agreed that the Bible could not be appropriately applied to a society with such a religiously diverse population. Religious, ethnic, and ideological differences, many believed, required a public order that was neutral, nonreligious, or secular.

While secularism descended upon American society after 1920 like a horde of locusts, devouring everything in its path, the foundation for this onslaught was largely laid, as we have seen, in the years between 1870 and 1915. Secular ideals were developed by the Greeks, advanced by key Renaissance leaders, and further elaborated by Enlightenment philosophers. Prior to 1870, however, few Americans had accepted these ideals and even fewer understood their full implications for public life. Only between 1870 and 1915 did American thinkers consistently begin to develop secular understandings of public life and attempt to apply them systematically to American society.

In this concluding chapter we will analyze why Calvinists (and indirectly other evangelicals) responded to secularization as they did. In doing so, we will examine other approaches that Christians living during these years might have used in their struggles against secularism. We will also trace the decline and subsequent resurgence of both Calvinism and evangelicalism in the twentieth century, evaluate the development of secularism in this century, and briefly compare the conflicting worldviews offered by these two ideologies.

THE DECLINE OF CALVINISM

During the years from 1870 to 1915 the face and character of American society changed dramatically. Technological and industrial innovations, massive immigration, rapid urbanization, smoldering racial conflict, growing nationalism, and the rise of new ideologies all powerfully affected American society. Calvinists and many other evangelical Christians responded to these developments by opposing those forces which sought to shift public life from biblical to secular foundations. Because God was supreme over both cultural and spiritual matters, Reformed Christians insisted, scriptural principles must guide political, economic, and social life.

Although Calvinists continued to proclaim that their theology was the most effective weapon against secularism and theological liberalism, it was clear even to them that after 1900 belief in their doctrines had decreased and their impact on culture had lessened. At the same time, Americans' diminishing commitment not only to Calvinism but also to a holistic biblical understanding of life helped secular views win increasing acceptance, especially as a philosophy for public life. Ineffective strategies that Calvinists and other evangelicals employed in battling against secularism undoubtedly promoted this result.

At the turn of the century, Calvinists were continuing to insist that their theology could best meet the intensifying challenge of secularism. Numerous times they asserted, as Southern Presbyterian James Howerton did in 1901, that in the near future two great logical systems — naturalism and orthodoxy — would wage war over fundamental principles. Using an analogy drawn from English Calvinist Charles Spurgeon, Howerton declared that as the collision of two giant icebergs crushed all smaller ones, so the clash between atheism and Calvinism would destroy all intermediate systems of thought. Put another way, Calvinism was the citadel within the walls; when all other systems had surrendered to the atheist bombardment, its impregnable walls would still defy the assaults of unbelief.[1]

Although Reformed conservatives exaggerated the extent to which the strength of orthodox Christianity rested upon allegiance to their theology, it is striking that commitment to Calvinism specifically and evangelical Christianity generally declined simultaneously. Probably, however, the decline of one did not cause the decline of the other, but both became less accepted because of new cultural forces and ideologies hostile to their positions.

As discussed earlier, in 1901 English Methodist Frederick Platt predicted that Reformed orthodoxy would quickly reemerge as a major cultural force. A mere eight years later, however, as Calvinists around the world celebrated the 400th anniversary of John Calvin's birth, Platt sought to explain why Calvinism had remained "ineffectual in our generation." Although this theology had mastered Europe and molded America, Platt declared, its days of dominance were past; its creed and discipline had been discredited. Platt argued that several major cultural currents had combined to erode commitment to Calvinism: subjectivism in religion and philosophy; the doctrines of the Fatherhood and immanence of God; various teachings, such as that human beings are innately good and that ethics should rest exclusively on inner compulsion, as well as evolutionary theories, comparative religion, new developments in foreign missions, and determinism in philosophy.[2]

Platt considered philosophical subjectivism the primary architect of Calvinism's destruction. This philosophical tendency made human consciousness the primary agent for interpreting and establishing truth. Subjectivism underlay the work of Immanuel Kant, idealism, modern psychology, and even Arminianism. Kant depreciated the value of theoretic reason, but made humanity's moral nature, which Calvinists distrusted, the chief source of knowledge. Idealism and psychology also appealed to human experience as the ultimate basis of knowledge and therefore helped weaken belief in systems of doctrine based upon divine revelation, such as Calvinism. Arminianism, as a theological system, Platt claimed, had not caused decreasing commitment to Reformed theology. "But as a vitalizing and genial influence suffusing itself through all the discussions of the relation of God to man, its disintegrating force upon Calvinism" had been immense.[3]

According to Platt, liberal theology's exaltation of the Fatherhood and immanence of God also weakened adherence to Calvinism. These doctrines, he argued, arose partially as a protest against Reformed theology's exaggeration of divine transcendence and its subordination of God's love to his sovereignty. Theologians in the early twentieth century also repudiated the sharp antithesis between the natural and the supernatural, thus strongly challenging the Reformed understanding of opposition between the "divine and human, nature and grace, evolution and creation, miracle and causation, and revelation and psychological processes."[4]

Platt believed further that new views of human nature and ethics led some to reject Calvinism. Repudiating the Reformed conception of human moral depravity, humanists proclaimed people's innate goodness and grand possibilities. Platt claimed that glowing portraits of what people, endowed with literary charm and aesthetic sensibility, could become had done more to discredit Calvinism in the present age "than the profound arguments of many philosophies." And many declared that Reformed ethics could not inspire sound morality because it was based primarily on external authority rather than on internal compulsion.[5]

Evolution, comparative religion, and the modern missions movement, Platt insisted, also blasted the Calvinist ramparts. Evolutionary theories taught that humans were not fallen and alienated from God but rather were growing better and better. The new field of comparative religion also repudiated traditional Reformed views of human corruptness and the uniqueness of Christianity. Many modern missiologists rejected the Reformed concept of a limited atonement and insisted that only belief that all persons could be saved could evoke sufficient devotion and sacrifice to fuel the missions enterprise.[6]

Underlying all other objections to Reformed orthodoxy, Platt concluded, was the protest that it portrayed God as partial, unjust, and cruel. Better understanding of other religions and civilizations, "sympathetic reflection on the state of the unevangelized millions, the complexity of the problem of heredity, [and] the effect of psychological analysis on the significance of responsibility," Platt declared, all raised questions about the doctrines of unconditional election and limited atonement.[7]

Reformed Christians responded to these numerous criticisms by attempting to show either that opponents misunderstood their position or that their views conformed more closely to the Bible and human experience than those of their detractors. As explained earlier, Calvinists did teach the Fatherhood and immanence of God, although not to the exclusion of divine justice and transcendence, as they judged modern theology did.[8] We have also seen that many Reformed Christians strongly promoted foreign missions and that most Calvinists believed that ethical practice was to rest upon both outward rules and inward motivation.[9] And they continually argued that history illustrated innate human sinfulness and that the Bible taught a final judgment.

Whether or not opponents misrepresented their position, however, Platt was correct that the masses no longer believed it. Even postmillennialist B. B. Warfield, who contended that when Reformed theology was clearly and persuasively presented it would conquer all opposition, admitted in 1909 that its fortunes were not at their zenith. Many had rejected it. Many of those who still formally professed it, did not always "illustrate it in life or proclaim it in word."[10]

Finally, decreasing commitment to Calvinism as a distinctive doctrinal system was also due to the vast amount of time and energy its advocates spent in defending broader evangelical Christianity against the arguments of liberalism, skepticism, and secularism. With such strong opposition, Reformed Christians needed all allies. Thus they usually defended what they considered the heart of the gospel, upon which all evangelicals agreed — the infallibility of the Scriptures, the divinity of Christ, the substitutionary atonement, and the new birth. Within their own denominations, they often used Reformed theology and rhetoric to oppose those who espoused more liberal theological views. But when speaking to a wider audience, they often defended broader evangelical, rather than narrower Reformed, essentials. This is evident from their contributions to *The Fundamentals* of 1910 – 1915, the five points labeled indispensable by the Northern Presbyterian General Assemblies of 1910, 1916, and 1923, J. Gresham Machen's widely acclaimed book *Christianity and Liberalism* (1923), and the stream of articles that flowed from the presses of the *Princeton Theological Review* and other Calvinist periodicals during the first two decades of the twentieth century.

The apologetic task of evangelical Christianity in the early twentieth century was immense. Most of the developments mentioned above, which challenged Calvinism, also threatened evangelicalism. Secular ideas were becoming increasingly accepted among elites in politics, jurisprudence, education, economics, business, and science. Historicism, a new relativistic methodology, was producing conceptions of history, psychology, sociology, and political science that were antithetical to orthodox views, and was slowly eroding confidence in biblical inspiration. Assaulted from without by hostile, relativistic ideologies and from within by subjective, mediating theologies, evangelical Christianity's task of defending a religion based upon actual historical events and transcendent, ultimate authority was huge.[11] The idea that standards and values were fixed forever by supernatural design was gradually being undermined not only in religion but also, as we have seen, in science, philosophy, law, social analysis, history, and economics.[12]

How one regards the progressive secularization of American society during the twentieth century depends on his or her perspective. Some, like Harvey Cox and William Clebsch, consider a secular society to be the ideal. They regard secularization as a positive process that extends the benefits and privileges previously enjoyed by the few to the whole community. At the same time, as society becomes secular, humans are freed from preoccupation with another world and become able to focus their attention exclusively on this world.[13]

If, however, one believes that God is ultimately supreme over society, then he or she will judge secularization a detrimental process because it denies God's jurisdiction over the world. Most Calvinists, of course, continued to affirm God's sovereignty over all cultural activity. Many Americans, on the other hand, eventually concluded that public life should be secular. They accepted this view either because they believed God to be nonexistent or unconcerned about cultural arrangements, or because they thought that the practical necessities of mediating between competing creeds, religions, and groups required such an arrangement.

Given Calvinists' desire to keep secularizing trends from reshaping American society, what courses of action could they have followed? They could have endorsed the Medieval view that society should be monolithically Christian and that all cultural activity should be under the jurisdiction of the institutional church. John Calvin had, however, rejected the long-standing practice of unifying church and state and had argued for their separation. Moreover, the belief that individuals should be free to worship or not worship God as they pleased, which developed during the eighteenth and nineteenth centuries, made the Constantinian-Thomistic ideal of a totally Christian society, enforced by law, both impossible to achieve and undesirable to most Americans living in the late nineteenth century.

Second, Calvinists could have accepted the view, which was becoming influential during the late nineteenth century, that religion was a personal and private matter with little relevance to public life. Those holding this view assumed that public life was either neutral or nonreligious or else governed by a civil religion common to all. Rooted in the Enlightenment, this position asserted that the Bible dealt almost exclusively with spirituality and individual morality. Scriptural principles were in no way normative for structuring political, economic, or social arrangements; only the moral teachings of the Bible were relevant to social life. During the early twentieth century many fundamentalists and proponents of the holiness movement accepted this position, at least in part. These Christians tended to emphasize individuals' inward experience rather than social change, and they often narrowed the areas of life that sanctification affected to " 'spiritual' activities, especially personal devotions, testimony about one's experience, and the avoidance of select symptoms of worldliness."[14]

As we have seen, most Calvinists vehemently resisted this position. They insisted that religion was more than a personal and private affair. Believing with John Calvin that all human beings are "incurable religious," that all people live by a philosophy of life whether they recognize it or not, many Reformed Christians declared that religion could not be divorced from any of life's activities. To them, separation of church and state did not mean and could not properly require that religious values and norms be removed from public affairs. Public life could not properly rest upon secularism because this philosophy is not neutral, as some claimed, but injects naturalistic and humanistic ideas into cultural development. Even legal systems, Calvinists insisted, could not be religiously impartial because statutes are always based upon underlying moral principles.

Calvinists, believing that all people are innately religious creatures who inevitably express their religious convictions in public as well as in private activities (or put another way, people's religious beliefs shape all public policies), had two remaining options. They could have continued to insist that Judeo-Christian values dominate and control public institutions and practices — schools, business and industry, politics and government, marriage and family, and the Sabbath. Or Calvinists could have advocated structural and confessional pluralism as Abraham Kuyper did in the Netherlands. As we have seen, most Reformed Christians sought to rest society as completely as possible on biblical norms. They attempted to do so not as medieval Catholics did, by placing social institutions and practices under the jurisdiction of the institutional church, but primarily by using the coercive power of the state to enforce their way of life.

The approach Reformed Christians employed seemed to many Americans to contradict New Testament teachings and historical testimony that believers should not expect to dominate society, especially through government. Although Calvinists did not attempt to force people to attend church services or to worship God, they did seek to compel all citizens to submit to Christian principles and practices in all areas of life. This strategy seems counter to New Testament teachings that Christians are not to attempt to establish a political community that forces Christian doctrines upon non-Christians.[15] Moreover, as Americans living during the late nineteenth century increasingly came to believe that religion should be relegated to private affairs and that public life should be neutral, support needed for Christian beliefs to control public policy dwindled.

Had Calvinists supported the option of structural and confessional pluralism their efforts to keep secularism from dominating public life might have been more successful. As advocated by Kuyper and some contemporary Calvinists, structural pluralism means that God has created a number of associations in human society, each with its own identity, integrity, and right of existence. Each association has its own unique function and its own proper area of jurisdiction. Confessional pluralism, which is more pertinent to our discussion, means that all faith communities with divergent philosophical assumptions should have equal rights in the public order. Each community should have the same opportunity under the law to promote its conceptions of life through voluntary associations, schools, labor unions, political parties, and businesses. This position seeks to safeguard "public legal rights as well as the private rights of all groups in society . . . within a common democratic order."[16]

Advocates of confessional pluralism argue that one religious orientation, secular humanism, should not have an exclusive right to propound its peculiar worldview through public institutions as it does presently in elementary and secondary education. When various groups advance different visions of life and reality, the most just and effective arrangement would be to allow each group to develop its own unique principles in the public areas of government, business, education, and social relations. This system would permit all people to express their convictions freely and would trample on no one's liberties. By encouraging each person to choose which set of principles he supports, this approach would challenge the current practice of many Americans who divide their lives into public and private sectors with appropriate philosophies for each. It could enhance respect for individual faith-commitments, and it could stimulate people to conduct politics on the basis of principles rather than on personality and patronage.

Confessional pluralism recognizes that people who hold divergent perspectives of life often share basic convictions about public policy. Many humanists, existentialists, socialists, and naturalists accept aspects of biblical morality while eschewing biblical theology and anthropology. Although they may not recognize God as the ultimate lawgiver, many non-Christians live by the same ideals the Bible teaches because they are convinced that doing so promotes social good. Since the Fall, God's common grace has operated to restrain sin and to promote civilization and thus has helped to effect this result. Augustine, Luther, and Calvin all taught that God actively produces civil righteousness through those who do not know him.[17]

Calvinists, unfortunately, did not endorse this pluralistic plan. There were several reasons for this. Their historical success in shaping and sometimes controlling the governments of Scotland, Holland, England, several Swiss cantons, and a few American colonies made it difficult for them to consider this pluralistic approach appropriate or necessary. Because they were convinced that whole societies should as directly as possible be under God's control and the Bible's laws, most Reformed Christians considered confessional pluralism unbiblical. Many of them continued to believe, as Calvin and the Puritans had, that they should seek to create a holy commonwealth, under God's direct control.[18] Like other Protestants, they found it hard to adjust to the ideologically and culturally heterogeneous society emerging in late-nineteenth-century America. They had exercised such great influence for so long that they were unprepared to live in a highly competitive situation in which many of their basic values were sharply challenged.[19] Moreover, Calvinists disliked the relativism that cultural pluralism implied.[20] If people with different ideological beliefs and ethical values could live together harmoniously, did this not suggest that there were no eternal verities on which values should be based? At the same time, like many other Protestants, Calvinists thought that all immigrants should quickly and eagerly conform to the standard Anglo-American pattern so as to assure unity, patriotism, and social advancement.[21] This commitment undoubtedly also made it very difficult for them to endorse the kind of cultural heterogeneity that pluralism seemed to suggest.

Furthermore, like many American Christians living during the late nineteenth century, Calvinists frequently underestimated the impact of secularism upon their nation and persisted to believe that Christian values and ideals would always control their culture. Abraham Kuyper himself did not realize how strongly secularism was battering America's biblical foundations as the twentieth cen-

tury approached. In his *Lectures on Calvinism* given at Princeton
Theological Seminary in 1898 and in his *Varia Americana* (1899)
in which he reflected on his visit to America, Kuyper praised the
United States as a Christian country. He was very impressed by
America's public symbols of religiosity — chaplains in Congress,
state universities, and the armed forces, Bible reading and prayer
in the public schools, strict Sabbath observance, national days of
prayer, and pious observances by Presidential candidates.[22] Thus
Kuyper himself did not encourage Americans to adopt the pluralistic plan being used in the Netherlands. Agreeing with Kuyper,
some Calvinists maintained at the turn of the century that America
had developed consistently from its Reformed sources and continued to be a strongly Christian nation.[23] The nature of secularization
in America was quite different from that in England and on the
European continent, and its more gradual, subtle change was much
harder to apprehend than the overt skepticism and attacks on
Christianity across the Atlantic. But the seeds of secularization had
been planted so successfully in our earlier history and especially
during the years from 1870 to 1915 that the flower was bound to
bloom widely during the next generation. In fact, as we have seen,
Calvinists repeatedly warned of this possibility. The strategy employed against secularism — repeated efforts to make Christian values dominate public life — slowed but did not stop its growth.

Some contemporary Calvinists, especially in Canada and in
the Netherlands, have argued and worked to bring about a genu-
inely pluralistic society. They believe that this approach allows
them to critique cultural development, denounce social and economic injustices, and present better alternatives for cultural life.
Their commitment to pluralism has also led some of them to attempt to establish distinctively Christian communities within the
larger culture. At the same time, they have developed Christian
alternatives to secular labor unions, media, schools, and companies. Such communities and organizations, they insist, demonstrate
that following biblical principles and practices enriches life. By ar-
ticulating and embodying their convictions, these Calvinists believe
they can create a good community for themselves and also raise
the quality of society's life. As more and more people willingly
practice scriptural norms and patterns, they contend, social life will
improve significantly.[24]

THE GROWTH OF SECULARISM

While commitment to Calvinism as a worldview was declining during the late nineteenth and early twentieth centuries, the secular

understanding of life was winning growing endorsement. Two widely heralded books published in 1929 sounded the bugle for secular humanism. In *The Modern Temper,* Columbia University professor Joseph Wood Krutch declared that new scientific and intellectual developments made it necessary for Americans to reject the old Christian worldview and adopt instead a secular understanding of life.[25] Similarly, political analyst Walter Lippmann insisted that "the acids of modernity" had so eroded the traditional worldview that educated persons could no longer believe it. He addressed *A Preface of Morals* to those who were "perplexed by the consequences of their own irreligion," who were troubled by the "vacancy in their lives."[26] He believed that few Americans were still motivated by the conviction that they could attain "eternal happiness by obedience to God's will on earth."[27] Religious teachings no longer guided business, art, or even the family. Scientists had replaced clergymen as the leading intellectual arbiters. "Their authority in the realm of knowledge," Lippmann declared, had become "virtually irresistable."[28] In the twentieth century, he claimed, science had become supreme everywhere. Since modern scholarship had undermined belief in traditional theistic religions, people needed to develop a new humanistic religion. Repudiating conceptions of God "as master of fate, creator, providence and King," human beings must consider "God" to be the "highest good at which they might aim."[29]

In order to win adherents to this new humanistic religion, thirty-four leading Americans, including John Dewey, Harry Elmer Barnes, R. Lester Mondale, and Roy Wood Sellars, issued the Humanist Manifesto I in 1933. Frankly religious in rhetoric and intention, the declaration sought to explain humanist principles systematically and winsomely. Its signers agreed with Lippmann that traditional religions had failed to adjust to "new conditions created by a vastly increased knowledge and experience" and were, therefore, "powerless to solve the problem of human living in the twentieth century." Because science had made "unacceptable any supernatural or cosmic guarantees of human values," people must embrace a new humanistic religion that defended "abiding values," not by resting them upon an imaginary metaphysical dimension, but by showing how significant and beneficial they were in human experience. Religion must be based upon scientific experimentation, not revelation. Since there is no God, these humanists argued, the universe is self-existing. Man therefore is a "part of nature" who "has emerged as the result of a continuous process." His ultimate goal is to reach his highest potential in "the here and now."[30]

Since 1940, humanists have become increasingly organized and self-conscious. Secular (sometimes also called scientific or naturalistic) humanists founded the American Humanist Association in 1941 and today express their views principally through two periodicals, *The Humanist* and *Free Inquiry,* and a steady flow of books issued by their publishing house, Prometheus Press. Outstanding modern proponents of this view include philosophers Betrand Russell, Corliss Lamont, A. J. Ayer, and Sidney Hook, psychologists Erich Fromm, Abraham Maslow, and B. F. Skinner, and scientists Julian Huxley and Francis Crick.

Secular humanists receive support from religious humanists. This latter group is quite diverse, including clergy and laity affiliated with a wide range of congregations, synagogues, and fellowships such as the humanistic wing of the Unitarian Universalist Association, the Ethical Culture Societies, the Fellowship of Religious Humanists, and the Society for Humanistic Judaism. Through their chief voice, *Religious Humanism,* these humanists express deep concern about morality and find much value in Judeo-Christian teaching. Yet they repudiate Christian theology and accept a naturalistic worldview. Secular and religious humanists joined together in 1973 to publish the Humanist Manifesto II to update their views. While the religious tone of the first manifesto was eliminated, both statements are apologies for a secular worldview.[31] In 1982 conferees of seven different groups largely representing these two varieties of humanism created the North American Committee for Humanism. Numerous other related humanist organizations such as the Association for Humanistic Psychology and the Society for Humanistic Anthropology exist today in America.[32]

Contemporary humanists agree with their predecessors in the late nineteenth century (and earlier times) that people cannot believe in the metaphysical dimension because it cannot be measured or tested by empirical methods. They insist that anthropological, sociological, and psychological factors explain the origin and persistence of religion. "Man created the gods," declares leading British humanist Julian Huxley, "to protect himself from loneliness, uncertainty and fear."[33] Human beings devised religions to help them relate to powers that seem unpredictable and mysterious. Feelings of impotence and dependence led people to project their own noblest traits onto the universe and to call this ideal image "God."[34]

Repeatedly, leading humanists declare that religion is declining and will eventually die. "The god-hypothesis, invented by man to provide an explanation of the meaning of existence," one of them writes, "has served its purpose and is destined to disappear."[35] Echoing Lippmann, contemporary humanists insist that Christianity cannot survive because its worldview has been rendered implausible and obsolete by modern science. Moreover, they maintain that all traditional religious remedies have been tried and have failed to solve the problems of Western culture.[36]

Because there is no God, man is the supreme being in the universe, they say. While Christians assert that human dignity rests upon their creation in the image and likeness of God and their relationship with him, humanists contend that "God" necessarily impairs instead of improves man's initiative, responsibility, and dignity. If God is omnipotent, argues Paul Kurtz, editor of *Free Inquiry*, then people are "helpless creatures." Rather, humans are their own authority. They respond to no will but their own; they are subject to no superior powers.[37] While man is an integral part of nature who cannot be, in the words of Corliss Lamont, "separated from it by any sharp cleavage or discontinuity," he has value because he is the pinnacle of the evolutionary process as is most evident in his rational abilities.[38]

For humanists, people are neither sinful as Christians contend, nor alienated as Marxists maintain, nor inauthentic as existentialists claim. People are fundamentally good as they are. They do not need to become their true selves by obeying the divine will, by conforming to the cosmic design, by participating in the historical process, or by assuming their autonomy in the continuous exercise of choice. Human beings are their own authority. They are free to create the kind of world they want, governed only by their own desires. Since there is no god, people must rely upon themselves.[39] As humanist psychologist Erich Fromm writes, "there is only one solution to his [man's] problems: to face the truth, to acknowledge his fundamental aloneness and solitude in a universe indifferent to his fate, to recognize that there is no power transcending him to solve his problem for him."[40]

Many humanists do insist that people must "save" themselves. By this they generally mean that people must strive to achieve their own highest potential or "self-actualization" and labor to build a world order where barriers to individual growth are removed and peace and liberty prevail. "There is no meaning to life," Fromm declares, "except the meaning man gives his life by the unfolding of his powers, by living productively."[41] According to the Humanist Manifesto I, "the end of man's life" is the "complete realization of human personality."[42] Those who obtain "fullness of being" experience joy, community, love, creative fulfillment, and freedom and live courageously and rationally.[43]

From roots in ancient Greece, the Renaissance, the Enlightenment, and the nineteenth century, secular humanism has developed into a powerful force in modern society. Yet what I argued about the years before 1920 is also generally true of those after 1920. While humanism has been systematically stated and explicitly promoted during the past fifty years, few Americans completely and enthusiastically endorse its principles as explained in its manifestos. Only 15,000 people subscribe to *The Humanist* and fewer still receive either *Free Inquiry* or *Religious Humanism.* Yet support for key humanistic ideas in America is much greater than the membership of avowedly humanist organizations. For numerous reasons, many Americans accept humanistic conceptions of humanity, morality, and social relations and even more are guided by an amalgamation of Christian and humanist principles.

Calvinists, as we have seen, continuously challenged secular views of man's nature, condition, and function. Humanist ideology, they argued, unlike Reformed theology, could not provide people with the security, significance, and love they deeply desired. While Reformed orthodoxy taught human depravity, it also asserted human dignity. Humans' worth rested in their creation in God's image and their capacity for reflecting his glory and character. God's provision of redemption through Christ further testified to their value. The humanist conviction that people evolved by chance and have no future beyond death made humans insignificant; the Christian conviction that people came from God and would spend eternity with him made humans important. Belief in election assured individuals that God loved them and would preserve them forever. Their confidence that God guided the universe and provided daily for their individual needs was to Reformed believers a tremendous source of comfort.[44] Summing up Reformed views, J. I. Vance asserted in 1909 that no philosophy had "ever proclaimed the dignity of man so substantially as the Calvinistic doctrine of election, assurance, and final happiness. The world needs the Calvinistic doctrine of man — he is not a freak of evolution, not the spawn of chance, but the offspring of the living and eternal purpose of God."[45]

After five decades of war, cruelity, crime, economic privation, and disillusionment, people may be ready to come full circle to the understanding of humanity that dominated the sixteenth and seventeenth centuries. Contemporary existentialist plays, poems, and prose have powerfully portrayed the gloomy implications of the naturalistic doctrine that humans are simply part and parcel of nature. An increasing number of philosophies affirm that people are insignificant, simply "a drop of water in an endless sea." Pessimism, cynicism, and hopelessness are rampant. History testifies to the limitations of the secular vision. Nietzsche searched for ultimate values and found nihilism; Marx called for a classless society and spawned rigid totalitarianism. Confusion over who man is paralyzes contemporary society. Secular ideologies have largely failed to convince people that they are valuable. Communism promised hope but delivered fear. Humanism proclaimed self-actualization but promoted selfishness. Modern man lives in a cultural crisis, groping for a moral vision sufficient to illumine his path and inspire his future. His emancipation from ultimate accountability has not proved to be the blessing he anticipated.[46] Perhaps the Bible does paint a true picture of humanity's condition and offer the correct remedy for our malady.

THE RESURGENCE OF CALVINISM

By 1920 the influence of Calvinism in America and worldwide had reached low tide. Upon his induction into the Charles Hodge Chair of Didactic and Polemic Theology at Princeton Seminary in 1921, his grandson, Caspar W. Hodge, acknowledged that Reformed orthodoxy had few "representatives among the leaders of religious thought."[47] The death in 1920 of Abraham Kuyper, the widely influential Dutch statesman-scholar, and the passing away the next year of B. B. Warfield, the outstanding American theologian and biblical expositor, left the Reformed community with no leaders of great stature.

During the late 1930s and early 1940s some thought they saw signs of Calvinism's reemergence as a cultural force. A South African claimed that Reformed orthodoxy was reviving in England, Scotland, Holland, France, Germany, Hungary, and the United States as well as in his own country, spurred by the disillusionment caused by World War I, the disintegration of modern Protestant theology, and the belief that Calvinism was the best weapon to fight humanism, theological modernism, and the autocracy of the state.[48] Auguste Lecerf, professor of dogmatics at the University of Paris, argued in 1939 that the world's spiritual malaise promised the quick resurgence of Calvinism.[49] In the middle of World War II, an English Baptist pastor insisted that Reformed orthodoxy's exaltation of God, holistic understanding of life and the universe, and view of human depravity, which seemed vindicated by human experience, explained its growing acceptance.[50]

Despite these predictions, Calvinism did not reemerge as a prominent theological power or societal influence during the 1940s and 1950s, especially in America. Neo-orthodoxy, which was widely accepted during these years, did agree substantially with Reformed views of human sinfulness and the transcendence and sovereignty of God. Yet few Americans accepted Calvinism as a doctrinal system. In 1947 a Christian Reformed spokesman concluded that only his own denomination and the Orthodox Presbyterians, a product of a 1937 schism from the Northern Presbyterian Church led by J. Gresham Machen, held consistently to Reformed theology. Although there were strong parties of Calvinists among United, Northern and Southern Presbyterians, German Reformed, and the Reformed Church of America, he believed that these bodies as a whole no longer strictly adherred to Reformed orthodoxy.[51] He could have also added that Baptists, North and South, had largely abandoned Calvinism for fundamentalism, premillennialism, and dispensationalism.

The emergence of modern evangelicalism in the 1940s through such organizations as the National Association of Evangelicals, founded in 1942, however, was vitally connected to the renaissance of Calvinism. Both orientations have grown steadily since that decade and in many ways have reinforced and supported one another. Today both movements, which are still intertwined, are showing their greatest vitality and strength since the beginning of the twentieth century. The revival of Calvinism is evident in many places — denominations, seminaries, para-church organizations, publications, and the leadership of the evangelical community.[52] Today there are nineteen Presbyterian and Reformed denominations in America with a combined membership exceeding five million.[53] While members and ministers of these communions have varying degrees of commitment to Reformed theology, these bodies provide a strong base for American Calvinism. In addition, substantial Reformed parties exist among Congregationalists, Episcopalians, Northern and Southern Baptists, and independent churches. Seminaries with a decidedly or basically Calvinistic orientation such as Calvin in Grand Rapids, Michigan; Westminster and Biblical in Philadelphia; Covenant in St. Louis; Reformed in Jackson, Mississippi; Gordon-Conwell in South Hamilton, Massachusetts; Trinity in Chicago; and Fuller in Pasadena, California have been among the fastest-growing in America. Interchurch organizations and conferences such as the Reformed Ecumenical Synod, the National Association of Presbyterian and Reformed Churches, and the Philadelphia Conferences on Reformed Theology have promoted Calvinistic unity and development. Puritan and Reformed, Eerdmans, Banner of Truth Trust, InterVarsity Press, and other major publishers have been pouring forth reprints of Calvinist classics and new articulations of Reformed positions. Such periodicals as *Christianity Today*, the *Reformed Journal*, the *Westminster Theological Journal*, and *The Reformed Review* have been controlled or strongly influenced by Calvinists. Such Reformed scholars and pastors as J. I. Packer, John Stott, Cornelius Van Til, Francis Schaeffer, G. C. Berkouwer, Harold John Ockenga, Carl Henry, and Harold Lindsell have promoted both evangelicalism and Calvinism.

CONCLUSIONS

As we have seen, by 1920 the groundwork had been laid for sweeping changes in American public life. The process of secularization that increasingly affected American society after 1870 grew even stronger after 1920. During the sixty years after that date, our political, economic, social, educational, and moral life became more and more secular. Yet America has not become as secular as most European nations. Our religious roots are deeper and firmer than those of most other nations. The fact that our nation was originally settled by Christians who sought to build a biblical commonwealth makes us unique. From the beginning, America was strongly shaped by biblical presuppositions and values. We can endlessly debate whether the fathers of our country and the framers of our Constitution were Christians or deists or whether America was ever a consistently Christian nation. It is clear, however, that basic biblical conceptions and ideals underlay a considerable portion of our early political, social, educational, and moral institutions and practices. It also seems apparent that in the twentieth century our common understanding of these dimensions of life has shifted dramatically and that the biblical consensus of earlier days on these matters has been significantly eroded. Christians can no longer count on the culture to promote their social and moral standards.

Today our public life is based chiefly upon secular rather than Christian values. Social relationships, economic transactions, legislative decisions, moral choices, educational curriculum and methodology, and modern communications rest largely upon secular perspectives and principles. Biblical teachings that marriage is a divinely ordained, permanent institution, that business enterprises should strive to glorify God by serving human needs, that political policies and practices should promote righteousness and justice, that human laws should be based upon God-given moral principles, that education should teach children to love and obey God, and that the media should present God's truth in all areas of life are often discarded. Instead, marriage is considered a contract between two people, which can be dissolved whenever one party is not fulfilling its duties or is not meeting the needs of the other. Consequently, divorce has risen to unprecedented levels. Many business, commercial, and industrial enterprises seek primarily to make profits and to benefit stockholders rather than to promote the public good. Huge transnational corporations have arisen which, driven by their desire to maximize profits, have frequently exploited their employees and sometimes interfered in the political affairs of developing nations. Occupational life increasingly has been separated from religious considerations. Many Americans think that their religious faith has little or nothing to do with their vocations. Political strategies and decisions are usually based on pragmatic considerations rather than on eternal moral principles. Likewise, moral choices increasingly rest upon situational, contextual factors rather than upon divine absolutes. Most court cases are decided on purely legal bases or on grounds provided by rationally trained experts who pay little attention to religion.

Much of public education inculcates humanistic values. Alternative, biblical approaches to history, morality, and science are ruled sectarian by the courts and thus disallowed by school administrators. Theistic approaches are rooted in faith not fact. They are not neutral, objective, and empirical like the instructional methodology and curriculum of the public schools supposedly are. As numerous critics have documented, however, the public schools do not simply present facts; they interpret those facts. Many teachers and textbooks base their lessons upon humanistic worldviews. Value free education is impossible. When biblical assumptions about life ceased to underlie public education, other religious ideas quite naturally replaced them. The public schools have become the chief agency in our country for spreading the established cultural religion; they seek to instill society's norms and to discredit deviant ideas.

Many today also insist that schools should not teach particular moral values. They should only help students clarify their own values, that is, help them learn how to evaluate different ethical systems. Such an approach, however, teaches students that all values are relative. It teaches them that values do not rest upon any absolute norms but that each person is free to select those guidelines which seem best to him from the smorgasboard of available values.

Many of the colleges and universites that were founded by

Christians and for years taught a biblical worldview now inculcate a secular understanding of life. Christian perspectives are sometimes ridiculed and more often ignored in American academia, and few distinctively evangelical universities exist in our country.[54]

Much of the media neglects, mocks, or even denounces Christianity. God's relationship to the world is generally considered irrelevant to analyzing news. Rarely does a major television network or a Hollywood movie present an avowed biblical perspective or portray Christian persons sympathetically.

Yet to say that America has become a secular society is only partially correct. Secularism has made deep inroads into all dimensions of American public life. At the same time, however, widespread private expression of religiosity has continued unabated from the early nineteenth century. Numerous independent polls from the 1940s to the present day have consistently revealed that 97 percent of Americans believe in God (although these polls rarely define the term "God"). Over 60 percent of Americans belong to Christian or Jewish congregations, and over 40 percent of us attend worship services on a typical weekend. And about one third of all adult Americans testify that they have been born again.[55]

Many Americans, however, seem to separate their lives into categories — to operate by one philosophy in their private lives and another in their public activities. This dichotomy is reinforced by the fact that the Bible is more revered than read in America. Polls have repeatedly demonstrated that few Americans understand the basic doctrines of their religious communions.[56] Because many Americans do not know what the Bible teaches about social, economic, political, and moral issues, they unwittingly accept secular understandings of these areas. Others realize that many of their political, social, economic, and moral beliefs and practices are inconsistent with Scripture, but they insist that biblical teachings are products of earlier cultural settings and therefore are irrelevant in our modern context. To enhance their reputation in the community or to maintain their family traditions, many continue to affirm religious doctrines that contradict or at least have little effect upon their public behavior.

By the 1970s it was obvious that the foundations for American sociocultural life had shifted fundamentally. Behaviors that were socially acceptable and publicly approved had changed markedly between the 1880s and the 1980s. Living by biblical values was much more expected, and deviation considered much more loathesome in the 1880s than a century later. By the 1970s surveys revealed that many Americans had repudiated such biblical norms as premarital chastity, sexual faithfulness within marriage, life-long marriage, strict observance of the Sabbath, and tithing.[57] The social context made it more difficult to live by biblical standards in the 1970s and 1980s than it had been in the 1870s and 1880s.

Yet in the midst of the hedonism and affluence of the 1970s, termed the "Me-Generation" by cultural historian Thomas Wolfe and the "Culture of Narcissism" by social critic Christopher Lasch, evangelical Christianity has once again risen to public prominence.[58] Millions claim to be born again, theologically conservative denominations and congregations are growing rapidly, Christian television and radio shows have proliferated, attendence at evangelical colleges and seminaries has risen dramatically. Presidential candidates and even presidents themselves profess to be genuine followers of Christ, numerous celebrities claim to have encountered Jesus personally, and the media has given considerable attention to all these developments.[59]

Evaluations of this evangelical renaissance are mixed. Some call it a third (or fourth) great awakening, comparing the development to two earlier outpourings of God's spirit (in the 1740s and the 1820s and '30s) that brought many conversions and significant social changes.[60] Jewish social historian Jeremy Rifkin predicts that evangelical Christianity will be instrumental in shaping the direction of American politics and culture in the 1980s and beyond and warns that only wide acceptance of its social and ethical commitments can sustain humanity in the twenty-first century. Along with Christopher Lasch and Daniel Yankelovich, Rifkin predicts a new age of scarcity, an age in which our expectations for greater affluence cannot possibly be fulfilled. He insists, however, that the hope of the future lies in a new life-style of conservation, sacrifice, and service, which he believes evangelical Christians will promote.[61]

Others, though, sharply criticize the evangelical resurgence. They note that while millions claim to have experienced the risen Christ personally, American moral conduct has not improved significantly. Divorce, child and spouse abuse, drug addiction, alcoholism, and aberrant sexual practices are at high levels. Dishonesty remains prevalent; selfishness and hedonism run rampant. Exploitation, discrimination, and racism persist. Our foreign policy continues to be shaped more by pragmatic considerations than by a desire to promote international justice; businessmen offer bribes, evade taxes, produce inferior products, and seek to cajole people into buying products that bring few benefits. Clearly, these critics argue, the evangelical renewal, at least thus far, is superficial. It has not penetrated to the depths of American society and begun to shift our cultural foundations back once again toward biblical positions. The revival is doing little to alter individual behavior significantly or to restructure institutions, redirect social relationships, build an economic order more sensitive to diminishing resources or more attuned to global needs, or to reevaluate our political priorities and practices. Unlike the first two great awakenings, the current revival has yet to begin to change social norms. For many evangelicals, conversion is simply an event or a decision that guarantees respectibility, self-worth, and eternal life but does not radically reorient their thinking or reshape their conduct.[62]

Prominent leaders today urge evangelical Christians to labor to re-cement America to its original biblical foundation or even to build stronger foundations than were laid originally. They challenge us to work to make our public life conform once again to scriptural standards.[63] We can do this effectively only if we understand what values previously underlay our sociocultural life and how these values have shifted.

It is probably impossible in this present age to develop a truly Christian culture. History demonstrates that all previous attempts, including those of Calvin's Geneva and Puritan New England, have been fundamentally marred. Biblical values and perspectives have always been amalgamated to some degree with various anti-Christian forces and thus have been somewhat distorted.[64] American society as it existed in 1870 was certainly not consistently Christian. Yet as Winthrop Hudson, Robert Handy, and other scholars have demonstrated, biblical ideals were deeply stamped into many dimensions of our culture at that time.[65] As we seek a Christian transformation of culture, our principal model ought to be the Scriptures — not a particular period of history. Yet history can teach us the possibilities and pitfalls inherent in various approaches to culture. Only by understanding such things can we avoid the errors of the past.

Unfortunately, many of the evangelicals who today challenge us to rebuild America's biblical foundations suggest the same strategies that Calvinists did in the late nineteenth century. Francis Schaeffer, Jerry Falwell, John W. Whitehead, and others insist that the United States should and can become a consistently Christian nation. Those advocating "theonomy," led by R. J. Rushdoony, contend further that our nation should practice every detail of Old Testament civil law. As George Marsden has perceptively pointed out, these men confuse the political principles of the Reformation with the ideals embodied in the Declaration of Independence and the Constitution. While the influence of the Reformation was powerful in colonial America and helped inform the thinking of those who wrote our nation's founding documents, other influences — Greek, Medieval, and Enlightenment — were also strong. Neither the Declaration nor the Constitution directly mentions Christianity or even the Bible. Although America's religious heritage has been substantially Christian, our political system was not built upon the idea that our nation should be a distinctly Christian one. Nor, according to the Scriptures, should it be. While we should strive to bring biblical values to bear upon all public policies and practices, we must guarantee all religious viewpoints, including secular humanism, the right to participate in shaping public life.[66]

Where does the New Testament teach that God's kingdom is political? Where does it command believers to build a distinctly Christian state? Since the New Testament was written in a pre-Christian age, a period in which believers did not direct sociocultural life, is it surprising that it does not instruct Christians to use political power to force nonbelievers to follow its principles? The New Testament does teach us to work to win hearts and souls to Jesus Christ. It tells believers to be salt and light to a world in great need. This is best done by proclaiming and embodying biblical principles in public life, not by seeking to force these principles upon others through the use of government. Since God's law is written on the hearts of all, even those who suppress it are influenced by hearing it. So let us create a society where there is genuine pluralism, where all have the opportunity to speak and participate in all public institutions. In this context, let us present biblical truth and seek to persuade others to accept it and to help us implement it in society.

In retrospect, during the years from 1870 to 1920 American Christians had an excellent opportunity to create a social structure and climate that rested largely upon biblical values but gave all people equal rights and opportunities under the law. Christians' ability to shape society diminished significantly after 1920 as Protestants divided into liberal and conservative camps, and the forces of secularism grew stronger. As evangelicals today begin to regain some of the cultural power and influence they had in the late nineteenth century, it is imperative that we do not repeat the mistakes of that era.

America today stands at a crossroads. Two roads lay before us. One road has been laid by Greek thinkers, Enlightenment philosophers, and secularists of the nineteenth and twentieth centuries. To travel this road, we must repudiate completely the biblical ideals upon which much of our public life has long rested. Signs along this first road declare that because no transcendent standards exist, man is autonomous, ethics is situational, and the state's laws are ultimate.

A second road has been built by Jews and Christians using the Scriptures as a blueprint. To follow it we must believe in the sovereignty and grace of God; and because God rules there are absolute standards for ethics and society. Signs along this road proclaim that God seeks to redeem individuals and the social order.

For three centuries most Americans traveled this second road. While more and more Americans have begun to take the first road during the past sixty years, important vestiges of the biblical path have remained. As Herbert Schlossberg writes, "these remnants are the smile of the Cheshire cat, remaining for a time after the disappearance of the entity in which it was incarnated."[67] Today we have reached a point of decision. The roads are increasingly diverging. The first road leads to disaster and demoralization; the second leads to life and hope. The choice of paths grows more important because disillusionment, doubt, and moral confusion have become increasingly prevalent in America. Few continue to see science and technology as man's savior. Diminishing natural resources, the threat of nuclear annihilation, and the persistence of racism, hunger, poverty, and brutality trouble many. Only as people experience the risen Christ in a personal way and rest social structures and practices more fully on divine principles will we solve our perplexing individual and social problems.

NOTES

INTRODUCTION

[1]Joseph W. Krutch, *The Modern Temper* (1929; New York, 1956), pp. 9, 16.

[2]Walter Lippmann, *A Preface to Morals* (New York: Macmillan, 1929), pp. 8, 12, and passim.

[3]See George Marsden, *Fundamentalism and American Culture: The Shaping of Twentieth Century Evangelicalism, 1870 – 1925* (New York: Oxford University Press, 1980), pp. 3-4, 199-205.

[4]Donald Meyer, "The Dissolution of Calvinism," in *Paths of American Thought*, ed. Arthur M. Schlesinger, Jr. and Morton White (Boston: Houghton Mifflin, 1963), pp. 80-85. Sidney Ahlstrom, in *A Religious History of the American People* (New Haven: Yale University Press, 1972), p. 844, insists that by the end of the nineteenth century unconditional election was the "pet doctrine of the Hard-Shell Baptists, a declining number of Old School Presbyterians, and a few small groups." Cf. Winthrop Hudson, "The Methodist Age in America," *Methodist History* (April 1974):1-15; idem., *Religion in America* (New York: Scribner's, 1973), pp. 178-80; John M. Blum et al., *The National Experience* (New York: Harcourt, Brace and World, 1963), p. 240.

[5]Stow Persons, *American Minds: A History of Ideas* (Huntington, NY: Robert E. Krieger, 1975), pp. 361ff.

[6]See Christopher Lasch, *The Culture of Narcissism: American Life in An Age of Diminishing Expectations* (New York: W. W. Norton and Co., 1979); Daniel Yankelovich, *New Rules: Searching for Self-Fulfillment in a World Turned Upside Down* (New York: Bantam, 1982).

[7]See George Marsden, "America's 'Christian' Origins: Puritan New England as a Case Study," in *John Calvin: His Influence in the Western World*, ed. W. Stanford Reid (Grand Rapids: Zondervan, 1982), pp. 241-62.

CHAPTER 1

[1]I came across this metaphor in Daniel Yankelovich, *New Rules: Searching For Self-Fulfillment in a World Turned Upside Down* (New York: Bantam, 1982), pp. xi-xii.

[2]Charles Hodge and Lyman Atwater, "The Presbyterian Church — its Position and Work," *BRPR* (Jan. 1870):146.

[3]Winthrop Hudson, "The Methodist Age in America," *Methodist History* (April 1974):1-15. See also idem., *Religion in America* (New York: Scribner's, 1973), pp. 178-80; Sydney Ahlstrom, *A Religious History of the American People* (New Haven: Yale University Press, 1972), p. 844; Donald Meyer, "The Dissolution of Calvinism," in *Paths of American Thought*, ed. Arthur M. Schleisinger, Jr. and Morton White (Boston: Houghton Mifflin, 1963), pp. 80-85.

[4]These membership statistics are from Philip Schaff and Samuel I. Prime, eds., *History, Essays, Orations and Other Documents of the Evangelical Alliance* (New York: Harper and Row, 1874), p. 752.

[5]Statistics from *History, Essays, Orations*, pp. 753-54. It seems valid to use

these same percentages, as consistent Calvinists were generally well-educated, usually very interested in higher education, and almost always deeply concerned about the theological orientation of schools under their control or subject to their influence.

[6]Hodge and Atwater, "Presbyterian Church," pp. 136-46, quotations from pp. 136, 139.

[7]Robert Aikman, "The Position of Calvinism," *Methodist Quarterly Review* (April 1873):291-92.

[8]Ibid., pp. 292-93.

[9]Ibid., pp. 294-97, quotations from pp. 294, 297.

[10]Ibid., pp. 307-19.

[11]In 1884 the Alliance did admit the Cumberland Presbyterians, well known for their Arminianism. But they were admitted on historical and technical grounds, in spite of theological objections against their doctrinal position.

[12]James Tadlock, "The Churches that Hold the Westminster Symbols . . . ," in *Memorial Volume of the Westminster Assembly, 1647 – 1897* (Richmond: Presbyterian Committee of Publication, 1897), pp. 173-74; William Roberts, "Calvinistic Forces in the Formation of National Life in the United States," in *Proceedings: Seventh General Council,* ed., G. D. Mathews (Washington: McGill and Wallace, 1899), p. 96; "The Calvinistic Century," *PQ* (Jan. 1901):145-50. Methodists viewed the theological landscape differently. "Does Calvinism Dominate Protestantism?" the editors of the *Christian Advocate* asked in 1901. They answered "No," while acknowledging that its influence was great and widespread. Many Baptist and Congregationalist ministers denied one or more fundamental points of Reformed theology, they argued; and a large percentage of Episcopal clergymen and the overwhelming majority of Lutherans were avowedly anti-Calvinist. Methodists, who in America were almost as numerous as Baptists and Presbyterians combined, were not Calvinists at all. See "Does Calvinism Dominate Protestantism?" *Christian Advocate* (July 25, 1901):1167.

[13]Frederic Platt, "The Renaissance of Calvinism," *London Quarterly Review* (July 1901):219-42; the quotation is from p. 220.

[14]"The Renaissance of Calvianism [sic]," *UP* (Feb. 6, 1902):11; "The Calvinistic Century," *PSt* (Jan. 1, 1902):3-5; Dunlap Moore, "The Renaissance of Calvinism," *Pres* (Nov. 13, 1901):12-13; "The Revival of Calvinism," *Review of Reviews* (Dec. 1901):726-27; *PSt* (Jan. 15, 1902):13; John Fox, " Is the Presbyterian Church Calvinistic?" *Pres* (Oct. 31, 1900):20-21.

[15]See Ephraim Emerton, "Why We Commemorate Calvin," *The Nation* (July 8, 1909):28-29; Benjamin B. Warfield, *Calvin as a Theologian and Calvinism Today* (Philadelphia: Presbyterian Board of Publication, 1909), pp. 29-30; Frederic Platt, "Calvinism and Criticism," *London Quarterly Review* (July 1909):67-89.

[16]Ernest Thompson, *Presbyterians in the South, 1890 – 1972* (3 vols.; Richmond: John Knox, 1973), 3:215.

[17]Ibid., 3:208-9, 257, 446-560. Cf. Thomas C. Johnson, "The Southern Presbyterians," in *The American Church History Series,* ed. Philip Schaff (14 vols.; New York: The Christian Literature Co., 1894), 11:478; G. H. Baskette, "Presbyterian Loyalty," *PQ* (Jan. 1896):91-93.

[18]See David Miller, *UP* (Jan. 28, 1904):4.

[19]J. C. McFeeters, *The Covenanters in America: The Voice of Their Testimony on Present Moral Issues* (Philadelphia: Spangler and Davis, 1882), pp. 61-64, 113ff., 147-66, 177-81; J. M. Foster, *Reformation Principles: Stated and Applied* (Boston, 1890), p. 314; *Reformation Principles Exhibited by the Reformed Presbyterian Church in the United States of America* (New York: J. W. Pratt, 1899), pp. 242-63.

[20]See Wallace Jamison, *The United Presbyterian Story* (Pittsburgh: The Geneva

Press, 1958), pp. 97-112; "Report by the Committee on Industrial Relations to the General Assembly of the UPCNA," quoted in Jamison, *The UP Story,* pp. 108-9; H. H. Marlin, *A Handbook of Christian Social Service* (1911); *Minutes of the General Assembly of the UPCNA,* 1900, pp. 27-29; 1911, p. 966; 1912, pp. 180ff.; 1913, pp. 521ff.

[21]See Ray King, *A History of the Associate Reformed Presbyterian Church* (Charlotte, NC: Board of Christian Education, 1966); "Overture to the Associate Reformed Church," *POS* (July 6, 1910):1.

[22]Henry Zwaanstra, *Reformed Thought and Experience in a New World: A Study of the Christian Reformed Church and its American Environment, 1890–1918* (Kampen: J. H. Kok, 1973), pp. 2-3.

[23]Ibid., pp. 14, 21. The following chapters deal very little, however, with the view and actions of the Christian Reformed Church because before World War I the denomination exercised little national influence. The bulk of its 76,000 members in 1910 were farmers or unskilled laborers who spoke Dutch exclusively and lived in close proximity to Grand Rapids, Michigan. Two recent studies have very closely described the denomination's contributions during the late nineteenth century: Zwaanstra's book and that by James Bratt, *Dutch Calvinism in Modern America: A History of a Conservative Subculture* (Grand Rapids: Eerdmans, 1984).

[24]David J. Burrell, "Church Union," *PQ* (Oct. 1902):384-88; the quotation is from p. 385. Cf. S. M. Woodbridge, "Why I am a Calvinist," *CI* (June 22, 1881):2; J. A. DeBaun, "The Current Theology and the Theology of the Reformed Church in America," *PRR* (July 1896):459-74; E. T. Corwin, "History of the Reformed Church, Dutch," in *American Church History Series,* 8:205.

[25]*PSt* (May 14, 1902):2-3; "A Federal Union," *CO* (June 11, 1890):1. Cf. James McNeilly, "Church Union," *PQ* (Jan. 1903):531-36. Reformed Church leaders maintained that both their demand that ministers be well educated and the rigid terms requiring ministers to subscribe to the Canons of Dort and the Heidelberg Catechism were responsible for their group's attachment to Calvinism. See, e.g., D. D. Demarest, "Reformed Church in America," *SPR* (April 1873):249-69; Cornelius Edgar, "Thoroughly Furnished," *Centennial Discourses,* p. 400.

[26]Lefferts Loetscher, *The Broadening Church: A Study of Theological Issues in the Presbyterian Church since 1869* (Philadelphia: University of Pennsylvania Press, 1954), pp. 1, 155, and passim. See also Robert E. Thompson, *A History of the Presbyterian Churches in the United States* (New York: Scribner's, 1895), pp. 287-88.

[27]See Henry B. Smith, "The Relations of Faith and Philosophy," in *Faith and Philosophy: Discourses and Essays by Henry B. Smith,* ed. George L. Prentiss (New York, 1877), pp. 20-27; Edward Morris, *The Theology of the Westminster Symbols* (Columbus, OH: The Champlin Press, 1900), pp. vii, 7-9, and passim; W. Andrew Hoffecker, *Piety and the Princeton Theologians: Archibald Alexander, Charles Hodge and Benjamin Warfield* (Phillipsburg, NJ: Presbyterian and Reformed, 1981).

[28]George Marsden, *The Evangelical Mind and the New School Presbyterian Experience* (New Haven: Yale University Press, 1970), pp. 213ff.

[29]Edward Morris, "The Doctrinal Platform of Our Church" (Cincinnati: Elm St., 1882), pp. 17, 19. See Marsden, *Evangelical Mind,* pp. 219ff. Two other reasons suggest that it is an oversimplification to assume that the doctrinal inclinations of New School Presbyterians led directly to theological liberalism. One is that some former New Schoolers, such as Edward D. Morris, either opposed all revision of the Westminster Confession after 1890 or supported only moderate changes that would not impair the integrity of the Calvinistic system. On the other hand, such former Old Schoolers as James McCosh, J. T. Duffield, Theodore Cuyler, Henry

McCook, and William Campbell advocated some type of creedal revision. Second, as George Marsden has shown, the New School had nearly as many affinities with later Fundamentalism as it had with theological liberalism.

It seems more likely that the attempt after 1885 to revise the Westminster Confession and the departure of some Northern Presbyterians from their historic beliefs was a response to new intellectual and cultural developments rather than the continuation of old alignments. This is especially clear, as I will explain in the next chapter, from the fact that one party of Northern Presbyterians did not argue merely for a different or broader interpretation of the Westminster Confession but repudiated many of its basic tenets. See Thompson, *History of the Presbyterian Churches*, p. 240; Marsden, *Evangelical Mind*, pp. 246-49.

[30]See Morris, "Doctrinal Platform," p. 14; Stephen W. Dana, "Presbyterianism" (Philadelphia: Patterson and White, 1880), p. 20: C. C. Hemenway, *Why I am a Presbyterian* (Auburn, NY: Warren S. Towner, 1882); Thomas Murphy, *Presbyterianism in History* (Germantown, PA: The Guide Job Print, 1885); William Alexander, "The Reformation We Need," *PRR* (April 1890):304-6; Scott F. Hershey, *Is Calvinism Doomed?* (Washington: J. L. Pearson, 1890), pp. 21-23.

[31]See Charles Briggs, *The Authority of the Holy Scripture* (New York, 1891); *The Case Against Professor Briggs, Part II* (New York, 1893), pp. 29-45; Loetscher, *Broadening Church*, pp. 51ff.

[32]In the long run the controversy brought to the surface currents of thought which by the mid-1920s made theological liberalism tolerated in the denomination. After 1900 opponents of Calvinism gained increasing influence over Northern Presbyterian seminaries. The proportion of ministers trained in non-Presbyterian seminaries grew steadily. The 1906 merger with the basically Arminian Cumberland Presbyterians made doctrinal compromise seem respectable. And secularizing trends in the culture made the environment favorable.

[33]*Baptist Advance: The Achievements of the Baptists of North American for A Century and a Half* (Nashville: Boardman, 1964), p. 13; Kenneth H. Good, *Are Baptists Calvinists?* (Oberlin, OH: Regular Baptist Heritage Fellowship, 1975), pp. 173-76; Robert Torbet, *A History of the Baptists* (Philadelphia: The Judson Press, 1950), pp. 231, 272.

[34]W. G. T. Shedd, *PR* (April 1885):372; "Reception of Baptist Delegation," in *Proceedings: Fifth General Council* (1892), p. 399; William Roberts, *The Presbyterian System: Its Characteristics, Authority and Obligation* (Philadelphia: Presbyterian Board of Publication, 1895), p. 17; "The Calvinistic Century," *PQ* (Jan. 1901):149.

[35]See Francis Beattie, reviewing "*The Sovereignty of God*: A Discussion by President G. W. Northrup, Chicago and Professor Robert Watts, Belfast," *PQ* (Jan. 1895):156-61. Cf. Albert Newman, "Recent Changes in the Theology of Baptists," *American Journal of Theology* (Oct. 1906):594.

[36]Thomas Armitage, *History of Baptists* (New York: Bryan and Taylor, 1887), pp. 777-84; Good, *Are Baptists Calvinists?* p. 185.

[37]Carl Henry, *Personal Idealism and Strong's Theology* (Wheaton, IL: Van Kampen Press, 1951), p. 19. See also J. L. Girardeau, "Strong's Systematic Theology," *PQ* (Jan. 1890):122.

[38]Ernest Reisinger and Fred Malone, "Publishers' Introduction to *Abstract of Systematic Theology* by James P. Boyce" (n.p., n.d.), pp. 2-8; Beattie, *PQ* (Jan. 1897):102.

[39]E. E. Folk, *Baptist Reflector*, quoted in "Publishers' Introduction," p. 21. Compared with Presbyterians, Baptists were more likely to live in rural areas, were more preoccupied with conversion and piety, and lacked a historical tradition of

responsibility for directing national culture. These factors combined to make Baptist Calvinists less active than Presbyterian and Reformed Calvinists in addressing cultural issues. See Rufus B. Spain, *At Ease in Zion: A Social History of Southern Baptists* (Nashville: Vanderbilt University Press, 1967).

[40]George Harris, *A Century's Change in Religion* (Boston: Houghton Mifflin, 1914), pp. 24-26.

[41]Williston Walker, *A History of the Congregational Churches in the United States,* in *The American Church History Series,* 3:397-98, 410-11.

[42]Frank H. Foster, *A Genetic History of the New England Theology* (Chicago: University of Chicago Press, 1907), p. 543; G. B. Smith, "Theological Thinking in America," in *Religious Thought in the Last Quarter-Century,* ed. G. B. Smith (Chicago: University of Chicago Press, 1927), p. 95.

[43]See Edward A. Lawrence, "The Theology of Calvin — Is It Worth Saving?" *Bibliotheca Sacra* (July 1883):449-62, the quotation from p. 450; Avan Tobey, "The Salvation of Infants," ibid., p. 385; Leonard Withington, "Is Theology an Improvable Science?" *Bibliotheca Sacra* (Oct. 1864):800-1; Granville S. Abbott, "Calvin and Calvinism," *Bibliotheca Sacra* (April 1873):401-21.

[44]Henry M. Dexter, *The Congregationalism of the Last 300 Years* (New York: Harper and Brothers, 1880), p. 711; C. Cushing, "What Congregationalism has Accomplished," *Congregational Quarterly* (Oct. 1876):541-52; "The Congregational Theology of the Future," *Pres* (July 29, 1891):4; Williston Walker, *The Creeds and Platforms of Congregationalism* (New York: Scribner's, 1893), p. 584; George N. Boardman, *A History of New England Theology* (New York: A. D. F. Randolph, 1899), pp. 293-98.

[45]Charles C. Tiffany, *A History of the Protestant Episcopal Church in the United States of America,* in *The American Church History Series,* 3:464-67 and James T. Addison, *The Episcopal Church in the United States, 1789–1931* (New York: Scribner's, 1951), p. 250.

[46]Ross Foster, "The Origin and Development of the Reformed Episcopal Church in America, 1873–1973" (Ph.D. diss. Clarksville School of Theology, 1979), pp. 12ff. Cf. "The Reformed Episcopal Church," *CI* (Aug. 10, 1876):4.

[47]Thomas G. Apple, "The Position of the German Reformed Church in Relation to Calvinism," *Mercersburg Review* (July 1872):450-54; John Sykes, "Why Are We Reformed?" *Mercersburg Review* (Oct. 1872):577-79; C. Clever, "Why Am I Reformed?" *Reformed Quarterly Review* (April 1891):224.

[48]Rupp, "The Reformed Church and Her Creed," *Reformed Quarterly Review* (Jan. 1895):11-15; J. I. Swander, "Calvinism. Our Relation Thereto" (1893), p. 3; Thomas G. Apple, "The Theology of the German Reformed Church," in *Proceedings: Second General Council* (Philadelphia: 1880), p. 490.

[49]James Good, "The German Reformed Coetus, 1747–1792," *PRR* (Oct. 1897):634-35; idem., "The Synod of Dort and the German Reformed," *CI* (Sept. 26, 1900):616.

[50]David Van Horne and James Good in "The Proposition For Federal Union Between the Two Reformed Churches," *PRR* (April 1891):283, 286; T. W. Chambers, "The General Synod of the RC in A," *PR* (Oct. 1886):716.

[51]*SPR* (Oct. 1877):769-72, the quotation from p. 769. Cf. "Views of the Cumberland Presbyterians," *Cath P* (March 1881):236-37; Darby, "Cumberland Presbyterian Church," in *Proceedings: Third General Council,* ed. G. D. Mathews (Belfast: Assembly Offices, 1884), p. 443.

[52]J. H. Martin in "Cumberland Debate," in *Proceedings: Third General Council,* pp. 137, 140, 146, 148, 153, 156. For a discussion of this debate, see Hubert W.

Morrow, "Admission of the Cumberland Presbyterian Church to the World Alliance of Reformed Churches," *Journal of Presbyterian History* (Spring 1977):58-73.

[53]A. A. Hodge, "Recent Theological Literature," *PR* (July 1884):564. Despite this view, also held later by B. B. Warfield and other Northern Presbyterian conservatives, in 1906 the Cumberland Presbyterians were allowed to rejoin their parent denomination. Clearly practical considerations outweighed theological ones in this merger. See John Ames, "Cumberland Liberals and the Union of 1906," *Journal of Presbyterian History* (Spring 1974):3-18.

CHAPTER 2

[1]J. I. Vance, "The World-Wide Mission of Calvinism," *Proceedings: Ninth General Council,* ed. G. D. Mathews (New York: Office of the Alliance, 1909), pp. 162-63. Cf. Moses Hoge, "The Educational Influence of Presbyterianism on National Life," in *Proceedings: Sixth General Council* (London, 1896), p. 152.

[2]Robert Ingersoll, as quoted in Orvin Larson, *American Infidel: Robert G. Ingersoll, A Biography* (New York: The Citadel Press, 1962), p. 28.

[3]Ingersoll, "What Must We Do to Be Saved?" (1880), quoted in Larson, *American Infidel,* p. 160. See Martin Marty, *The Infidel: Freethought and American Religion* (New York: World, 1961), p. 165. Cf. "Ingersoll and Calvinism," *Pres* (June 5, 1880):9; "Ingersoll's Scheme," *PB* (Nov. 24, 1880):1; and "The Popular Refutation," *PB* (Aug. 3, 1881):1, for the Calvinist response to Ingersoll's broadsides.

[4]Cited by F. F. Ellinwood, "Calvinism and Fatalism," *The Homiletic Review* (June 1890):483-84. Cf. *CI* (Jan. 29, 1890):1.

[5]Cited by Ellinwood, "Calvinism and Fatalism," p. 484. For similar attacks on Calvinism, cf. *Pres* (Sept. 3, 1890):1; *PB* (July 11, 1888):1; *CI* (Feb. 10, 1881):1; "Orthodoxy," *CI* (Jan. 13, 1880):1.

[6]James A. Bell, *John Calvin: His Errors, Ignorance, Misconceptions, and Absurdities and the Errors of Presbyterianism, Disclosed and Exposed* (New York, 1891), pp. 7-21.

[7]Joseph Allen, *Three Phases of Modern Theology: Calvinism, Unitarianism, Liberalism* (Boston: George H. Ellis, 1880), pp. 7-25.

[8]Oliver Wendell Holmes, "The Pulpit and the Pew," *NAR* (Feb. 1881):117-38.

[9]John Miller, *Fetish in Theology or Doctrinalism Twin to Ritualism* (Princeton, NJ, 1875), pp. 15-59 and passim. Soon after the publication of this book, the New Brunswick Presbytery of New Jersey removed Miller from the Presbyterian ministry, having concluded that he denied the Trinity. See Robert Thompson, *A History of the Presbyterian Church in the United States* (New York: Scribner's, 1895), p. 225.

[10]John Miller, "Seven Failures of Ultra Calvinism," *Bibliotheca Sacra* (July 1890):491-502.

[11]David Swing, "The Ideal Church," *Forum* (April 1886):199-208.

[12]See "Progressive Orthodoxy," *Andover Review,* 1-8 (May 1885 – Dec. 1885):467-72, 554-64, 56-68, 143-63, 568-81, and "The Present Tendency in Theology," *Andover Review* (Sept. 1890):298-303.

[13]George A. Gordon, *Ultimate Conceptions of Faith* (Boston: Houghton Mifflin, 1903), p. 34. While noting that Beecher was not a professional theologian, Gordon believed that he accurately represented the views of the Andover Progressives (pp. 34-35). Cf. Lyman Abbott, "No Theology and New Theology," *Forum* (March 1890):187; Sydney Ahlstrom, *A Religious History of the American People* (New Haven: Yale University Press, 1972), p. 771.

[14]Quoted by Paxton Hibben, *Henry Ward Beecher: An American Portrait* (New

York: George H. Doran, 1927), pp. 309-10; Henry Ward Beecher, "Progress of Thought in the Church," *NAR* (Aug. 1882):110ff.

[15]Cited by Hibben, *Henry Ward Beecher,* p. 310.

[16]Beecher, "Progress of Thought in the Church," pp. 112-17.

[17]Beecher, "Spiritual Barbarism," cited in *Henry Ward Beecher: A Sketch of His Career,* ed. Lyman Abbott (Hartford, CT: American, 1887), p. 482. Cf. Beecher, "Progress of Thought in the Church," pp. 106, 112.

[18]Beecher, "Spiritual Barbarism," p. 482.

[19]Cited in Lyman Abbott, *Henry Ward Beecher* (New York: Houghton Mifflin, 1903), p. 12.

[20]Hibben, *Henry Ward Beecher,* p. 235.

[21]Gordon, *Ultimate Conceptions,* p. 38. Cf. Gordon's *The New Epoch for Faith* (Boston: Houghton Mifflin, 1901), p. 261; and *The Christ of Today* (Boston: Houghton Mifflin, 1900), p. 184.

[22]Gordon, "The Contrast and Agreement between the New Orthodoxy and the Old," *Andover Review* (Jan. 1893):5.

[23]Ibid., p. 5. Cf. Gordon, *New Epoch,* p. 262; idem., *Ultimate Conceptions,* p. 38; Newman Smyth, *Orthodox Theology of Today* (New York: Ward Lock and Co., n.d.), pp. 36-38; "Progressive Orthodoxy — VIII," *Andover Review* (Dec. 1885):572.

[24]Gordon, *Ultimate Conceptions,* pp. 39-40. Cf. idem., "Contrast and Agreement," p. 6; *New Epoch,* p. 275.

[25]Gordon, *New Epoch,* pp. 276-77; idem., *Christ of Today,* p. 186. Cf. George N. Boardman, *A History of New England Theology* (New York: A. D. F. Randolph, 1899), p. 297.

[26]George A. Gordon, "The Theological Problem for Today," *Outlook* (Dec. 4, 1897):868-73.

[27]Lyman Abbott, "The Spirit of Calvinism," *Outlook* (July 9, 1904):585-86; idem., "Paul's Doctrine of Election," ibid., pp. 866-71; Charles Gore, "Legitimate Reactions from Calvinism," *Outlook* (Oct. 9, 1897):365-68.

[28]Quoted by Charles A. Dickey, "American Impressions of the Alliance," *Cath P* (Dec. 1880):452.

[29]*Christian Advocate* (June 14, 1888):390; L. W. Munhall, "Not 'Converted to Calvinism'," *Christian Advocate* (June 23, 1898):1094.

[30]W. L. Nourse, "Calvinism," *PQ* (Oct. 1891):572; A. A. Hodge, *Popular Lectures on Theological Themes* (Philadelphia: Presbyterian Committee of Publication, 1887), p. 214; G. D. Mathews, "Presbyterian and Methodist Union," *Cath P* (Oct. 1883):302; W. J. R. Taylor, "American Methodism in 1876," *PQPR* (Oct. 1876):591, 607.

[31]D. Fisk Harris, *Calvinism: Contrary to God's Word and Man's Moral Nature* (1880), pp. 111, 126ff., 279, 321ff., 374ff., 392ff., 404; *Christian Advocate* (Feb. 5, 1891):84, and *Christian Advocate* (March 20, 1890):177.

[32]C. B. Stoddard, "Some Misinterpretations of Scripture," *Christian Advocate* (Aug. 20, 1876):557-58; See also "Predestination Doctrine Misrepresented," *BT* (March 24, 1910):180-81; *Misrepresentations of Calvinism Briefly Corrected* (Philadelphia: Presbyterian Board of Publication, n.d.), p. 1; Madison G. Peters, "Popular Lies Concerning Calvinism" (Philadelphia: A. T. Zeising, 1885), pp. 4-5; Thorton C. Whaling, "The Condescension of Some Apostles of Modern Thought," *PQ* (July 1900):444.

[33]*Christian Advocate* (June 25, 1891):415. Cf. J. B. Mann, "Why Change Their Creed?" *Christian Advocate* (July 24, 1890):483; *Christian Advocate* (March 9, 1893):156.

[34]Stoddard, "Some Misinterpretations," pp. 557-58. Cf. John A. Faulkner, "What is the Real Difference between Calvinism and Arminianism?" *Christian Advocate* (Aug. 1, 1901):1220; "Calvinism Past and Present," *Christian Advocate* (Nov. 16, 1899):1822.

[35]James Orr, "Calvin and His Doctrinal System," in *Proceedings: Ninth General Council*, pp. 86-89; Peters, "Popular Lies Concerning Calvinism," pp. 3-5; "Misrepresentations of Calvinism," p. 1; "An Uncalled For and Baseless Charge," *Pres* (May 6, 1891): p. 4; "Predestination Doctrine Misrepresented," pp. 180-81.

[36]"Ignorance of What Calvinism Is," *SP* (March 23, 1905):6; "Calvinism," *SWP* (March 22, 1888):1; W. L. Nourse, "Calvinism; Calvinism and Infant Salvation," *PQ* (Oct. 1891):586; "Predestination Doctrine Misrepresented," pp. 180-81; "Of Course," *Pres* (June 5, 1880):9.

[37]B. B. Warfield, "Recent Reconstructions of Theology," *The Homiletic Review* (March 1891):202ff. Cf. Henry Beets, "The New vs. the Old Theology," *BT* (March 1902):130; Francis Patton, "Is Andover Romanizing?" *Forum* (June 1887):334; Samuel Smith, "The Andover Renaissance in Theology," *PQ* (July 1887):36.

[38]J. A. DeBaun, "The Current Theology and the Theology of the Reformed Church in America," *PRR* (July 1886):461-65.

[39]DeBaun, "Current Theology," pp. 466-67; Beets, "New vs. the Old," pp. 130-31; G. D. Mathews, "Mr. Beecher's Theology," *Cath P* (Oct. 1883):302; A. A. Hodge, *PR* (Oct. 1883):874-75.

[40]DeBaun, "Current Theology," pp. 468-69.

[41]Warfield, "Recent Reconstructions," pp. 205-6, 208; Patton, "Is Andover Romanizing?" pp. 335, 337; Smith, "Andover Renaissance," p. 60; Beets, "New vs. the Old," pp. 130ff.

[42]"Strength of Calvinism," *Banner* (May 12, 1905):197-99; A. A. Hodge, *Popular Lectures*, p. 161; Peters, "Popular Lies," pp. 1-2; William Breed, "Memories and Duties," in *Addresses Delivered at the Centennial Celebration of the General Assembly of the Presbyterian Church* (Philadelphia: MacCalla and Co., 1888), p. 214; "The Closing Year," *CO* (Jan. 1, 1890):4.

[43]The Adopting Act made the Westminster Confession and Catechisms the official standard for American Presbyterians, but it also stated that some doctrines in them were not necessary and essential to the whole and that even the essential doctrines of the standards might be understood and stated differently by some. See Leonard Trinterud, *The Forming of an American Tradition* (Philadelphia: Westminster, 1949), pp. 48-49.

[44]See George Marsden, *The Evangelical Mind and The New School Presbyterian Experience* (New Haven: Yale University Press, 1970), pp. 213ff.

[45]William Hutchison, *The Modernist Impulse in American Protestantism* (Cambridge, MA: Harvard University Press, 1976), pp. 51-64. Several circumstantial factors help account for Swing's acquittal. His trial occurred only three years after the reunion of the New and Old School parties in 1870, and the spirit of brotherhood and the inclination to tolerate moderate theological differences remained strong. Most Presbyterians in Chicago respected Swing's long and successful ministry in that city. His accuser, Francis Patton, on the other hand, was young and a newcomer to Chicago. The concluding report of the trial emphasized that Patton had not "proved from the published writings of Swing that he discarded any essential doctrine of the Presbyterian Church." At the trial Swing explicitly denied that he opposed any of "the Evangelical Calvinist doctrines" of his communion. These considerations make untenable the conclusion that Swing's acquittal proves that liberalism was widespread among Presbyterians in Chicago or anywhere else during the 1870s. See *The Great Presbyterian Conflict: Patton vs. Swing* (Chicago:

MacDonald and Co., 1874), p. 164. See also pp. 92-105, 138-45, 161-63. The report also added that "Swing is accused on almost every point, on the ground of inferences which do not seem to follow unavoidably from his language. It is a just maxim in our ecclesiastical law that no man should be convicted of an offense, so long as there can be any doubt of his guilt" (p. 167).

[46]Lefferts Loetscher, *The Broadening Church: A Study of Theological Issues in the Presbyterian Church since 1879* (Philadelphia: University of Pennsylvania Press, 1954), pp. 1, 155, and passim.

[47]Philip Schaff, *Creed Revision in the Presbyterian Church* (New York: Scribner's, 1890), p. 42. Cf. David S. Schaff, *The Life of Philip Schaff* (New York: Scribner's, 1897), pp. 286, 321, 426-28; Thomas Hall, "Presbyterianism and Calvinism," *Interior* (Sept. 20, 1900):1158.

[48]E.g., T. K. Davis, *The Calvinistic System* (1900), p. 6.

[49]Hall, "Presbyterianism and Calvinism," p. 1158. Hall claimed that the first time the Northern Presbyterian Church "ever officially attached itself to the name of Calvin" was in the directions the General Assembly gave to its revision committee in 1889. See also "The Westminster Confession," *Outlook* (Oct. 20, 1900):436-37; *New York Independent* (Oct. 11, 1900); John Fox, "Is the Presbyterian Church Calvinistic?" *Pres* (Oct. 31, 1900):20-21.

[50]"The Westminster Confession," *Outlook* (April 28, 1900):942-43.

[51]Francis Patton, "The Revision of the Confession of Faith," in *Addresses and Sermons*, vol. 24, p. 8.

[52]Edward Morris, *Theology of the Westminster Symbols* (Columbus: The Champlin Press, 1900), pp. 808-9. For a conservative Calvinist's endorsement of Morris' orthodoxy, see William Craven, *PRR* (July 1900):542-46.

[53]Patton, "Revision," p. 12.

[54]Warfield, "1903 Revision of the Confession of Faith" (Richmond, 1904), in *Selected Shorter Writings of B. B. Warfield – II*, ed. John E. Meeter (Nutley, NJ: Presbyterian and Reformed, 1973), pp. 398ff. Cf. Southern Presbyterian theologian Samuel A. King who stated in *How Far Has Original Calvinism Been Modified By Time?* (Richmond: Whittet and Shepperson, 1909), p. 25 that the Northern Presbyterian revision of 1903 did not materially "impair the integrity of the system of doctrine set forth in the Confession."

[55]Davis, *Calvinistic System*, pp. 3, 4, 6; Arthur Bierbower, "Corporate Orthodoxy and Personal Heresy," *Ind* (Sept. 21, 1899):2546.

[56]Philip Schaff, "The Calvinistic System in the Light of Reason and the Scripture," *Andover Review* (April 1892):333; Davis, *Calvinistic System*, pp. 4-6.

[57]Philip Schaff, "What is the Calvinistic System?" *Ind* (July 31, 1890):1-2; Philip Schaff, *Creed Revision in the Presbyterian Church* (New York: Scribner's, 1890), pp. 13-14.

[58]George Mott, "A Revised Confession," *Pres* (Sept. 2, 1891):12-13; "The Westminster Confession," *Outlook* (March 16, 1901):614; Schaff, *Creed Revision*, pp. 11, 14, 30.

[59]B. B. Warfield, "The Significance of the Westminster Standards as a Creed" (New York: Scribner's, 1898), pp. 18, 34-36. Cf. B. B. Warfield, "Revision Movement in the Presbyterian Church," *Ind* (Aug. 9, 1900):1908; "The Situation," *Pres* (May 16, 1900):3; W. G. T. Shedd, *Calvinism: Pure and Mixed* (New York: Scribner's, 1893), p. 14.

[60]Patton, "Revision," p. 11. Cf. "The Presbyterian Creed," *Outlook* (May 5, 1900):11, quoting the *Herald and Presbyter*: "the proposition to construct a new creed which shall put in the faith of the Gospel and leave out Calvinism is like the proposition 'to write a sermon and leave out religion.' "

[61]Warfield, *On the Revision of the Confession of Faith* (New York: Anson D. F. Randolph and Co., 1890), pp. 71-73.

[62]Shedd, *Calvinism: Pure and Mixed,* pp. 153-56. Cf. James Ramsey, "The Effect of Revision on the Standards of the Church," *PB* (March 28, 1901):12.

[63]"The Question Which Must Be Settled," *Pres* (April 18, 1900):9.

[64]Warfield, *On the Revision,* pp. 38-40.

[65]J. Ritchie Smith, "The Westminster Confession and Catechism," *PQ* (July 1899):406.

[66]Morris, *Theology of the Westminster Symbols,* p. 802. Cf. Warfield, "Revision Movement," p. 1908; Henry C. Minton, "The Ideal Presbyterian Confession," *Pres* (Aug. 1, 1900):9; "The Situation," p. 3.

[67]Schaff, *Creed Revision,* pp. v, 146. Cf. Howard Crosby, *The Good and Evil of Calvinism* (New York: Anson D. F. Randolph and Co., n.d.), p. 13.

[68]B. B. Warfield, "The Final Report of the Committee on Revision of the Confession," *PRR* (April 1891):329-30; "The Question," p. 9; "Dr. Hillis' Sensation," *Pres* (April 4, 1900):6; "Calvinism," *CI* (July 9, 1890):2; Charles Martindale, "Sovereignty of God and Liberty of Man," *PQ* (Jan. 1903):351-59; "Foreordination," *PB* (March 28, 1901):5.

[69]Davis, *Calvinistic System,* p. 6; "The Presbyterian Creed," *Outlook* (April 21, 1900):897-98.

[70]Schaff, *Creed Revision,* pp. 13-14. Cf. "What is Essential to a Reformed Church?" *Interior* (July 12, 1900):863-64; Mott, "A Revised Confession — No. 2," p. 12.

[71]" 'Saving the Face' of the Creed," *Ind* (June 6, 1901):1330. Cf. "The Westminster Confession," *Outlook* (April 21, 1900):893-94; "The Westminster Confession," *Outlook* (March 16, 1901):614.

[72]Warfield, "Revision Movement," p. 1906; "Revision a Probable Failure," *PB* (June 12, 1889):1; "The Westminster Standards," *Outlook* (Nov. 20, 1897):729; W. S. P. Bryan, "The Proposed Revision of the Standards," *PQ* (Oct. 1889):596.

[73]" 'Saving the Face' of the Creed," p. 1331.

[74]Davis, *Calvinistic System,* p. 6; "Westminster Confession," p. 614.

[75]Quoted in "A Pulpit Blast," *Pres* (June 3, 1891):4.

[76]"The Westminster Standards," *Outlook* (Oct. 20, 1900):436-37. Cf. *New York Independent* (Oct. 11, 1900); John Fox, "Is the Presbyterian Church Calvinistic?" *Pres* (Oct. 31, 1900):20-21.

[77]"The Westminster Standards," *Outlook* (Nov. 20, 1897):729. Cf. Bierbower, "Corporate Orthodoxy," p. 2545; "A Pulpit Blast," p. 4; Hall, "Presbyterian and Calvinism," p. 1158.

[78]"The Westminster Confession," *Outlook* (Nov. 20, 1897):699-700. Cf. Schaff, "The Theology for Our Age and Country," *PQPR* (Jan. 1872):36.

[79]E.g., "Troublers of Israel," *Ind* (May 25, 1911):1123; "A Presbyterian Exodus?" *Ind* (Dec. 22, 1898):1876; "Revision a Probable Failure," p. 3. Cf. R. A. Webb, *PQ* (Oct. 1900):652.

[80]John J. McCook, "Modern Tendencies in the Church," *Pres* (May 16, 1900):7. Cf. Shedd, *Calvinism: Pure and Mixed,* pp. vi, 156.

[81]Patton, "The Revision," pp. 11, 14. Cf. Henry B. Smith, *Faith and Philosophy: Discourses & Essays,* edited and with an introductory note by George L. Prentiss (New York: Scribner, Armstrong & Co., 1877).

[82]Shedd, *Calvinism: Pure and Mixed,* p. 156; Robert Kerr, *Presbyterianism for the People* (Philadelphia: Presbyterian Board of Publication, 1883), pp. 68ff; Warfield, "Significance of the Westminster Standards," p. 36.

[83]Warfield, "Revision Movement," p. 1908.

[84]Warfield, "Presbyterians and their Creed," *Ind* (July 11, 1901):1615.

[85]Warfield, "Final Report," p. 330; idem., *On the Revision*, p. 39.

[86]E.g., Morris, *Theology of the Westminster Symbols*, pp. 805-6; Patton, "The Revision," p. 11.

[87]"Revision in the Northern Church," *CO* (May 7, 1890):4; Steffens, "Proper Attitude," pp. 474, 489; James Harper, "The Revision of the Westminster Confession of Faith," *Evangelical Repository* (Aug. 1891):452-54; "The Northern Assembly," *CO* (May 14, 1890):4; "An Echo of the New Theology," *PSt* (May 15, 1900):4-5; R. A. Webb, "The Revised Confession," *PQ* (April, 1904):451-65.

[88]"The Agitation for the Revision of the Westminster Confession," *Christian Advocate* (May 3, 1900):686-87; "President Patton's Tremendous Paper," *Christian Advocate* (Feb. 6, 1890):81; *Christian Advocate* (April 27, 1893):263.

CHAPTER 3

[1]Bryan Wilson, *Religion in Secular Society* (London, 1966), p. xiv. In "The Meanings of Secularization," in *Secularization and the Protestant Prospect*, ed. James Childress and David Harned (Philadelphia: Westminster, 1970), pp. 31-40, Larry Shiner identifies five ways that social scientists use the term *secularization*. It is the process whereby: 1) religious values decline in social importance; 2) religious groups conform to the world; 3) humanity and nature come to be interpreted solely as the result of mechanistic processes; 4) society rejects the religious understanding that has previously informed its life, considers itself autonomous, and consequently limits religion to the sphere of private life; and 5) beliefs and patterns of behavior are transferred from the "religious" to the "secular" sphere. Although all these meanings inform my use of the word, definitions one and four are primary.

[2]For succinct discussions of the meaning of secularism, see Georgia Harkness, *The Modern Revival of Christian Faith: An Analysis of Secularism* (New York: Abingdon-Cokesbury, 1952), pp. 11-16, who defines secularism as "the organization of life as if God did not exist" (p. 11); and Lesslie Newbigin, *Honest Religion For Secular Man* (London: SCM, 1966).

The term *secularism* was coined by British thinker George J. Holyoake in his *Secularism, the Practical Philosophy of the People* (1845). His definition of secularism as "the doctrine that morality should be based on regard to the well-being of mankind in the present life, to the exclusion of all other considerations drawn from belief in God or a future state" is used by the *Oxford English Dictionary*.

In this chapter, secular humanism and Modernism will be used interchangeably to denote this same complex of ideas.

[3]John M. Bonham, *Secularism: Its Progress and Its Morals* (New York: G. P. Putnam's Sons, 1894), p. 191.

[4]A. O. Lovejoy, "Religious Transition and Ethical Awakening in America," *Hibbert Journal* (July 1908):501. Lovejoy analyzed Shailer Mathew's *The Church and the Changing Order* (1907), Joseph Leighton's *Jesus Christ and the Civilization of Today* (1907), and E. A. Ross's *Sin and Society* (1907), all of which argued that the trends toward secularization made the early twentieth century "a transitional period big both with peril and possibilities for church and society" (pp. 502-14).

[5]Frederick Woodbridge, "Naturalism and Humanism," *Hibbert Journal* (Jan. 1908):6, 14-17. Cf. Robert MacKintosh, "Are We Part of Nature?" ibid., pp. 37ff., and J. H. Muirhead, "Religion a Necessary Constituent in all Education," ibid., pp. 344-45.

[6]B. B. Warfield, *Calvin as a Theologian and Calvinism Today* (Philadelphia: Presbyterian Board of Publication, 1909), pp. 39ff.

⁷Martin Marty, *The Great Schism: Three Paths to the Secular* (New York: Harper and Row, 1969). For a discussion of secularization in Europe and England, see Franklin Baumer, *Religion and the Rise of Skepticism* (New York: Harcourt, Brace and Co., 1960), pp. 10-13, 96ff.

⁸Sidney Mead, *The Old Religion in the Brave New World* (Berkeley, CA: University of California Press, 1977), pp. 1-4, 29-30, 51-53, 55-57, argues that Sectarian Christianity "has survived at the expense of migrating out of the public realm" that its proponents had "dominated for centuries and into the impregnable because ultimately inaccessible recesses of individual hearts." This "internalization" or "privatization" of Christianity is "one of the most momentous changes that has ever taken place in Christendom." Mead notes that unlike their Puritan ancestors, many later Christians did not believe that the "sovereignty of God could be made manifest on earth only by full incarnation in social, political and economic as well as ecclesiastical institutions." As this study will demonstrate, however, while Calvinists and other evangelicals accepted the separation of church and state, significant numbers of them continued to believe that God's kingdom intended to transform public life. Mead exaggerates the extent to which Americans converted religion from a worldview that totally directed their individual and corporate lives into an experience that affected only their private lives. Yet he does describe a trend that has strongly influenced American religion during the past one hundred years. See also Thomas Luckmann, "The Invisible Religion," in *Secularization and the Protestant Prospect,* pp. 71-92, esp. pp. 75-78, 80-81; and Paul Carter, *The Spiritual Crisis of the Gilded Age* (DeKalb, IL: Northern Illinois University Press, 1972).

⁹In *A Common Faith* (New Haven: Yale University Press, 1934), p. 48 and passim John Dewey summarizes the naturalistic views he had expounded in numerous works written after 1890. "There are values, goods, actually realized upon a natural basis. . . . We need no external criterion and guarantee of their goodness. They are had, they exist as good, and out of them we frame our ideal ends." In *Drift and Mastery: An Attempt to Diagnose the Current Unrest* (1914; Englewood Cliffs, NJ: Prentice-Hall, 1961), p. 91, Walter Lippmann wrote: "we are unsettled to the very roots of our being. We don't know how to behave when eternal authority has disappeared."

¹⁰E.g., T. H. Huxley, *Evolution and Ethics* (London, 1893), pp. 26-29, 34 and passim; Herbert Spencer, *Data of Ethics* (New York, 1880), pp. 123, 126. Both Huxley and Spencer lectured widely across America in the late nineteenth century. See also John Dewey, *Moral Principles in Education* (Boston: Houghton Mifflin, 1909), p. 58; idem., *The Influence of Darwinism on Philosophy and Other Essays in Contemporary Thought* (New York, 1910), pp. 263, 267-68; Antonio Llano, "Morality the Last of the Dogmas," *Philosophical Review* (July 1896):386ff.; W. R. Sorley, *Ethics of Naturalism* (1904).

¹¹Marty, *The Great Schism,* pp. 99-141, quotation from p. 115.

¹²Robert Handy, *A Christian America: Protestant Hopes and Historical Realities* (New York: Oxford University Press, 1971). Winthrop Hudson's judgment that by the middle of the nineteenth century "Protestantism had established undisputed sway over almost all aspects of the nation's life" is much more characteristic of scholarly opinion than Marty's view. Hudson adds that "among the populace at large the patterns of belief and conduct — both private and public, individual and corporate — were set by the churches" (*American Protestantism* [Chicago: University of Chicago Press, 1961], pp. 109-10).

¹³Stow Persons, *American Minds: A History of Ideas* (Huntington, NY: Robert E. Krieger, 1975), pp. 237-362. Cf. Henry May, *The End of American Inno-*

cence: A Study of the First Years of Our Own Time, 1912–1917 (New York: Knopf, 1959), pp. 121-216.

[14]See May, *End of American Innocence*, pp. 169-212, and Persons, *American Minds*, pp. 241-362.

[15]George Santayana, "Warning Against Spiritual Shipwreck," *Current Opinion* (Aug. 13, 1913):120.

[16]Herbert Spencer, *First Principles* (1862), Part I, p. 60. Cf. Bonham, *Secularism*, p. 248.

[17]See James Bixby, *The Ethics of Evolution* (Boston: Small, Maynard and Co., 1900), pp. 16-19 and passim; Minot Savage, "Natural Ethics," *NAR* (Sept. 1881):237ff.; John Dewey, "Evolution and Ethics," *Monist* (April, 1898):325-26.

[18]A. A. Hodge, "Adaptation of Presbyterianism to the Wants and Tendencies of the Day," *Proceedings: First General Council*, ed. J. Thompson (Edinburgh: Thomas and Archibald Constable, 1877), pp. 56-58.

[19]Ibid., pp. 58-60.

[20]T. D. Witherspoon, "The Work of Presbyterianism for the Future," in *Addresses Delivered at the Centennial Celebration of the General Assembly of the Presbyterian Church* (Philadelphia: MacCalla and Co., 1888), pp. 25-26, 29-32.

[21]William T. Herridge, "Christianity and Culture," *PR* (July 1888):404.

[22]Donald Tewksbury, *The Founding of American Colleges and Universities Before the Civil War* (Hamden, CT: Archon Books, 1965), pp. 90-91, reports that Calvinists sponsored almost half of all American colleges established before 1860. For Calvinists' influential role in the voluntary societies of this period, as well as for their cultural prestige and power, see Charles I. Foster, *An Errand of Mercy: The Evangelical United Front, 1790–1837* (Chapel Hill, NC: University of North Carolina Press, 1960), pp. 123, 143, 240-42. For Calvinists' leadership in science during the antebellum period, see Theodore Bozeman, *Protestants in An Age of Science: The Baconian Ideal and Antebellum American Religious Thought* (Chapel Hill, NC: University of North Carolina Press, 1977), chap. 1.

[23]Abraham Kuyper, *Lectures on Calvinism* (1898; Grand Rapids: Eerdmans, 1931), "Biographical Note," pp. i-vii; Frank Vandenberg, *Abraham Kuyper* (Grand Rapids: Eerdmans, 1960), pp. 203-4; Jan Van Lonkhuyzen, "Abraham Kuyper—A Modern Calvinist," *PTR* (Jan. 1921):131-47; "Dr. Kuyper," *Pres* (Oct. 26, 1898):7; Henry Beets, "Dr. Abraham Kuyper," *BT* (Feb. 26, 1904):65-68.

[24]Kuyper, *Lectures on Calvinism*, pp. 11-17.

[25]Ibid., pp. 17-19.

[26]Ibid., pp. 21-26.

[27]Ibid., pp. 26-28.

[28]Ibid., pp. 29-31. Cf. Lyman Atwater, "Calvinism in Doctrine and Life," *PQPR* (Jan. 1875):86; William Hastie, *The Theology of the Reformed Church in its Fundamental Principles* (Edinburgh: T. and T. Clark, 1904), pp. 239-41; Herman Bavinck, "Calvin and Common Grace," *PTR* (July 1909):460-63.

[29]Kuyper, *Lectures on Calvinism*, pp. 11, 19, 41, 172-80.

[30]Ibid., pp. 173-82, 199.

[31]Ibid., pp. 183-87.

[32]Ibid., pp. 187-95.

[33]*Outlook* (Nov. 18, 1899):694.

[34]*Methodist Review* (Jan. 1900):174.

[35]William N. Clarke, *American Journal of Theology* (July 1900):634-35.

[36]Henry Beets, "Calvinism," *BT* (Sept. 1899):47-48.

[37]Francis Beattie, *Calvinism in Modern Thought* (Philadelphia: Westminster, 1901), pp. 4-47.

[38]Henry C. Minton, *PRR* (July 1900):536-39.

[39]Nicholas M. Steffens, "Calvinism and the Theological Crisis," *PRR* (April 1901):222-23; Cf. Henry Beets, "Calvinism as a Life-System," *BT* (May 20, 1904):161-63; Robert H. Fleming, "The Alliance of Reformed Churches," *CO* (June 29, 1910):6; John C. Monsma, *What Calvinism Has Done for America* (Chicago: Rand McNally and Co., 1919).

[40]Frederic Platt, "The Renaissance of Calvinism," *London Quarterly Review* (July 1901):219-23.

[41]Hastie, *Theology*, pp. 129, 159, 162-63; Herman Bavinck, "The Future of Calvinism," *PRR* (Jan. 1894):3-5. Cf. J. I. Vance, "The World-Wide Mission of Calvinism," in *Proceedings: Ninth General Council*, ed. G. D. Mathews (London: Office of the Alliance, 1909), p. 165; A. M. Hunter, "Has Calvinism a Future?" *Biblical World* (Oct. 1914):233, 238; B. B. Warfield, *Calvin and Calvinism* (New York: Oxford University Press, 1931), p. 355; T. V. Moore, "The Power and Claims of a Calvinistic Literature" (Philadelphia: Presbyterian Board of Publication, 1859), pp. 6ff.; Francis Beattie, "Some Salient Features of Presbyterian Doctrine," *PQ* (Oct. 1899):667. See also H. Henry Meeter, *The Fundamental Principle of Calvinism* (Grand Rapids: Eerdmans, 1930).

[42]Ernst Troeltsch, "Calvin and Calvinism," *Hibbert Journal* (Oct. 1909):104-5.

[43]Hastie, *Theology*, p. 164. Cf. Troeltsch, "Calvin and Calvinism," p. 108; Platt, "Renaissance of Calvinism," p. 233.

[44]Kuyper, *Lectures on Calvinism*, pp. 50-54. Cf. Warfield, *Calvin as a Theologian*, p. 37; David Woodside, "The Influence of Calvinism on the World Today," in *Proceedings: Ninth General Council*, p. 162; S. L. Morris, "The Relation of Calvin and Calvinism to Missions," in *Calvin Memorial Addresses* (Richmond: Presbyterian Committee of Publication, 1909), pp. 132ff.

[45]Geerhardus Vos, *The Kingdom and the Church* (1904; Grand Rapids: Eerdmans, 1951), pp. 27, 29, 87-88. Cf. J. M. Foster, *Christ the King* (Boston, 1894), pp. 201-5; "The Onward Kingdom," *UP* (Sept. 30, 1880):631; Edward Morris, "The Future of Humanity on Earth," *PR* (July 1880):438.

[46]For a fuller development of Calvinistic views of culture, see H. Henry Meeter, *The Basic Ideas of Calvinism* (Grand Rapids: Grand Rapids International Publications, 1960), pp. 70-226, and Henry VanTil, *The Calvinistic Concept of Culture* (Philadelphia: Presbyterian and Reformed, 1959), pp. 18-50, 94-110, 191-245.

[47]See Paul Scotchner, "Reformed Foundations for Social Concern: A Comparison of Sixteenth Century European Ideas," *Westminster Theological Journal* (Spring 1978):323-25.

[48]See George Marsden, *Fundamentalism and American Culture: The Shaping of Twentieth Century Evangelicalism, 1870 – 1925* (New York: Oxford University Press, 1980), pp. 125-38.

[49]Kuyper, *Lectures on Calvinism*, pp. 50-51.

[50]Warfield, *PTR* (Jan. 1903):139-41. Cf. Warfield, *Faith and Life* (New York: Longmans, Green and Co., 1916), pp. 49, 204, 207; Kuyper, *Lectures on Calvinism*, pp. 30-31.

[51]See Marsden, *Fundamentalism and American Culture*, pp. 31-32, 62ff. Marsden observes that the abolition of individual vices such as playing cards, dancing, drinking, and attending the theater almost totally replaced earlier efforts to build a glorious civilization for such evangelicals as Charles Blanchard (who served as the president of Wheaton College from 1882 until 1925) and Dwight L. Moody.

[52]Hodge, "The System of Theology Contained in the Westminster Shorter Catechism Opened and Explained" (Philadelphia: Westcott and Thomson, 1886), Part I, pp. 25, 51; William Blaikie, "Christianity, Calvinism and Culture," *Cath P* (May

1879):323-27, 329; Emil Doumergue, "Calvin, an Epigone of the Middle Ages or an Initiator of Modern Times?" *PTR* (Jan. 1909):95-96, 100-101; William Griffis, "The Vicious Distinction Between the Sacred and the Secular," *CI* (Aug. 1, 1900): pp. 495-96.

[53]Warfield, *PTR* (Jan. 1903):140.

[54]A. A. Hodge, *Popular Lectures on Theological Themes* (Philadelphia: Presbyterian Board of Publication, 1887), pp. 10, 19, 26, 293, 296-97, 324, with the quotation from p. 327. In the typology of H. Richard Niebuhr, Anabaptists and dispensationalists adopt a stance of "Christ against culture," stressing the antagonism between the demands of Christ and the development of society. Liberal Protestants endorse "the Christ of culture," believing that there is a fundamental agreement between the claims of Christ and the pattern of society. Catholics place "Christ above culture," seeing him as the fulfillment of all cultural aspirations and the church as the central institution of society. Lutherans and many Fundamentalists see "Christ and culture in paradox." They perceive a tension or a polarity between the demands of Christ and those of society and tend to compartmentalize life into secular and sacred activities. Calvinists, as well as Methodists, generally understand Christ to be the "transformer of culture." While recognizing human depravity and social transmission of sin, belief in the opposition between Christ and all human institutions and customs does not lead them to separate from the world or simply to endure "in the expectation of a transhistorical salvation," as does the fourth position. Rather, Christ is seen as converting human beings *in* their culture. The primary difference between Methodists and Calvinists is that the former are more individualistic and have not developed as fully as Calvinists have the corporate implications of Christ's lordship. See H. Richard Niebuhr, *Christ and Culture* (New York: Harper and Row, 1951), pp. 39-44, 219, and passim.

[55]Kuyper, *Lectures on Calvinism*, pp. 50-51, 187-89. Cf. Platt, "Renaissance of Calvinism," pp. 235-36.

[56]Warfield, *Calvin as a Theologian*, p. 31; Kuyper, *Lectures on Calvinism*, p. 69. Cf. Hodge, *Popular Lectures*, pp. 160-61; "Unconscious Calvinism," *BT* (July 8, 1909):448.

[57]Warfield, *Calvin and Calvinism Today*, pp. 23, 33.

[58]See H. J. Kuiper, "Calvinism versus Humanism," *BT* (Sept. 9, 1915):556-57. See also Luther Gerlach, *People, Power, Change: Movements of Social Transformations* (Indianapolis: Bobbs-Merrill, 1970), pp. 4, 36-42, 53, 55, 65ff.

[59]Stow Persons points out that in late-nineteenth-century America, naturalism as a philosophy emphasizing materialism, determinism, atheism, or antitheistic humanism was not widely accepted. But humanistic theists often promoted secular premises. See "Religion and Modernity, 1865 – 1914," in *The Shaping of American Religion*, pp. 376-80.

[60]See Henry May, *Protestant Churches and the Industrial America* (New York: Harper and Brothers, 1949), pp. 205-35, and James Timberlake, *Prohibition and the Progressive Movement* (Cambridge, MA: Harvard University Press, 1963), pp. 7-36, 130-48.

[61]Bonham, *Secularism*, p. 305; Henry S. Commanger, *The American Mind* (New Haven: Yale University Press, 1950), pp. 9, 162, 179; Merle Curti, *The Growth of American Thought* (New York: Henry Holt and Co., 1953), p. 325.

[62]George Marsden argues that the shift from an emphasis on the Old Testament age of law to one on the New Testament age of the Spirit produced a more "private" view of Christianity. While the Holiness movement in some cases stimulated great efforts to improve society, it generally led to an inward, private religiosity. In addition, the kingdom was no longer seen as a kingdom of laws; "hence civil law

would not help its advance." Marsden, *Fundamentalism and American Culture*, pp. 87-88.

[63]See Handy, *Christian America*, pp. 165-66, 183; Hudson, *American Protestantism*, p. 124, 135; and Sidney Mead, *The Lively Experiment: The Shaping of Christianity in America* (New York: Harper and Row, 1963), pp. 142, 154.

[64]Nathaniel West, a leading nineteenth-century dispensationalist, declared that it was a "gigantic" misconception to expect the church "to reform the world." *The Thousand Years: Studies in Eschatology in Both Testaments* (1889; Fincastle, VA, n.d.), pp. 445-52.

[65]While it is true, as Marsden states and Norris Magneson documents, that Holiness advocates did much social work in the late nineteenth century, their pessimistic view of culture often kept them from addressing larger structural ideals such as the nature of economic enterprise, public education, and social and political arrangements and affairs. See Marsden, *Fundamentalism and American Culture*, pp. 87-88; Norris Magneson, *Salvation in the Slums: Evangelical Social Work, 1865 – 1920* (Metuchen, NJ: Scarecrow Press, 1977).

[66]See Warfield, "The Millennium and the Apocalypse" (1904), in *Biblical Doctrines* (New York, 1929), pp. 647, 662-64, and J. Gresham Machen, "Christianity and Culture," *PTR* (Jan. 1913):1-15. See also Marsden, *Fundamentalism and American Culture*, pp. 136-38.

[67]See Gordon Spykman, et al., *Society, State and Schools: A Case for Structural and Confessional Pluralism* (Grand Rapids: Eerdmans, 1981), pp. 30-50; James Skillen, ed., *Confessing Christ and Doing Politics* (Washington, D.C.: Association for Public Justice, 1982), pp. 54-62; Rockne McCarthy et al., *Disestablishment a Second Time: Genuine Pluralism for American Public Schools* (Grand Rapids: Eerdmans/Christian University Press, 1982).

CHAPTER 4

[1]See John Bennett, *Christians and the State* (New York: Scribner's, 1958), p. 3.

[2]John Calvin, *Institutes of the Christian Religion*, ed. John T. McNeill (2 vols.; Philadelphia: Westminster, 1960), 2:1485ff.

[3]J. M. Foster, *Christ the King* (Boston: James H. Earle, 1894), pp. 8, 11, 68, 77ff.; A. A. Hodge, in *Proceedings of the National Convention to Secure the Religious Amendment to the Constitution of the United States* (Philadelphia: Christian Statesman Association, 1874), p. 81; A. W. Miller, "Christ and the State," *SPR* (April 1870):233-36; Alfred Jones, "Church and State; their Relations," *PQ* (April 1890):209-10.

[4]Abraham Kuyper, *Lectures on Calvinism* (Grand Rapids: Eerdmans, 1931), p. 78. Cf. Lyman Atwater, "Religion and Politics," in *Proceedings: Second General Council* (Philadelphia, 1880), p. 326.

[5]Foster, *Christ the King*, pp. 38, 70; A. B. Curry, "Civil Government," *PQ* (April 1904):582, 584; J. M. Wylie, *Political Science: Its Study Necessary to the Gospel Minister* (1892), pp. 8-11; "Christianity and Politics," *BT* (June 10, 1915):360; Arthur Link, "Woodrow Wilson: Presbyterian in Government," in *Calvinism and the Political Order*, ed. George Hunt (Philadelphia: Westminster, 1965), p. 164.

[6]Kuyper, *Lectures on Calvinism*, p. 85.

[7]R. W. Sloane, "The Bible a Law for Nations," *Cath P* (April 1879):242.

[8]Kuyper, *Lectures on Calvinism*, pp. 87-88.

[9]Robert Dabney, *Syllabus and Notes of the Course of Systematic and Polemic*

Theology (Richmond: Presbyterian Committee of Publication, 1890), pp. 865-66. Cf. "The National Reform Convention," *UP* (April 30, 1885):279.

[10]Kuyper, *Lectures on Calvinism,* pp. 88-89.

[11]Robert Thompson, *The Divine Order of Human Society* (Philadelphia, 1891), pp. 128-29.

[12]Lyman Atwater, "The State in Relation to Morality," *PQ* (March 1878):397-98.

[13]Foster, *Christ the King,* p. 56.

[14]C. R. Vaughan, "The Non-Secular Character of the Church," *PQ* (Oct. 1888):436-41; David McAllister, *The National Reform Movement* (Philadelphia: Aldine Press, 1870), pp. 172-74; Lyman Atwater, "Civil Government and Religion," *PQPR* (April 1876):213-16; A. A. Hodge, *Popular Lectures on Theological Themes* (Philadelphia: Presbyterian Board of Publication, 1887), pp. 273-78.

[15]Sloane, "Bible a Law for Nations," pp. 242-43; Lyman Atwater, "Taxation of Churches, Colleges and Charitable Institutions," *PQPR* (April 1874):374; H. H. George, "National Reform in America," in *First International Convention of the Reformed Presbyterian Churches* (n.p., Alexander Malcolm and Co., 1896), p. 425. Sidney Mead argues that Sectarian Christianity cannot conceive of a "religiously neutral civic authority. If it is not overtly 'Christian' it must be infidel, godless, atheist, or, as the sophisticated now commonly say, 'secular.' " See *The Old Religion in the Brave New World: Reflections on the Relation Between Christendom and the Republic* (Berkeley, CA: University of California Press, 1977), p. 41.

[16]"Religion and the State," *Pres* (July 22, 1915):6; Hodge, *Popular Lectures,* p. 275. For Lincoln's views, see Sidney Mead, *The Lively Experiment: The Shaping of Christianity in America* (New York: Harper and Row, 1963), pp. 73-86.

[17]A. B. Curry, "Civil Government," p. 581. See also William Strong, *Two Lectures Upon the Relations of Civil Law to Church Polity, Discipline and Property* (New York, 1875), pp. 15, 25ff., and Jon Teaford, "Toward a Christian Nation: Religion, Law and Justice Strong," *Journal of Presbyterian History* (Winter 1976):429-30.

[18]Thompson, *Divine Order,* pp. 129-31.

[19]Joseph Jones, "The State is Responsible," *SWP* (Aug. 30, 1888):1; Foster, *Reformation Principles,* pp. 78-83; Sylvester Scovel, "Call for the Conference," in *Report of the World's Christian Citizenship Conference* (Pittsburgh: National Reform Association, 1911), pp. 5ff.; Dabney, *Syllabus and Notes,* pp. 869-70.

[20]McAllister, *National Reform Movement,* pp. 106-10, 181-82; Hodge, in *Proceedings of the National Convention,* p. 84; "The Responsibility of Nations," *CO* (March 26, 1890):1; J. S. Milligan, "Christian Government," *UP* (March 5, 1885):147.

[21]A. A. Hodge, in *Proceedings of the National Convention,* p. 85.

[22]Atwater, "Religion and Politics," p. 325; idem., "Civil Government," p. 202.

[23]Atwater, "Civil Government," pp. 212-13. Cf. Sloane, "Bible a Law for Nations," pp. 242-43; "Are We a Christian Nation?" *BT* (Nov. 24, 1905):498-99; "Questions to Be Met," *PB* (Nov. 14, 1888):1.

[24]William B. Greene, Jr., *PTR* (April 1905):339-40; Atwater, "Civil Government," pp. 198-99.

[25]Atwater, "Religion and Politics," p. 328; "Political Duty," *UP* (Feb. 5, 1880):88; "The Presidential Election," *PB* (Nov. 14, 1888):1; "Inauguration Prayer-Meeting," *PB* (Feb. 20, 1889):1; "1894," *UP* (Jan. 3, 1895):8; W. C. Campbell, "Civic Righteousness," *PSt* (April 23, 1902):7-8.

[26]Atwater, "Religion and Politics," p. 328.

27David Wallace, "Letters to Young Christians," *UP* (Sept. 23, 1880):602. Cf. "Thoughts for the Time," *PB* (July 4, 1888):1.

28W. G. T. Shedd, *Orthodoxy and Heterodoxy: A Miscellany* (New York: Scribner's 1893), p. 260.

29"Dishonesty in Politics," *UP* (Nov. 11, 1880); p. 750; "Projected Reform," *PB* (Aug. 3, 1881):1; "Issues to be Met," *PB* (July 11, 1888):1; "The Next President," *UP* (Feb. 19, 1880):120-21.

30"Not an Agreeable Spectacle," *PB* (April 13, 1881):1; *CI* (April 21, 1881):1.

31G. J. Coulson, "The Draft of American Politics," *SPR* (April 1881):323-34. Cf. Foster, *Reformation Principles,* pp. 7-11; "Our Country," *CI* (July 9, 1890):1-2.

32Shedd, *Orthodoxy and Heterodoxy,* p. 263.

33W. H. McMaster, "Municipal Reform," *PSt* (June 14, 1905):10; "Problem of the Cities," *POS* (April 13, 1910):450.

34"A National Need," *PB* (April 6, 1881):1; "Civil Service Reform," *CI* (July 20, 1881):2-3; "Under Way," *UP* (Sept. 3, 1885): 568; "A Non-Partisan Civil Service," *PSt* (March 12, 1902):2-3.

35Atwater, "The Assassination of the President," *PR* (Dec. 1881):775-78. Cf. "The Perils of Partisanship," *Pres* (Feb. 7, 1900):5.

36"Reform in Southern Cities," *PSt* (Sept. 24, 1902):3. Cf. John Prugh, "The Great Cities of the United States," in *Proceedings: Sixth General Council,* p. 345; Ira Landrith, "The Men of Our Church, and Civil Affairs," in *Presbyterian Brotherhood* (Philadelphia: Presbyterian Board of Publication, 1907), pp. 239, 243.

37Mark Matthews, "Municipal Reform," in *Second World's Christian Citizenship Conference,* pp. 162, 164-66. See C. Allyn Russell, "Mark Allison Matthews: Seattle Fundamentalist and Civic Reformer," *Journal of Presbyterian History* (Winter 1979):453-58.

38See W. M. Greer, "Christianity and American Politics," in *National Reform Documents* (Philadelphia: Aldine Press, 1889), pp. 89-91; Robert P. Kerr, "National Reform," *PQ* (Jan. 1888):585.

39*Proceedings of the Fifth National Reform Convention to Aid in Maintaining the Christian Features of the American Government . . .* (Philadelphia, 1874), p. 10.

40Teaford, "Toward a Christian Nation," p. 431.

41Noticeably absent from the NRA's supporters were Southern Presbyterians. While agreeing with many of the organization's aims, the growing adherence of Southern Presbyterians to the doctrine of the spiritual character of the church gave priority to the notion that a democratic government should not pass laws based solely on Christian premises.

42McAllister, *National Reform Movement,* p. 154.

43Foster, *Christ the King,* pp. 66-67; R. C. Wylie, "Christian Principles of National Fundamental Law," in *National Reform Documents* (Allegheny, PA: National Reform Association, 1900), p. 81; Stephen Tyng, in *Proceedings of the National Convention,"* p. 25.

44Robert Ingersoll, *Arena* (Jan. 1890):124-25.

45McAllister, *National Reform Movement,* pp. 141-53. Cf. Wylie, "Christian Principles," pp. 78-79; Foster, *Christ the King,* pp. 68-71.

46McAllister, *National Reform Movement,* pp. 106-34.

47McAllister, "Brief History of the National Reform Movement," in *National Reform Documents,* pp. 13ff.; "The Religious Amendment to the United States Constitution," *UP* (Nov. 11, 1880):744; S. M. Campbell, "Is This a Christian Nation? *American Presbyterian Review* (April 1870):235ff.; "1789, A Christian Nation, 1889," *PB* (April 17, 1889):1.

48Atwater, "Taxation," p. 347.

[49]See "National Reform," *UP* (Feb. 5, 1880):83-84.

[50]McAllister, *National Reform Movement*, pp. 136-39. Cf. Sloane, "The Bible," pp. 244-45; "National Reform" (June 24, 1880):417; Thompson, *Divine Order*, p. 216.

[51]J. H. McIlvaine, "Our National Obligations to Acknowledge God in the Constitution of the United States" (1868), pp. 1-8.

[52]A. M. Milligan, in *Proceedings of the National Convention*, pp. 73-75.

[53]Foster, *Reformation Principles*, p. 25; "National Reform Convention," pp. 279-80; McAllister, "Brief History," pp. 13ff.

[54]Hodge, in *Proceedings of the National Convention*, p. 81.

[55]"Hearing Before the Committee on the Judiciary, House of Representatives" (Washington, 1896), pp. 12-22.

[56]Ibid., pp. 12-13.

[57]Ibid., pp. 18, 22.

[58]John Alexander, "Introduction," in Foster, *Christ the King*, p. 34. Cf. McAllister, *National Reform Movement*, pp. 166-69.

[59]See George, "National Reform in the United States," pp. 248-49; McAllister, *National Reform Movement*, pp. 181-82.

[60]Kerr, "National Reform," pp. 535-40; "Our National Religion," *Pres* (April 30, 1870):4. See Robert Handy, *A Christian America: Protestant Hopes and Historical Realities* (New York: Oxford University Press, 1971), pp. 100ff., and Winthrop Hudson, *The Great Tradition of the American Churches* (New York: Harper and Brothers, 1953), pp. 33-39 and passim.

[61]*Proceedings of the Fifth National Reform Convention*, pp. 69, 14. Cf. Wylie, "Christian Principles," p. 81; H. H. George, "The Revival of National Religion," in *Report of the World's Christian Citizenship Conference* (Pittsburgh: National Reform Association, 1911), pp. 142-45.

[62]Foster, *Christ the King*, pp. 77-79; McAllister, *National Reform Movement*, pp. 134-39.

[63]See William McLoughlin, *Isaac Backus and the American Pietist Tradition* (Boston: Little, Brown and Co., 1967), p. xii.

[64]Greene, *PTR* (April 1904):352.

[65]Atwater, "Religion and Politics," p. 326. Cf. Benjamin Abbot, "Religion in the Government," *CI* (Jan. 13, 1881):8; "Our National Religion," *Pres* (April 30, 1870):4.

[66]"National Reform," *UP*, p. 417; Sloane, "Bible a Law for Nations," pp. 243, 245-47; Foster, *Reformation Principles*, p. 24; Wylie, "Christian Principles," p. 81.

[67]McAllister, *National Reform Movement*," pp. 172-75; McIlvaine, "Our National Obligations," p. 2.

[68]*Proceedings of the Fifth National Convention*, p. 12.

[69]Sloane, "The Bible," pp. 242-43.

[70]E.g., McAllister, *National Reform Movement*, p. 175.

[71]W. F. Jamieson, *The Clergy—A Source of Danger to the American Republic* (Chicago, 1872), pp. 9-11, 147, 155, 166-69, 189-220, 297-98.

[72]Ibid., pp. 317-31. See also "Hearing Before the Committee," pp. 12, 17.

[73]McAllister, *National Reform Movement*, pp. 175-76.

[74]Ibid. See William Henry Roberts, *Law Relating to Religious Corporations* . . . (Philadelphia: Presbyterian Board of Publication, 1896), p. vii.

[75]"Christian Nations," *POS* (May 18, 1910):610; Handy, *Christian America*, pp. 95ff.; Hudson, *Great Tradition*, pp. 80-136; Arthur S. Link, "Woodrow Wilson," in *Calvinism and the Political Order*, ed. George L. Hunt (Philadelphia: Westminster, 1965), pp. 169-70.

[76]Norris Magnuson, *Salvation in the Slums: Evangelical Social Work, 1865–1920* (Metuchen, NJ: Scarecrow Press, 1977); Charles Hopkins, *The Rise of the Social Gospel in American Protestantism* (New Haven: Yale University Press, 1940); Henry May, *Protestant Churches and Industrial America* (New York: Harper and Brothers, 1949); Aaron Abell, *American Catholicism and Social Action: A Search for Social Justice, 1865–1950* (Garden City, NY: Hanover House, 1960).

[77]McAllister, *National Reform Movement*, pp. 193-206.

[78]J. C. McFeeters, *The Covenanters in America* (Philadelphia: Spangler and Davis, 1892), pp. 180-81.

[79]In *Twilight of the Saints: Biblical Christianity and Civil Religion in America* (Downers Grove, IL: Inter-Varsity Press, 1978), pp. 164ff., Robert Linder and Richard Pierard suggest that Christians today can approach politics in any one of five ways. (1) Believing politics to be dirty, they can totally ignore it in order to carry on more spiritual pursuits. This is largely what Southern Presbyterians did, based upon their conviction that the church as an institution would compromise and neglect its primary mission to save souls if it engaged in political activity. (2) Christians can work to impose evangelical faith on the nation. This was the basic approach taken by Calvinists who supported the NRA. (3) They can embrace and encourage a civil religion based upon a least common denominator of theistic and humanistic convictions, which can provide a cultural consensus to hold our political life together. Some opponents of the NRA supported such a position. (4) Christians can accept the fact that the majority of Americans are secular in their basic outlook and "thus prepare to live in a society which does not reflect Christian values or influence." However, secularization had not advanced this far in the late nineteenth century. (5) Christians can concentrate on practicing the teachings of the New Testament in a modern American setting. They can continue to proclaim biblical truths for every social and political context without demanding that their view dominate American society. This is the option that Pierard and Linder advocate, as do I and as did many evangelicals living in the late nineteenth century, including some Calvinists. This approach seems most faithful to New Testament teachings and most sensitive to the political realities of contemporary America. Moreover, it avoids the pitfalls of inactivity, coercion, compromised faith, or pessimism evident in the other approaches.

[80]See William J. Wolf, "Abraham Lincoln and Calvinism," in *Calvinism and the Political Order*, pp. 141-56; Link, "Woodrow Wilson," pp. 157-74; idem., "The Higher Realism of Woodrow Wilson," *Journal of Presbyterian History* (March 1963):1-13.

[81]Foster, *Christ the King*, p. 65; "Resolutions Adopted by the Convention," in *First International Convention*, p. 314; *Manual of Doctrine of the Reformed Presbyterian Church of North America* (1912), pp. 16-17.

[82]McFeeters, *Covenanters of America*, p. 124. Cf. R. J. George, "The Blighting Effect upon Spiritual Life . . . ," in *A Report of the Christian Citizenship Conference* (1902), pp. 47-52; Trumbull, "Distinctive Principles," p. 147; F. M. Foster, *The Witnessing Church* (New York: J. W. Pratt and Son, 1890), pp. 190-99.

[83]D. M. Sleeth, "Should Christians Vote?" *UP* (March 21, 1895):182.

[84]A. Kilpatrick, "The Attitude of Protest—the Attitude of Power," in *Report of the Christian Citizenship Conference*, pp. 94ff.; T. P. Stevenson, "Unfinished Aspects of the Covenanting Struggle," in *First International Convention*, p. 239.

[85]Greene, *PTR* (April 1904):352.

[86]Kilpatrick, "Attitude of Protest," pp. 94ff.; R. C. Wylie, "Dissent from Unscriptural Political Systems," in *First International Convention*, pp. 259-60.

[87]McFeeters, *Covenanters in America*, p. 113; *Manual of Doctrine*, p. 18.

[88]Ernest Thompson, *The Spirituality of the Church* (Richmond: John Knox Press, 1961), pp. 24-25; Jack Maddex, "From Theocracy to Spirituality: The Southern Presbyterian Reversal on Church and State," *Journal of Presbyterian History* (Winter 1976):438-57.

[89]James Waddell, "Political Religion," *SPR* (April 1883):375-80; Vaughan, "Non-Secular Character of the Church," p. 412.

[90]William Bogg, "Church and State in their Reciprocal Relations and Fundamental Contrast," *SPR* (Jan. 1884):164-66, 176. Cf. Vaughan, "Non-Secular Character of the Church," pp. 413-18.

[91]Ernest Thompson, *Presbyterians in the South, 1890–1972* (3 vols.; Richmond: John Knox Press, 1973), 3:358.

[92]Thomas C. Johnson, "A History of the Southern Presbyterian Church," in *The American Church History Series*, ed. Philip Schaff (14 vols.; New York: The Christian Literature Co., 1894), 11:423, 478.

[93]Boggs, "Church and State," pp. 142-53, 176-80; Waddell, "Political Religion," p. 373; W. C. Clark, "Church and State," *PQ* (Jan. 1900):116-17; "The Church and State Again," *PSt* (Jan. 5, 1910):2.

[94]Johnson, "A History," p. 478.

[95]Angus McDonald, "The Spirituality of Christ's Kingdom," *SWP* (June 14, 1905):5-6; "Morals and Politics," *CO* (Sept. 14, 1910):2.

[96]"The Presbyterian Council," *PQ* (Oct. 1899):734.

[97]E. C. Gordon, "A Distinction with a Difference," *PSt* (June 15, 1900):6; Vaughan, "Non-Secular Character of the Church," pp. 428-33; Waddell, "Political Religion," p. 385.

[98]"Presbyterian Council," p. 734; McDonald, "Spirituality of Christ's Kingdom," p. 5; Jones, "Church and State," pp. 209, 217-18; Miller, "Christ and the State," p. 259.

[99]"Religion and the State," *Pres*, p. 6; Abbott, "Religion in the Government," p. 8; "Social Service," *UP* (Feb. 1, 1912); Henry Zwaanstra, *Reformed Thought and Experience in a New World* (Kampen: J. H. Kok, 1973), pp. 95-129. Around 1900 some Southern Presbyterians began to question their denomination's intense commitment to the doctrine of the spirituality of the church. See e.g., Alexander McKelway, "Shall They Remain Distinctive?" *PSt* (Nov. 15, 1905):11-12.

[100]Rockne M. McCarthy et al., *Disestablishment a Second Time: Genuine Pluralism for American Schools* (Grand Rapids: Eerdmans/Christian University Press, 1982), pp. 108-23, quotation from p. 112.

[101]See Rockne M. McCarthy, "American Civil Religion," in *Confessing Christ and Doing Politics*, ed. James W. Skillen (Washington, D.C.: Association for Public Justice, 1982), pp. 63-87.

[102]See Robert Webber, *The Moral Majority: Right or Wrong?* (Westchester, IL: Crossway Books, 1981); Robert Zwier, *Born-Again Politics: The New Christian Right in America* (Downers Grove, IL: InterVarsity, 1982); John L. Kater, Jr., *Christians on the Right: The Moral Majority in Perspective* (New York: Seabury, 1982).

CHAPTER 5

[1]A. A. Hodge, *Popular Lectures on Theological Themes* (Philadelphia: Presbyterian Board of Publication, 1887), p. 283.

[2]W. M. Sloane, "The Renascence of Education," *PR* (July 1885):464-65, concluded it was not likely that Americans could make their government secular without also making their public education secular.

³See "Recent Publications on the School Question," *BRPR* (April 1870):313-25; David Wylie, "Three Views of the Public School Question," *PRR* (July 1890):465-73; Robert Sample, "Romanism and the Public Schools," *PQ* (Oct. 1892):523; Herman Horner, *Biblical World* (Jan. 1906):58.

⁴Edward Morris, "Presbyterianism and Education," in *Proceedings: Second General Council* (Philadelphia, 1880), pp. 280-83; Simon McPherson, "Presbyterianism and Education," in *Addresses Delivered at the Centennial Celebration of the General Assembly of the Presbyterian Church* (Philadelphia: McCalla and Co., 1888), pp. 76-79; Joseph Wilson, "Presbyterianism and Education," *PQ* (July 1889):326; George Denny, "Calvin's Influence on Educational Progress," in *Calvin Memorial Addresses* (Richmond: Presbyterian Committee of Publication, 1909), pp. 150, 156.

⁵Morris, "Presbyterianism and Education," pp. 284-86; Denny, "Calvin's Influence on Educational Progress," pp. 151-55; Sylvester Scovel, "The Sympathy of Presbyterianism with the Popular Education and the Christian Training of Youth," in *Proceedings: Sixth General Council* (1896), pp. 207-11.

⁶McPherson, "Presbyterianism and Education," pp. 80-82; A. A. Taylor, "Presbyterian Colleges, as related to the Growth of our Ministry," *PQPR* (Jan. 1877):187ff.; J. G. Van Den Bosch, "A Plea for Higher Education," *BT* (July 29, 1904):288-90.

⁷See Robert Handy, *A Christian America: Protestant Hopes and Historical Realities* (New York: Oxford University Press, 1971), pp. 101-5.

⁸A. A. Hodge, "Religion in the Public Schools," *The New Princeton Review* (Jan. 1887):28.

⁹David McAllister, *Constitutionality of the Reading of the Bible in the Public Schools* (Pittsburgh: National Reform Association, 1902), p. 18; Sylvester Scovel, "Sympathy of Presbyterianism," p. 210.

¹⁰Scovel, "Our National Religion as Foundation for Teaching in Our Schools," in *National Reform Documents* (Allegheny, PA: National Reform Association, 1900), p. 42; R. C. Wylie, *Our System of Public Education: Is It Christian or Secular?* (Allegheny, PA: National Reform Association, 1901), p. 52.

¹¹E.g., Robert Dabney, "Secularized Education," *PQ* (Sept. 1879):377-400, esp. pp. 396-97. See also Lewis J. Sherrill, *Presbyterian Parochial Schools 1846 – 1870* (New Haven: Yale University Press, 1932), p. 40.

¹²E.g., Hodge, "Religion in the Public Schools," p. 28; Wylie, *Our System of Public Education,* p. 53; Sloane, "Renascence of Education," p. 464.

¹³Charles Hodge, *Systematic Theology* (3 vols.; New York: Scribner's, 1874), 3:356. Charles Hodge, "Parochial Schools," in *Discussions in Church Polity* (New York: Scribner's, 1878), pp. 449-50.

¹⁴J. M. Foster, *Christ the King* (Boston, 1894), p. 107; Wylie, *Our System of Public Education,* p. 61; Henry C. Minton, "Report on Public Education," in *Second World's Christian Citizenship Conference* (Pittsburgh: National Reform Association, 1913), p. 107.

¹⁵Hodge, *Systematic Theology,* 3:354. Cf. Thomas Barksdale, "Shall the Bible Be Excluded from the Public Schools?" *PQ* (July 1888):314.

¹⁶"Recent Publications," p. 319; Robert Thompson, *The Divine Order of Human Society* (Philadelphia, 1891), p. 185.

¹⁷Dabney, "Secularized Education," p. 383. Cf. William Radcliffe, "Church and Public Education," in *Proceedings: Ninth General Council* (London: Office of the Alliance, 1909), p. 239; Charles Knox, "Problems for Educated Minds in America in the New Century," *PQPR* (April 1877):211-13; P. R. Law, "Schools and

Colleges and the Church," *PQ* (July 1893):571; "Education and the Bible," *CI* (Jan. 20, 1876):9.

[18]E.g., *In Defense of the Public Schools* (Philadelphia: Aldine Press, 1888), pp. 94-95; H. D. Jenkins, "Are Our Public Schools Godless?" *PQ* (Jan. 1889):26-28; Thompson, *Divine Order*, p. 176; "The Assembly on Popular Education," *Pres* (July 2, 1870):4.

[19]A. A. Hodge, "Religion in the Public Schools," p. 32. Cf. Scovel, "Our National Religion," p. 38; David Burrell, "Our Godless Schools — II," *CI* (Jan. 12, 1910):19.

[20]"Recent Publications," *BRPR*, p. 320; "Unjustifiable Neglect," *PB* (Dec. 15, 1880):1; Wylie, "Three Views," p. 470; Foster, *Christ the King*, p. 383; "Education and Educators," *POS* (Aug. 24, 1910):896.

[21]Burrell, "Our Godless Schools — III," *CI* (Jan. 19, 1910):34; William Roberts, "Higher Education in the West," *PR* (April 1888):211.

[22]"Education and National Life," *UP* (Sept. 9, 1880):576; "The Divorce of Religion and Education," *SPR* (April 1877):226-27; Robert P. Kerr, "The Religious Element in Education — Parochial Schools," *PQ* (April 1898):220; Henry C. Minton, "National Christianity and Public Education," *Report of the World's Christian Citizenship Conference* (Pittsburgh: National Reform Association, 1911), pp. 163-64; "Education and the Bible," *CI* (Jan. 20, 1876):9.

[23]Quoted by Sample, "Romanism," pp. 536-37.

[24]"Education and National Life," p. 576; Simon Blocker, "Religious Instruction in the Schools," *CI* (Sept. 28, 1910):616; Foster, *Christ the King*, p. 377; Scovel, "Our National Religion," p. 38; Minton, "Report on Public Education," p. 107.

[25]See, e.g., "Liberal Christianity," *BRPR* (Jan. 1868):131; W. G. T. Shedd, *Theological Essays* (New York: Scribner's, 1887), pp. 122-23.

[26]Henry Utterwick, "Religion in the Public Schools," *CI* (Feb. 23, 1910):115-16; "Religion and School," *Pres* (Sept. 14, 1910):3-4; K. M. McIntyre, "Secular Education Must Be Christianized," *PSt* (Dec. 10, 1902):13-14.

[27]Dabney, "Secularized Education," p. 385. Despite these convictions, Calvinists did not develop a holistic educational philosophy and wrote few textbooks grounded in biblical presuppositions for use in the schools. See Edward Rian, *Christianity and American Education* (San Antonio, TX: Naylor, 1949), p. 235.

[28]C. Hodge, "Parochial Schools," p. 452. Cf. Andrew F. West, *PR* (April 1887):384; Louis Berkhof, "Unity in Education," *BT* (Aug. 6, 1913):510-11; Lyman Atwater, "Proposed Reforms in Collegiate Education," *PR* (July 1882):112-13.

[29]Sample, "Romanism," p. 527.

[30]Dabney, "Secularized Education," p. 387. Cf. "Universal Education," *PSt* (May 7, 1902):3-4.

[31]Thompson, *Divine Order*, pp. 189-90. Cf. Robert Thompson, "National Christianity and Public Education," in *Report of the World's Christian Citizenship Conference*, p. 171.

[32]Thompson, *Divine Order*, p. 179. Cf. Knox, "Problems for Educated Minds," p. 211; Hodge, *Popular Lectures*, pp. 275, 286; "Religion in the Public Schools," p. 37.

[33]Handy, *Christian America*, pp. 98ff., 110ff.; Sidney Mead, *The Lively Experiment: The Shaping of Christianity in America* (New York: Harper and Row, 1963), pp. 57-71.

[34]M. J. Wallace, "Education," *SPR* (Oct. 1871):505-6.

[35]Hodge, *Popular Lectures*, pp. 281-82. Cf. "What Christianity is Not," *CI* (Sept. 21, 1881):2-3.

[36]Hodge, "Religion in the Public Schools," pp. 30-31. Cf. Thornton Whaling, "Our Church and Education," *PQ* (Oct. 1890):538; J. W. Stagg, "Should the Bible Be Used in Public Schools?" *PSt* (March 29, 1905):6.

[37]Hodge, "Religion in the Public Schools," pp. 30-31. Cf. J. A. Quarles, "Education and Christianity," *SPR* (Oct. 1871):476; Sample, "Romanism," p. 527; Ethelbert Warfield, "The Teaching of History," *School Review* (Jan. 1895):35, 38, 40.

[38]Hodge, "Religion in the Public Schools," pp. 30-31. Cf. "Religion in the Public Schools," *CI* (Dec. 3, 1890):4; D. H. MacVicar, "Social Discontent," *PR* (April 1887):272.

[39]"The Divorce of Religion and Education," *SPR*, pp. 229-30; Kerr, "Religious Element in Education," p. 218; Dabney, "Secularized Education," pp. 390-91.

[40]Francis Lieber, "The Necessity of Religious Instruction," *PQPR* (Oct. 1873): 653; Kerr, "Religious Element," p. 216; Knox, "Problems for Educated Minds," p. 211.

[41]Law, "Schools and Colleges," p. 584; *Pres* (July 23, 1890):1; Kerr, "Religious Element," p. 215; "The Failure of Our Common Schools," *CI* (Aug. 3, 1910):485-86; "Complete Education," *CI* (Sept. 28, 1910):614.

[42]Wylie, "Three Views," pp. 469-70. Cf. Scovel, "Sympathy of Presbyterianism," p. 210.

[43]Daniel W. LaRue, "The Church and the Public School," *Educational Review* (May 1909):468-76. For a similar perspective, see William T. Harris, *Moral Education in the Common Schools,* Circular of Information, No. 4 (U.S. Bureau of Education, 1888):85-86. Similarly, John Dewey urged educators to use the public schools to develop "the positive creed of life implicit in democracy and science." See John Dewey, "Education as a Religion," *The New Republic* (August 1922), and "Religion and Our Schools," *Hibbert Journal* (July 1908):809, 799. For the religious views of Dewey, see Harry M. Campbell, *John Dewey* (New York: Twayne, 1971), pp. 26-27, 34-37, 54, 63-76. Many Christians today believe that American public schools have for years been teaching a humanistic faith based upon the ideas of Rousseau, Jefferson, Comte, Dewey, and others. For an example of this view, see Rousas J. Rushdoony, *The Messianic Character of American Education* (Nutley, NJ: The Craig Press, 1979), pp. 316-17 and passim.

[44]Sample, "Romanism," p. 258. Cf. William H. Vroom, "The Contest for the Christian Faith in America," *L* (Feb. 6, 1907):226-27.

[45]Morris, "Presbyterianism and Education," pp. 290-92.

[46]Dabney, "Secularized Education," p. 393. Cf. Barksdale, "Shall the Bible Be Excluded?" p. 314; Vroom, "The Contest for Christian Faith," p. 226.

[47]Hodge, *Popular Lectures,* p. 283. Cf. Scovel, "Our National Religion," p. 45.

[48]New School Presbyterian and abolitionist George B. Cheever used almost all of these arguments as early as 1854 in his *Right of the Bible in our Public Schools* (New York: Robert Carter and Brothers, 1854), pp. 33-96, 124-39, 157-82, 194-215, 224ff. Many non-Calvinists offered similar arguments. See Kingsley Twining, "The State and Religion in its Schools," *Congregational Quarterly* (Oct. 1871):565-92; Julius Seelye, "Should the State Teach Religion?" *Forum* (July 1886):427-33; "Shall Education by the State Be Exclusively Secular?" *Methodist Quarterly Review* (April 1880):299-315; A. C. Coxe, "Theology in the Public Schools," *NAR* (March 1881):221-22.

[49]B. J. McQuaid, "Religion in the Schools," *NAR* (April 1881):338.

[50]John Higham, *Strangers in the Land: Patterns of American Nativism, 1860–1925* (New York: Atheneum, 1965), pp. 28, 59.

[51]Lorenzo J. Markoe, "Is There Any System of Public School That Would

Satisfy Catholics?" *Catholic World* (June 1902):329-34; Thomas Preston, "What Roman Catholics Want," *Forum* (April 1886):165-68.

[52]John F. Mullany, "Is Catholic Education a Menace to American Institutions?" *NAR* (Oct. 1905):545.

[53]Preston, "What Roman Catholics Want," pp. 161-63; McQuaid, "Religion in the Schools," pp. 334, 335; Edward Pace, "The Influence of Religious Education Upon the Motives of Conduct," *Educational Review* (Nov. 1903):332-38.

[54]Mullany, "Is Catholic Education a Menace?" p. 546; McQuaid, "Religion in the Schools," pp. 332-33. Cf. Robert D. Cross, "Origins of the Catholic Parochial Schools of America," *The American Benedictine Review* (June 1965):205, 209.

[55]"Roman Catholic Schools," *CO* (Dec. 7, 1910):1; Markoe, "Is There Any System?" p. 333; Mullany, "Is Catholic Education a Menace?" pp. 551-54.

[56]E.g, Francis Beattie, "The Place and Use of the Bible in the Public Schools of the United States," *PQ* (April 1904):514; Sample, "Romanism," pp. 530-31; Frank B. Lenz, "The Education of the Immigrant," *Educational Review* (May 1916):469-77.

[57]Mullany, "Is Catholic Education a Menace?" pp. 548, 550, 554; Preston, "What Roman Catholics Want," pp. 170-71.

[58]E.g., Hodge, "Religion in the Public Schools," p. 32; "The Bible in Our Public Schools," *Pres* (Jan. 22, 1870):4; Burrell, "Our Godless Schools — III," p. 34.

[59]J. A. Grier, "The Bible in the Schools of Pa.," *UP* (July 16, 1885):467; "Roman Catholic Church and the Public Schools," *PB* (Sept. 26, 1888):1; "The Assault Upon the Public Schools," *CI* (April 9, 1890):1-2. See Higham, *Strangers in the Land*, p. 60.

[60]Markoe, "Is There Any System?" p. 332.

[61]See "Divorce of Religion and Education," p. 232; David Burrell, "Our Godless Schools — I," *CI* (Jan. 5, 1910):4; "Teaching Religion in the Public Schools," *PSt* (Oct. 13, 1915):3.

[62]"Religion in the Public Schools," *Ind* (Dec. 18, 1902):3040-42.

[63]*Ind* (Aug. 28, 1902):2090, and *Ind* (Oct. 16, 1902):2489-90; "Christmas Without Christ," *Current Literature* (Jan. 1907):62-63.

[64]Cited in "Religion in the Schools," *Current Literature* (Jan. 1904):91. Stanley Matthews, a Presbyterian elder who defended the School Board of Cincinnati in 1870 when it prohibited Bible reading in that city, used this argument. See Matthews, *The Relation of the State to Religious Education: John Minor et al. Versus the Board of Education of the City of Cincinnati et al.* (Cincinnati: Robert Clark and Co., 1870).

[65]Thompson, *Divine Order,* pp. 175, 179, 182-86; Wylie, "Three Views," p. 469; Hodge, "Religion in the Public Schools," pp. 28, 30, 35, 37.

[66]Samuel Spear, "The Bible and the Public School," *PQ* (March 1878):364-65, 369, 371, 374, 377, 389-90. Cf. "Religion and Education," *Educational Review* (June 1901):101-3.

[67]Herbert W. Horwill, "The Bible in the Public Schools," *Atlantic Monthly* (Sept. 1903):298. He noted that if public school teachers treated the Bible as "a religious and ethical textbook" they violated "the principle of neutrality" (p. 299). See also H. H. Schroeder, "The Religious Element in the Public Schools," *Educational Review* (April 1909):385.

[68]LaRue, "Church and the Public School," pp. 468-70. Cf. John Dewey, "Teaching Ethics in High School," *Educational Review* (Nov. 1893):313-21; idem, *Moral Principles in Education* (Boston: Houghton Mifflin, 1909), pp. 2, 58; idem, "The Chaos in Moral Traning," *Popular Science Monthly* (Aug. 1894):433-43. Edward Goodwin, in "The Exclusion of Religious Instruction From the Public

Schools," *Educational Review* (Feb. 1908):136-37, protested that naturalistic ethics were being taught in the common schools.

[69]Wilbur Jackson, "Nature-Study and Religious Training," *Educational Review* (June 1905):13, 18, 20, 23-24, 26. Fortunately, he declared, a new religious system rooted in nature and "compatible with the scientific spirit of the times" increasingly was undergirding common school instruction.

[70]See Sloane, "Renascence of Education," p. 464; Hodge, "Religion in the Public Schools," p. 29.

[71]For a general discussion of forces abetting the secularization of the public schools, see Samuel W. Brown, *The Secularization of American Education: As Shown by State, Legislation, State Constitutional Provisions and State Supreme Court Decisions* (New York: Columbia University Press, 1912); Gerrit Verkuyl, *Christ in American Education* (New York: Revell, 1934), pp. 31ff.; V. T. Thayer, *Religion in Public Education* (New York: The Viking Press, 1947), pp. 39ff.; Renwick H. Martin, *Our Public Schools—Christian or Secular?* (Pittsburgh: National Reform Association, 1952), pp. 50ff.

[72]McQuaid, "Religion in the Schools," pp. 332, 336. Cf. Dabney, "Secularized Education," pp. 377-79; Whaling, "Our Church and Education," pp. 554-55.

[73]Hodge, "Religion in the Public Schools," p. 29. Cf. W. M. Grier, "Denominational Colleges," *PQ* (Oct. 1887):242; MacVicar, "Social Discontent," p. 272.

[74]Jenkins, "Are Our Public Schools Godless?" pp. 34-39. Cf. John Westerhoff III, *McGuffey and His Readers: Piety, Morality and Education in Nineteenth Century America* (Nashville: Abingdon, 1978). Westerhoff documents the shift from a primary stress on Christian motifs such as God, salvation, and righteousness in the first editions to strong support of the American gospel of success in later editions. According to Westerhoff, the theistic worldview slowly disappears until by the 1879 edition "none of the first edition emphasis on salvation and piety remains." In their study "Values Expressed in American Children's Readers, 1800–1950," *Journal of Abnormal and Social Psychology* (Feb. 1962):136-42, Richard de Charon and Gerald H. Moeller show that the emphasis on moral teaching in children's readers declined dramatically between 1840 and 1880. John A. Nietz, *Old Textbooks . . . As Taught in the Common Schools from Colonial Days to 1900* (Pittsburgh: University of Pittsburgh Press, 1961), pp. 253, 343, notes the decline of religious emphasis in history and music textbooks after 1870. Karl Wilson, "Historical Survey of the Religious Content of Geography Textbooks from 1784 to 1895" (Ph.D. diss. University of Pittsburgh, 1951) demonstrates the steady decline in the amount of space given to religious content in geography textbooks during the late nineteenth century.

[75]William Faunce, "Survey of Moral and Religious Progress," *Educational Review* (April 1905):366, 369, 371, 372. Cf. Charles C. Hall, "Progress in Religious and Moral Education," *Educational Review* (June 1904):5-7.

[76]See "Evolutionary Philosophy," *BT* (March 17, 1905):125-27.

[77]Goodwin, "Exclusion of Religious Instruction," pp. 129-38, quotation from p. 136.

[78]"Coeducational and Secular Education in the United States," *Educational Review* (Oct. 1908):301-3. William T. Harris, who later became the United States Commissioner of Education, declared in 1888 that each year more religious rites and ceremonies were set aside in the legislature, the town meeting, the public assembly, and the school. "If retained," Harris concluded, religious rites became "empty forms with no appreciable effect." See *Moral Education in the Common Schools*, pp. 81-82.

[79]Burrell, "Our Godless Schools—I," p. 4. Cf. "A Complete Education," *CI*

(Sept. 28, 1910):614; "Our Godless Schools," *POS* (Feb. 23, 1910):239; "Our Public School System: an Utter Failure?" *BT* (Sept. 5, 1912):556-57; "The Problem of Our Public School," *BT* (Aug. 18, 1910):508-9.

80Cited by Wylie, *Our System of Public Education,* p. 47.

81Ibid., pp. 2, 7, 24, 31, 34, 46-47. Cf. Beattie, "Place and Use of the Bible," p. 534; McAllister, *Constitutionality of the Reading of the Bible,* p. 1. For a discussion of the legal battles over religion in the schools, see Donald Boles, *The Bible, Religion and the Public Schools* (Ames, IA: Iowa State University Press, 1963).

82Timothy Smith, "Parochial Education and American Culture," in *History and Education: The Educational Uses of the Past,* ed. Paul Nash (New York: Random House, 1970), pp. 197, 201-2; idem., "Progressivism in American Education, 1880 – 1900," *Harvard Educational Review* (Spring 1961):180, 185-91; David Tyack, "The Kingdom of God and the Common School," *Harvard Educational Review,* pp. 447-69.

83Taylor, "Presbyterian Colleges," p. 145.

84Thompson, *Divine Order,* p. 182.

85"Unjustifiable Neglect," *PB,* p. 1; Wylie, "Three Views," p. 473; "The Schools We Need," *PSt* (Oct. 19, 1910):2; Burrell, "Our Godless Schools — I," p. 34.

86E.g., *CI* (Jan. 3, 1900):1; "Assault Upon the Public Schools," pp. 1-2; Sample, "Romanism," pp. 524, 529-31.

87See "Religion in the Public Schools," *CI* (Dec. 3, 1890):4; Dabney, "Secularized Education," pp. 377ff.; Kerr, "Religious Element," pp. 219ff.; "Recent Publications," pp. 317-18.

88Wylie, *Our System of Public Education,* p. 53. Cf. Minton, "Report on Public Education," p. 99.

89"Religion and the Public Schools," *PSt* (April 16, 1902):5. Cf. Burrell, "Our Godless Schools — III," p. 34.

90See Henry Zwaanstra, *Reformed Thought and Experience in a New World* (Kampen: J. H. Kok, 1973), p. 146.

91Dabney, "Secularized Education," p. 380. Dabney's argument anticipated later ones used by Supreme Court Justices, such as that of Thomas C. Clark in the case of *School District of Abington Township vs. Schempp* (1963). Against those who contended that to deny the majority in a community the right to participate in religious exercises in the public school is in itself a denial of religious freedom, he argued that "while the Free Exercise Clause prohibits the use of state action to deny the rights of free exercise to anyone, it has never meant that a majority could use the machinery of the state to practice its beliefs."

92P. Moerdyke, *CI* (March 2, 1910).

93Zwaanstra, *Reformed Thought and Experience,* p. 147.

94Blocker, "Religious Instruction in Schools," p. 616; "Assault Upon the Public Schools," pp. 1-2; Sample, "Romanism," p. 526; Wylie, "Three Views," p. 471.

95"Public Schools or Parochial Schools?" pp. 540-41. Cf. "The Public School Problem Solved?" *BT* (Aug. 25, 1910):524-25; Moerdyke, *CI,* p. 1.

96Hodge, *Popular Lectures,* p. 280.

97E.g., Utterwick, "Religion in the Public Schools," pp. 115-16; "Religion and the School," *Pres,* pp. 3-4; McIntyre, "Secular Education," pp. 13-14; Sample, "Romanism," p. 530.

98Dabney, "Secularized Education," p. 381.

99See C. Hodge, "Parochial Schools," pp. 452-53; A. A. Hodge, "Religion in the Public Schools," p. 47; "Public Schools or Parochial Schools?" pp. 540-41.

100See Sherrill, *Presbyterian Parochial Schools,* pp. 26-84. A major reason Presbyterians established few parochial schools after 1870 was undoubtedly the failure of their schools before that date (ibid., p. 185). Cf. William K. Dunn, *What Happened to Religious Education?* (Baltimore: Johns Hopkins University Press, 1958), p. 189. See also *Pres* (Jan. 7, 1891):3.

[101]On RCA schools, see J. Van Vlaarderen, "Our Christian Schools," *PSt* (Feb. 23, 1910):1. On Southern Presbyterian schools, see Kerr, "Religious Element," pp. 215-30 and J. M. Otts, "Our Educational Policy," *SPR* (Jan. 1872):50-63. On CRC schools, see I. Van Dellen, "The Primary School and the Nation," *BT* (April 28, 1905):185-87 and "Our Public School System An Utter Failure?" pp. 556-57.

[102]Wylie, *Our System of Public Education,* p. 53; Beattie, "Place of the Bible," pp. 534-37; John C. Hoekje, "Religious Education and the Public Schools," *L* (Dec. 15, 1915):131, 137; Sample, "Romanism," pp. 529-31.

[103]See Philip Schaff, "Progress of Christianity in the U. S. of A.," *PQ* (Sept. 1879):227-30.

[104]Morris, "Presbyterianism and Education," pp. 293-94.

[105]E.g., C. Wright Mills, *Sociology and Pragmatism* (New York: Oxford University Press, 1964), p. 43.

[106]Kerr, "Religious Element," p. 223; George Sumney, "The Denominational Colleges and the Higher Education," *PQ* (April 1903):209.

[107]Mills, *Sociology and Pragmatism,* pp. 44-53.

[108]Richard Hofstader, "The Revolution in Higher Education," in *Paths of American Thought,* ed. A. M. Schleisinger, Jr. and Morton White (Boston: Houghton Mifflin, 1963), pp. 278-79; "Do Not Lose the Gifts of the Fathers," *Pres* (Nov. 23, 1910):4; "Denatured Church Colleges," *POS* (Feb. 2, 1910):133; W. S. Plumer Bryan, "The Church and Her Colleges, and the Carnegie Foundation," *PTR* (April 1911):185-241; "Rockefeller and Carnegie Educational Funds," *Pres* (March 4, 1915):10-11.

[109]Mills, *Sociology and Pragmatism,* pp. 40-53; Martin Marty, *The Modern Schism: Three Paths to the Secular* (New York: Harper and Row, 1969), pp. 140-41; Hofstadter, "Revolution in Higher Education," pp. 275ff.

[110]See John Bascom, "Atheism in Colleges," *NAR* (Jan. 1881):32-40 and Laurence Veysey, *The Emergence of the American University* (Chicago: University of Chicago Press, 1965), pp. 203-4, 280-81, 311, 343.

[111]See William S. Elsbree, "Teacher Education in the United States," in *The Year Book of Education,* ed. G. Bereday and J. Gauwerys (New York: Harcourt, Brace and World, 1963), pp. 171-91; James Russell, "The Function of the University in the Training of Teachers," *Columbia University Quarterly* (Sept. 1899):327-33, 335-42; George Schmidt, *The Liberal Arts College* (New Brunswick, NJ: Rutgers University Press, 1957), pp. 167-68, 191-92.

[112]Taylor, "Presbyterian Colleges," pp. 144-46. Cf. Knox, "Problems for Educated Minds," pp. 209-12.

[113]James McCosh, "A Presbyterian College in America," *CP* (Aug. 1880):84-85. Cf. "Church Colleges," *Pres* (March 4, 1891):4-5; "Divisions in a Faculty," *Pres* (April 10, 1880):10.

[114]A. A. Hodge, "The General Assembly of the Presbyterian Church in the United States of America," *PR* (July 1883):603. D. W. Fisher, "Christianity in the Colleges," *PTR* (April 1903):259, noted that in 1902 only ten of Princeton Seminary's 137 students and only six of McCormick Seminary's 112 students did not come from distinctively Christian colleges.

[115]William C. Roberts, "The American Colleges," in *Proceedings: Third General Council,* p. 478. Cf. R. Q. Mallard, "Colleges and Universities in a Nation's Life," *PQ* (Jan. 1893):101.

[116]James McCosh, "The Place of Religion in Colleges," in *Proceedings: Third General Council,* p. 468.

[117]F. H. Gaines, "The Bible in the College Curriculum," *PQ* (April 1895):211.

[118]Cf. Edmund James, "The Function of the State University," *Science* (Nov. 17, 1905):617-18; W. N. Stearns, "Religious Education in State Universities," *Biblical World* (June 1906):447-52; G. Hodges, "Religious Life in American Colleges," *Outlook* (July 28, 1906):693-701; E. D. Ross, "Religious Influences in the Development of State Colleges and Universities," *Indiana Magazine of History* 46 (1950):343-62.

[119]E.g., William Matlock, "Religion in State Universities," *Educational Review* (Oct. 1910):258-63.

[120]Radcliffe, "Church and Public Education," p. 240; Warfield, "The Religious Aspect of American Education," in *Proceedings: Ninth General Council,* p. 246; "College Religion," *Pres* (Feb. 2, 1910):3-4; "The Denominational College," *Pres* (May 4, 1910):4; J. B. Shearer, "Bible Study in College," *PQ* (Jan., 1888):524-29; For the views of other observers who judged the state's universities lax or inadequate in their moral training, see Charles Fordyce, "College Ethics," *Educational Review* (May 1909):492-500; "Are the Colleges Undermining Faith and Morals?" *Current Literature* (Sept. 1909):300-3; and Harold Bolce, "Blasting at the Rock of Ages," *Cosmopolitan* (May 1909):665-76.

[121]William Clebsch, *From Sacred to Profane America: The Role of Religion in American History* (New York: Harper and Row, 1968), pp. 104-36, quotations from pp. 177, 136.

[122]See Wilson, "Presbyterianism and Education," p. 324; Bryan, "Church," p. 211; James McCosh, "What an American University Should Be," *Ind* (July 9, 1885):872-73; David Burrell, *For Christ's Crown and Other Sermons* (New York, 1896), pp. 171-72.

[123]Grier, "Denominational Colleges," pp. 244-45; Warfield, "Teaching of History," pp. 33-40; Welch, "Our Teachers," pp. 219-23; Law, "Schools and Colleges," p. 584.

[124]V. T. Thayer, *Religion in Public Education,* p. 42, and Samuel Brown, *Secularization of American Education,* both argued that the secular school was firmly established in the United States by 1910.

[125]See "Recent Publications," pp. 317-18; "Divorce of Religion and Education," p. 232; Thompson, *Divine Order,* p. 182.

[126]E.g., "Can the Schools Be Saved?" *Newsweek* (May 9, 1983):50-58; "What's Wrong With Our Teachers?" *U.S. News and World Report* (March 14, 1983):37-41; Tim LaHaye, *The Battle for the Public Schools: Humanism's Threat to Our Children* (Old Tappan, NJ: Revell, 1982); Rockne McCarthy et al., *Disestablishment a Second Time: Genuine Pluralism for American Schools* (Grand Rapids: Eerdmans/Christian University Press, 1982).

CHAPTER 6

[1]Edward Morris, "Presbyterianism and Education," *Proceedings: Second General Council* (Philadelphia, 1880), p. 293.

[2]Stuart Robinson, "The Pulpit and Sceptical Culture," *PQ* (Jan. 1879):136-38. Cf. James McCosh, "How to Deal with Young Men Trained in Science in This Age of Unsettled Opinion," *Proceedings: Second General Council,* p. 204. "Does the Evolution Theory Conflict with Christianity?" *PB* (Sept. 15, 1880):2.

[3]Theodore Bozeman, *Protestants in an Age of Science: The Baconian Ideal and*

Antebellum American Religious Thought (Chapel Hill, NC: University of North Carolina Press, 1977), pp. 166-69 and passim.

⁴Ibid., pp. 48, 87-88.

⁵Perry Miller, *American Thought: Civil War to World War I* (New York: Holt, Rinehart and Winston, 1954), pp. ix-xi.

⁶Bozeman, *Protestants in an Age of Science*, p. 21.

⁷Ibid., pp. 62-64, 103.

⁸W. G. T. Shedd, *Orthodoxy and Heterodoxy* (New York: Scribner's, 1893), pp. 101, 105.

⁹George Daniels, ed., *Darwinism Comes to America* (Waltham, MA: Blaisdell, 1968), pp. xii-xiii.

¹⁰See Lyman Abbott, *Reminiscences* (Boston, 1915), p. 456; John Duffield, "Evolutionism Respecting Man and the Bible," *PQ* (Jan. (1878):158-73; "Evolution," *Pres* (May 22, 1880):6.

¹¹See, for example, John Dillenberger, *Protestant Thought and Natural Science* (New York: Doubleday and Co., 1960), pp. 249-51 and James R. Moore, *The Post-Darwinian Controversies: A study of the Protestant struggle to come to terms with Darwin in Great Britian and America, 1870 – 1900* (London: Cambridge University Press, 1979), pp. 113-14.

¹²Daniels, *Darwinism Comes to America,* p. 33; Francis P. Weinsenberger, *Ordeal of Faith: The Crisis of Church-Going America, 1865 – 1900* (New York: Philosophical Library, 1959), p. 63.

¹³See George F. Wright, "Some Analogies between Calvinism and Darwinism," *Bibliotheca Sacra* (Jan. 1880):61-76; idem., "Calvinism and Darwinism," *Bibliotheca Sacra* (Oct. 1909):687-88; Arthur B. Reeve, "Is Evolution Calvinistic?" *Bibliotheca Sacra* (July 1905):560-65; and Asa Gray, *Natural Science and Religion: Two Lectures Delivered to the Theological School of Yale College* (New York: Scribner's, 1880), p. 102.

¹⁴Moore, *Post-Darwinian Controversies,* pp. 203-4, 251, 269, 280, 290-98, 304-7, 334-40, shows that many leading Calvinists accurately understood the major premises and metaphysical implications of developmental theories. See also Dennis R. Davis, "Presbyterian Attitudes Toward Science and the Coming of Darwinism in America, 1859 – 1929" (Ph.D. diss. University of Illinois, 1980).

¹⁵McCosh, "How to Deal with Young Men," p. 204; James McCosh, *The Developmental Hypothesis: Is it Sufficient?* (New York: Robert Carter and Brothers, 1876), pp. 75-77.

¹⁶Moore, *Post-Darwinian Controversies,* passim.

¹⁷Charles Hodge, *What is Darwinism?* (New York: Scribner, Armstrong and Co., 1874), p. 142.

¹⁸Charles Hodge, *Systematic Theology* (3 vols.; New York: Scribner's, 1874), 2:27-28. Cf. Robert Dabney, *Syllabus and Notes of the Course of Systematic and Polemic Theology* (Richmond: Presbyterian Committee of Publication, 1890), p. 31.

¹⁹George Armstrong, "Creation as a Doctrine of Science," *PQ* (July 1887):119-20; W. G. T. Shedd, *Dogmatic Theology,* (2 vols.; Grand Rapids: Zondervan, 1951), 1:501-2; McCosh, *Development Hypothesis,* p. 13.

²⁰Arnold H. Guyot, "Cosmogony and the Bible; The Biblical Account of Creation in the Light of Modern Science," in *History, Essays, Orations, and Other Documents of the Sixth General Council of the Evangelical Alliance* (New York: Harper and Brothers, 1874), p. 283.

²¹Shedd, *Dogmatic Theology,* 1:501-10; Cf. Hodge, *What is Darwinism?* pp. 26ff.; Robert Watts, "A Short Method with the Antitheistic Scientists," *PQ*

(Oct. 1888):388-94; J. B. Warren, "Evolution: As It Relates to Christian Faith," *Pres* (Nov. 11, 1915):8-9; James McCosh, *The Religious Aspect of Evolution* (New York: G. P. Putnam's Sons, 1888), p. 26; A. H. Strong, *Systematic Theology* (Rochester, NY, 1889), p. 191.

[22]Hodge, *Systematic Theology*, 2:10. Cf. Gordon M. Russell, *PTR* (July 1911):481-82.

[23]A. A. Hodge, "Introduction," in Joseph S. Van Dyke, *Theism and Evolution: An Examination of Modern Speculative Theories as Related to Theistic Conceptions of the Universe* (London: Hodder and Stoughton, 1886), p. xvii.

[24]McCosh, "How to Deal with Young Men," p. 207. Cf. idem., *Christianity and Positivism* (Reading, PA: Frank J. Boyer, 1871), pp. 344, 346-49, 352-53; George Macloskie, "Theistic Evolution," *PRR* (Jan. 1898):13; Hodge, *What is Darwinism?* p. 163.

[25]Hodge, *Systematic Theology*, 2:30.

[26]Dabney, *Syllabus and Notes*, pp. 35-36, 60. Cf. Hodge, *Systematic Theology*, 2:172; Shedd, *Dogmatic Theology*, 1: 152.

[27]McCosh, *Development Hypothesis*, pp. 18-19, 45.

[28]McCosh, "Is There Final Cause in Evolution?" *Ind* (Oct. 10, 1889):3.

[29]McCosh, *Development Hypothesis*, pp. 9-12.

[30]McCosh, "Present State of the Evolution Question — Wallace and Weismann," *Ind* (Oct. 3, 1889):2; McCosh, *Christianity and Positivism*, pp. 42, 63-64.

[31]Macloskie, "Theistic Evolution," pp. 2, 20. Cf. George Macloskie, "The Outlook of Science and Faith," *PTR* (Oct. 1903):601. McCosh repeatedly made this point in his many works on the subject.

[32]In addition to the views of McCosh and Macloskie, see Van Dyke, *Theism and Evolution*, pp. 24, 29, 33 and Francis Patton, "Evolution and Apologetics," *PR* (Jan. 1885):144.

[33]Hodge, *What is Darwinism?* pp. 175-77; Hodge, *Systematic Theology*, 2:15-16, , quotation from p. 15. Cf. Dabney, *Syllabus and Notes*, pp. 26-27 and Duffield, "Evolutionism," p. 150.

[34]See McCosh, *Development Hypothesis*, pp. 37-45.

[35]Ibid., p. 7.

[36]McCosh, *Religious Aspect of Evolution*, pp. 1, 2, 7, 59. McCosh also insisted that Genesis described a process of evolution in 1:2, 11, 21, 24, and 2:7. Cf. Macloskie, *PR* (Jan. 1883):214-16.

[37]McCosh, *Development Hypothesis*, pp. 37-45; George Macloskie, "Scientific Speculation," *PR* (Oct. 1887):624; idem., "Errors as to the Relations of Science and Faith," *PRR* (Jan. 1895):102; Asa Gray in *Darwiniana: Essays and Reviews Pertaining to Darwinism*, ed. A. Hunter Dupree (1876; Cambridge, MA: Belknap Press, 1963), pp. 304, 308-11.

[38]Macloskie, "Theistic Evolution," p. 7.

[39]McCosh, *Religious Aspect of Evolution*, pp. 7, 27, 60-67; idem., "Is There Final Cause?" pp. 2-3. Cf. George Macloskie, *Elementary Botany* (New York: Henry Holt and Co., 1883); Abraham Kuyper, *Lectures on Calvinism* (1898; Grand Rapids: Eerdmans, 1931), pp. 112-17.

[40]Candlish, "Reformation Theology," p. 233; Patton, "Evolution and Apologetics," p. 144; Van Dyke, *Theism and Evolution*, pp. 41-47.

[41]Macloskie, "The Outlook of Science and Faith," pp. 608-9.

[42]Guyot, "Cosmogony and the Bible," p. 276; R. T. Brumby, "Relations of the Bible to Science," *SPR* (Jan. 1874):5-6; Strong, *Systematic Theology*, pp. 105-6; James Orr, "Christianity and Modern Science," *The Bible Student and Teacher* (May 1910):349-51.

43McCosh, *Development Hypothesis*, p. 54.

44Duffield, "Evolutionism," pp. 156-59. Cf. a progressive creationist such as A. H. Strong who wrote in 1899 that "we do not admit the existence of scientific error in the Bible," *Systematic Theology*, p. 105. See also McCosh, *Religious Aspect of Evolution*, pp. 70-74 and Macloskie, "Science and Faith," p. 605.

45Duffield, "Evolutionism," pp. 156-59. George Armstrong, "The Pentateuchal Story of Creation," *PQ* (Oct. 1888):345-47.

46Guyot, "Cosmogony and the Bible," p. 276. Cf. Macloskie, "Outlook of Science and Faith," p. 605.

47McCosh, *Christianity and Positivism*, p. 353.

48McCosh, *Religious Aspect of Evolution*, p. 70.

49McCosh, "How To Deal with Young Men," p. 208.

50Armstrong, "Pentateuchal Story," pp. 350-68; Guyot, "Cosmogony and the Bible," pp. 278-86. See also McCosh, *Religious Aspect of Evolution*, pp. 70-74; J. S. Beekman, "The Development Theory," *PQPR* (Oct. 1877):605, 607; and Shedd, *Dogmatic Theology*, 1:512-23.

51McCosh, *Christianity and Positivism*, pp. 353, 359; Macloskie, "Theistic Evolution," p. 20; Patton, "Evolution and Apologetics," p. 144; Hodge, *What is Darwinism?* pp. 141-42; Duffield, "Evolutionism," pp. 153-54.

52Duffield, "Evolutionism," pp. 152-75; George Weldon and Charles Hodge, "Discussion on Darwinism and the Doctrine of Development," in *History, Essays, Orations*, pp. 317-20; Macloskie, "Theistic Evolution," p. 7.

53Duffield, "Evolutionism," p. 174. Cf. *PQPR* (Oct. 1872):800; McCosh, *Christianity and Positivism*, p. 353.

54Dabney, *Syllabus and Notes*, pp. 33, 260. Cf. E. D. Campbell, "Evolution and God," *UP* (Jan. 22, 1890):52-53.

55McCosh, *Development Hypothesis*, p. 89; idem., *Religious Aspect of Evolution*, p. 27. Cf. Patton, "Evolution and Apologetics," p. 141.

56McCosh, *Christianity and Positivism*, pp. 50-51, 346-49; idem., *Religious Aspect of Evolution*, pp. 52, 88.

57Macloskie, "Theistic Evolution," pp. 2, 3, 5, 20.

58Macloskie, "Errors," pp. 102-5; idem., "Theistic Evolution," pp. 10, 21, quotation from p. 10.

59Patton, "Evolution and Apologetics," pp. 142-44. Cf. Hodge, "Introduction," pp. xvii-xix.

60George Armstrong, *PQ* (Oct. 1888):501-4, quotation from p. 501. Cf. idem., "Darwin and Darwinism," *PQ* (July 1889):348.

61McCosh, "How to Deal with Young Men," p. 204; idem., *Religious Aspect of Evolution*, pp. xi, 6.

62Macloskie, "Errors," p. 104.

63Nicholas Steffens, "The Dangerous Character of Modern Theology," *CI* (Feb. 7, 1900):83-84.

64Robinson, "Pulpit and Sceptical Culture," p. 147.

65Cf. Bozeman, *Protestants in an Age of Science*, pp. 112, 116-17.

66In McCosh, *Development Hypothesis*, pp. 78-104.

67William Taylor, "Some Phases of Modern Thought," *PQPR* (Oct. 1877):620-21; Hodge, *What is Darwinism?* pp. 126ff.; Armstrong, "Pentateuchal Story," p. 345; Macloskie, "Errors," pp. 98-107; Alexander Mair, "The Contributions of Christianity to Science," *PR* (Jan. 1888):47-48; E. Blekkink, "The Large View of Things," *L* (Oct. 16, 1907):801-2.

68Kuyper, *Lectures on Calvinism*, pp. 130-35.

69Shedd, *Dogmatic Theology*, 1:35-45; Francis Patton, *PR* (Jan. 1885):167-68.

70Thomas Kuhn, *The Structure of Scientific Revolutions* (Chicago: University of Chicago Press, 1962), pp. 43ff., 143ff. Cf. S. G. Brush, "Should the History of Science Be Rated X?" *Science* (March 22, 1974):1166-67; David L. Hull, "Scientific Bandwagon or Travelling Medicine Show?" *Society* (Sept./Oct. 1978): 52, 58; Harry Cook, in the *Journal of the American Scientific Affiliation* (March 1973):34-38.

[71]Kuhn, *Structure of Scientific Revolutions*, pp. 52ff.; Brush, "Should the History of Science Be Rated X?" p. 1170; Hull, "Scientific Bandwagon," p. 53.

[72]Kuyper, *Lectures on Calvinism*, pp. 132-34.

[73]Ibid., pp. 136-37.

[74]Ibid., pp. 139-40.

[75]Ibid., pp. 140-41.

[76]B. B. Warfield, *PTR* (Jan. 1903):145-46.

[77]Webb, "Evolution Controversy," p. 283.

[78]D. W. Fisher, "Naturalism," *PRR* (Jan. 1896):56-65; Warfield, *PTR* (Oct. 1908):640-50; Hugh Scott, "Has Scientific Investigation Disturbed the Basis of Rational Faith?" *PTR* (Oct. 1906):441-44, 447-50.

[79]John Dewey, "The Influence of Darwin on Philosophy" (1909), in *American Thought*, pp. 214-24, quotations from pp. 214 and 219.

[80]Marty, *Righteous Empire*, p. 193; Cynthia E. Russett, *Darwin in America: The Intellectual Response, 1865–1912* (San Francisco: W. H. Freeman, 1976), pp. 27-28; Lefferts Loetscher, *The Broadening Church: A Study of Theological Issues in the Presbyterian Church Since 1869* (Philadelphia: University of Pennsylvania Press, 1954), p. 10.

[81]Bozeman, *Protestants in an Age of Science*, pp. 167-72.

[82]Davis, "Presbyterian Attitudes Toward Science," demonstrates that this was the case. See pp. 5, 74, 130, 241-42, 259, 392, and passim.

[83]*Minutes of the General Assembly of the Presbyterian Church in the U.S.A.* (1923), p. 212.

[84]See "In the Beginning; CT Joins the Origins Debate," *Christianity Today* (Oct. 8, 1982):22-26, 28-45; Henry Morris and John Whitcomb, Jr., *The Genesis Flood: the Biblical Record and Its Scientific Implications* (Philadelphia: Presbyterian and Reformed, 1961); Arthur C. Custance, *Evolution or Creation?* (Grand Rapids: Zondervan, 1976); and Davis A. Young, *Christianity and the Age of the Earth* (Grand Rapids: Zondervan, 1982).

CHAPTER 7

[1]"Are We Passing Through a Great Moral Crisis?" *Current Literature* (July 1907):87-88; "Blasting at the Rock of Ages," *Current Literature* (June 1909):654-55; "The Modern Assault on the Christian Virtues," *Current Literature* (Jan. 1906):49-50.

[2]"Are We Passing?" pp. 87-88.

[3]Quoted in "Blasting at the Rock of Ages," p. 654.

[4]"Humanism," *Nation* (Aug. 15, 1912):140-41.

[5]Some observers complained about or applauded this trend even earlier. John M. Bonham, in *Secularism: Its Progress and Its Morals* (New York: G. P. Putnam's Sons, 1894) praised a growing acceptance of secular ethics (see pp. 5, 21, 131-32, 170-74, 192, 372-73). James Bixby, in *The Ethics of Evolution: The Crisis in Morals Occasioned by the Doctrine of Development* (Boston: Small, Maynard, and Co., 1900) lamented that "the time honored principles of ethics that recognized the moral sense as innate, the verdict of the conscience as authoritative and the sanctions of morality as God-given are daily discredited" (p. 16). A. O. Lovejoy commented on the same trend in 1908, in "Religious Transition and Ethical Awakening in America," *Hibbert Journal* (July 1908):500-514.

[6]On the vital connection between the common schools and morality, see Lyman Atwater, "The State in Relation to Morality, Religion and Education," *PQ* (March 1878):413-15.

[7]Kenneth Cauthen, *Science, Secularization and God* (New York: Abingdon, 1969), pp. 19ff.: William Quillian, Jr., "Evolution and Moral Theory in America," in *Evolutionary Thought in America*, ed. Stow Persons (New York: George Braziller, 1956), pp. 398-417; John Dewey, "The Evolutionary Method as Applied to Morality. 1. Its Necessity," *Philosophical Review* (March 1902): 107-24, and "2. Its Significance for Conduct," *Philosophical Review* (July 1902):353-71; Stow Persons, *American Minds: A History of Ideas* (Huntington, NY: Robert E. Krieger, 1975), pp. 237-350.

[8]Charles Hodge, *Systematic Theology* (3 vols.; New York: Scribner's, 1874), 1:254-61. Cf. William B. Greene, Jr., "The Metaphysics of Christian Apologetics," *PRR* (Jan. 1898):72-75. Charles Cashdollar's survey of textbooks, exercise books, and extant lecture notes of Reformed scholars offers abundant evidence that these men frequently criticized Comte's ethical views in college and seminary classrooms. See "August Comte and the American Reformed Theologians," *Journal of the History of Ideas* (Jan.-March 1978):61-79.

[9]James McCosh, "What Morality Have We Left?" *NAR* (May 1881):497-98. Cf. *PQPR* (Jan. 1877):188-89. D. Campbell, "The Outcome of Evolution," *UP* (March 18, 1880):179.

[10]Robert Dabney, *Syllabus and Notes of the Course of Systematic and Polemic Theology* (Richmond: Presbyterian Committee of Publication, 1890), p. 63.

[11]T. P. Epes, "Authority in Revelation and Morals," *PQ* (July 1891):324.

[12]Atwater, "The State," p. 415; William B. Greene, Jr., "The Metaphysics of Christian Apologetics: Morality," *PRR* (Oct. 1898):678-80; Thomas Nichols, "Morality: Intuitive and Imperative," *PRR* (July 1899):511-16; James Coleman, *Social Ethics: An Introduction to the Nature and Ethics of the State* (New York: Baker and Taylor, 1902), pp. 180-88; William H. Johnson, "Pragmatism, Humanism and Religion," *PTR* (Oct. 1908):548-49.

[13]McCosh, "An Advertisement for a New Religion, By an Evolutionist," *NAR* (July 1878):50; Francis Patton, "The Metaphysics of Oughtness," *PR* (Jan. 1886):137-39; Greene, "Metaphysics," p. 680; James Orr, "Autonomy in Ethics," *PTR* (April 1908):271.

[14]Orr, "Autonomy in Ethics," p. 270; Patton, "Metaphysics of Oughtness," pp. 143-45.

[15]Patton, "Metaphysics of Oughtness," p. 139. Cf. Hodge, *Systematic Theology*, 1:279.

[16]McCosh, "Religious Conflicts of the Age," *NAR* (July 1881):36-37.

[17]See Henry May, *The End of American Innocence: A Study of the First Years of Our Own Time, 1912–1917* (New York: Knopf, 1959), pp. 153-64, 193-212. H. L. Mencken led the assault on the traditional view: "And what is the king of all axioms and emperor of all fallacies? Simply the idea of men—that all men, at all times and everywhere, have ever agreed, do now agree and will agree forevermore ... that certain things are right and certain other things are wrong ..." (*The Philosophy of Friedrich Nietzsche* [1908: Boston: Luce, 1913], p. 282). Such views were also expressed by William Frank Norris, Jack London, Theodore Dreiser, and James H. Robinson, to name a few.

[18]Greene, "Metaphysics," p. 664. Cf. George Patton, "Kidd's Social Evolution," *PQ* (July 1895):458; William Findley, "Two Divine Witnesses," *UP* (Sept. 9, 1880):1.

[19]Patton, "Metaphysics of Oughtness," pp. 141-46, 149, quotation from p. 146.

[20]McCosh, "What Morality Have We Left?" pp. 499-505.

[21]Nichols, "Morality," pp. 512-13.

[22]Francis Ferguson, "Evolution in Ethics — Mallock and Spencer," *Cath P* (July 1, 1880):36, 42-44. Cf. Hodge, *Systematic Theology*, 1:276-79. Hodge claimed that while materialism contradicted the facts of consciousness, the theistic solution satisfactorily accounted for all the facts of consciousness and observation, satisfying the mind and the heart.

[23]W. A. Cocke, "Moral Philosophy and Christianity," *SPR* (Jan. 1871):22; William B. Greene, Jr., "The Importance of Preaching the Ethics of Christianity," *PQ* (Oct. 1900): 517; "Can We Have Morality Without Religion?" pp. 49-50.

[24]Ferguson, "Evolution in Ethics," p. 44.

[25]Herbert Spencer, in *The Principles of Ethics* (2 vols.; New York: D. Appleton, 1898), 1:xiv declared that the primary reason he published *The Data of Ethics* in 1879 was because "the gap left by the dissappearance of the code of supernatural ethics" had to be filled by a "code of natural ethics." Cf. *The Data of Ethics* (New York: D. Appleton, 1893), p. 183; Henry C. Minton, "Theological Implications of the Synthetic Philosophy," *PRR* (July 1896):406, 408; *PQPR* (Jan. 1877):188-89. According to Perry Miller, in the years between 1860 and 1900 Americans enthusiastically recapitulated Spencer's thought to justify a competitive America. Miller, *American Thought: Civil War to World War I* (New York: Holt, Rinehart and Winston, 1954), p. xxiii. During these years Americans bought more than 350,000 copies of Spencer's books. See Nelson M. Blake, *A History of American Life and Thought* (New York: McGraw-Hill, 1963), p. 399.

[26]Spencer, *Principles of Ethics,* 1:79, 87; idem., *Data of Ethics,* pp. 123, 126; idem., *The Principles of Psychology* (2 vols.; New York, 1899), 1:279-80. Cf. Bonham, *Secularism,* pp. 170-74.

[27]Epes, "Authority," p. 321; Johnson, "Pragmatism," p. 549; *POS* (Feb. 23, 1910):225.

[28]McCosh, "What Morality Have We Left?" pp. 508-9.

[29]Ferguson, "Evolution in Ethics," p. 35. Cf. Lyman Atwater, "The State," p. 415; Patton, "Kidd's Social Evolution," p. 463. Evolutionists such as Thomas Huxley refuted this claim, arguing that morality was not dependent upon Christianity. Science alone could sustain upright morality. See "Science and Morals" (1886) in Thomas Huxley, *Evolution and Other Essays* (New York: D. Appleton, 1897), pp. 145-46.

[30]McCosh, "An Advertisement," pp. 50, 56, 58-59; Patton, "Metaphysics of Oughtness," p. 134; Cf. Charles Hodge, *Systematic Theology* 3:277. Hodge protested that man's knowledge of his own mind as a thinking substance "is the first and most certain and most indestructible of all forms of knowledge. It is impossible that the materialist can have any higher evidence of the existence of matter than he has of his own mind."

[31]Ferguson, "Evolution in Ethics," p. 36. Cf. "Rats Wiser Than Men," *Pres* (Jan. 3, 1880):4-5.

[32]Lyman Atwater, "Religion and Politics," in *Proceedings: Second General Council* (Philadelphia: Office of the Alliance, 1880). p. 325.

[33]Francis Patton, *PR* (Jan. 1886):199.

[34]Stow Persons, "Evolution and Theology," in *Evolutionary Thought in America,* pp. 434ff.; Eric Goldman, *Rendezvous with Destiny* (New York: Knopf, 1955), pp. 73-80, 90-91; Richard Hofstadter, *Social Darwinism in American Thought* (Boston: Beacon Press, 1955), pp. 67-84.

[35]Miller, *American Thought,* pp. ix-xiv, xxiii-xxxiii; Francis P. Weisenburger,

Ordeal of Faith (New York: Philosophical Library, 1959), pp. 150-52; Hofstadter, *Social Darwinism,* p. 123.

[36]Johnson, "Pragmatism," pp. 551, 560. Similarly, in 1909 the editors of *Current Literature* protested pragmatism's assault on Christian morality. Cf. "Modern Assault on the Christian Virtues" p. 68-69; Henry Minton, *PTR* (July 1903):466.

[37]Weisenburger, *Ordeal of Faith,* pp. 153-54; Johnson, "Pragmatism," pp. 548, 561-62; Greene, *PTR* (July 1911):475.

[38]See, for example, Bonham, *Secularism,* pp. 186, 192. As God could not be known, Bonham argued, the "objective manifestations of Nature are the only means of determining the whole relationship of men to Nature and of man to man" (p. 248).

[39]Cocke, "Moral Philosophy," p. 2.

[40]John Dewey, *Reconstruction in Philosophy* (New York: Henry Holt and Co., 1920), pp. 161-62. Dewey repeatedly denied the existence of transcendent or eternal values. See "Consciousness and Experience," in *The Influence of Darwin on Philosophy and Other Essays in Contemporary Thought* (New York: Henry Holt and Co., 1910), pp. 263, 267-68. Cf. *A Common Faith* (New Haven: Yale University Press, 1934), pp. 71-72, 77, 80. For Dewey's ethical views, see James H. Tufts and John Dewey, *Ethics* (New York, 1908). Dewey argued that ethics was a positive science analogous to the physical sciences. Rejecting the idea of antecedent fixed moral absolutes, he urged people to consider moral principles not as norms but as tools for analyzing ethical situations. In his many essays on morals for public schools Dewey consistently repudiated all ethical approaches rooted in an "a priori determination of morality," insisting rather that morals were a function of "the interaction between intrinsic human nature on the one hand and social customs and institutions on the other" (Dewey, *Human Nature and Conduct* [New York: Henry Holt and Co., 1922], pp. viii-ix). See also *Ethics* (New York: Henry Holt and Co., 1916).

[41]E.g., H. L. Minton, *PTR,* pp. 464-66; William B. Greene, Jr., *PTR* (July 1911):475-576.

[42]Dabney, *Syllabus and Notes,* p. 106.

[43]E.g., Nichols, "Morality," pp. 516ff.

[44]Epes, "Authority," pp. 330-31. Cf. George T. Purves, "Problems of the Twentieth Century," in *Twentieth Century Addresses* (Philadelphia: Presbyterian Board of Publication, 1902), p. 164.

[45]William B. Greene, Jr., *PTR* (Oct. 1913):656; James Howerton, *The Church and Social Reforms* (New York: Revell, 1913), pp. 34-36.

[46]McCosh, "Religious Conflicts," p. 38.

[47]E.g., Spencer, *Principles of Ethics,* 1:114-21, 127-29, 252-55, 300; 2:425. T. H. Huxley, however, had basic disagreements with Spencer. He believed that such institutions as "laws" and "the state" could civilize man. Cf. his *Evolution of Ethics and Other Essays,* pp. 62, 87-88, 91-92.

[48]McCosh, "What Morality Have We Left?" pp. 501-4; "The Morality of the Future," *Pres* (Nov. 13, 1880):10; Ferguson, "Evolution in Ethics," p. 44.

[49]E.g., Francis Patton, *PR* (Jan. 1886):199.

[50]Nicholas Steffens, "The Ethics of Natural Man," *PRR* (July 1900):469-70; Orr, "Autonomy in Ethics," pp. 271, 275; William B. Greene, Jr., *PTR* (April 1915):286-87.

[51]E.g., P. P. Flourney, "Evolutionary Ethics and Christianity," *SPR* (July 1884):436. For an example of the secular ethical view, see John Dewey, "Evolution and Ethics," *Monist* (April 1898):338 and *Human Nature and Conduct,* pp. 231, 234.

[52]Dabney, *Syllabus and Notes,* p. 105; McCosh, "An Advertisement," p. 51.

[53]G. J. A. Coulson, "God and Moral Obligations," *SPR* (April 1878):330; Minton, "Theological Implications," p. 408.

[54]Lyman Atwater, "Christian Morality, Expediency and Liberty," *PR* (Jan. 1881):70, 75; Steffens, "Ethics of Natural Man," p. 475; Carroll Cutler, *PRR* (July 1891):551.

[55]Patton, "Kidd's Social Evolution," p. 476.

[56]Francis Patton, *PR* (Jan. 1883):218.

[57]Ferguson, "Evolution in Ethics," p. 39.

[58]Flourney, "Evolutionary Ethics," pp. 437-38; James A. Quarles, "Two Current False Philosophies," *PQ* (April 1900):203.

[59]Patton, *PR* (Jan. 1883):218.

[60]Ferguson, "Evolution in Ethics," p. 43.

[61]Cutler, *PRR* (July 1891):551.

[62]Orr, "Autonomy in Ethics," pp. 276-77.

[63]Patton, *PR* (Jan. 1883): 217. Cf. S. L. Orr, "John Calvin and His Ethical System," in *Proceedings: Ninth General Council,* ed. G. D. Mathews (London: Office of the Alliance, 1909), pp. 127-30; Greene, *PRR* (Oct. 1896):699. Cf. Greene, *PTR* (July 1911), p. 500.

[64]A. H. Strong, *Systematic Theology* (Rochester, NY, 1899), p. 86.

[65]McCosh, "What Morality Have We Left?" pp. 500, 509. Cf. Goldwin Smith, "The Prospect of a Moral Interregnum," *Atlantic Monthly* (Nov. 1879):629-42; Hodge, *Systematic Theology,* 1:278; Greene, "Metaphysics," pp. 690-92.

[66]Strong, *Systematic Theology,* p. 86. Cf. W. G. T. Shedd, *Theological Essays* (New York: Scribner's, 1887), pp. 375-77. According to Shedd, the "utmost that Confucius, Sakyamuni and Socrates can do is give good advice. They cannot incline and enable men to obey it." See also Flourney, "Evolutionary Ethics," pp. 446-47; William B. Greene, Jr., *PTR* (Oct. 1908):688.

[67]McCosh, "What Morality Have We Left?" p. 509.

[68]Quarles, "Two Current False Philosophies," p. 203.

[69]E.g., "An Immoral Theory," *Pres* (April 3, 1880):10-11; Dabney, *Syllabus and Notes,* p. 98. For a prominent example of naturalistic reductionism and determinism, see Antonio Llano, "Morality: the Last of the Dogmas," *Philosophical Review* (July 1896):386ff. He insisted that people increasingly realized that their conduct was determined by their physical organization, which, in turn, was determined by inheritence, environment, and the laws of matter and force, moral feelings that were rooted in a sense of personal responsibility would disappear.

[70]E.g., Arthur B. Reeve, "Is Evolution Calvinistic?" *Bibliotheca Sacra* (July 1905):560-65; Mason Pressley, "Calvinism and Science," *Evangelical Repository* (Nov. 1891):666-68.

[71]Persons, *American Minds,* quotation from pp. 351-52. See also pp. 271-84, 318-35, 353-61.

[72]E.g., Atwater, "The State," p. 413. Atwater wrote that "large numbers of children receive no proper moral or religious instruction elsewhere" than in the common schools.

[73]Neil G. McCluskey, *Public Schools and Moral Education: The Influence of Horace Mann, William Torrey Harris and John Dewey* (Westport, CT: Greenwood Press, 1958), pp. 143, 217, 233, 266; Walter B. Jacobs, "Values in Secondary Education," *Educational Review* (Feb. 1895):136-37; A. E. Kellogg, "The Content of School Readers," *Educational Review* (Nov. 1894):339, 347. William Faunce, president of Brown University, complained in 1905 that the "absence of ethical instruction in many schools is having its inevitable result," as seen in "growing disrespect

for law" and increasing acceptance of egoistic moralities. See "Survey of Moral and Religious Progress," *Educational Review* (April 1905):371-72.

[74]See Richard Hofstadter, "The Revolution in Higher Education," in *Paths of American Thought,* ed. A. M. Schlesinger, Jr., and Morton White (Boston: Houghton Mifflin, 1963), pp. 276ff.; R. Freeman Butts, *The College Charts Its Course: Historical Conceptions and Current Proposals* (New York: Arno Press, 1971), pp. 182-83, 185-88, 196, 203, 221-24, 260-61. Charles Hall of Union Seminary in New York City lamented in 1904 that certain factors made it very difficult in secondary public schools, state universities, and many private colleges to provide "positive religious teaching." These schools did not have an adequate sense of their responsibility to provide religious training or "an adequate anxiety in view of the fact that education in this country so largely is non-religious" ("Progress in Religious and Moral Education," *Educational Review* [June 1904]:6-7).

[75]Harold Bolce, "Blasting at the Rock of Ages," *Cosmopolitan* (May 1909):665-76.

[76]Persons, *American Minds,* pp. 249-55, 271-84, 318-44.

[77]On the general effects of science, see Merle Curti, "The Delimitation of Supernaturalism," in *The Growth of American Thought* (New York: Harper and Brothers, 1943), pp. 531-55 and Edward A. White, *Science and Religion in American Thought: The Impact of Naturalism* (Stanford, CA: Stanford University Press, 1952), p. 110. John Dewey complained in *Philosophy and Civilization* (New York: Minton, Balch and Company, 1931) that the prestige of science was "so great that an almost superstitious aura gathers around its name and work" (pp. 320-22).

[78]E.g., Freeman Butts and Lawrence A. Cremin, eds., *A History of Education in American Culture* (New York: Henry Holt and Co., 1953), p. 325. Henry Steele Commager, *The American Mind* (New Haven: Yale University Press, 1950), p. 179.

[79]"Biblical Ethics," *PSt* (Jan. 5, 1910):1.

[80]Greene, "Importance of Preaching," pp. 503-5, 519. Cf. E. D. Morris, "Ethical Preaching," *Cath P* (March 1883):165-67; Faunce, "Survey of Morals," p. 366.

[81]See George Marsden, *Fundamentalism and American Culture: The Shaping of Twentieth Century Evangelicalism, 1870 – 1925* (New York: Oxford University Press, 1980), pp. 21, 24, 26-28, 35-37, 66-68, 73-74, 156-64.

[82]Robert Wiebe, *The Search for Order, 1877 – 1920* (New York: Hill and Wang, 1967), pp. 44-75, 133-64; Gerald Heard, *Morals Since 1900* (New York: Harper and Brothers, 1950), pp. 117-28; Marquis Childs and Douglass Cater, *Ethics in a Business Society* (New York: Harper and Brothers, 1954), pp. 63-100.

[83]Betrand Russell, *Why I am Not a Christian* (London: George Allen, 1957), p. 51. Cf. John Dewey, *Philosophy and Civilization,* p. 319. Dewey observed that the "earlier optimism which thought that the advance of natural science was to dispel superstition, ignorance and oppression, by placing reason in the throne, was unjustified." He also complained in *Democracy and Education* (New York, 1916), p. 394, that "men still want the crutch of dogma, of beliefs fixed by authority. . . ."

[84]Walter Lippmann, *Preface to Morals* (New York: Macmillan, 1931), pp. 3ff., 37ff., 314ff.

CHAPTER 8

[1]The first quotation is from Robert Thompson, *The Divine Order of Human Society* (Philadelphia: John D. Wattles, 1891), pp. 142-43; the second is from J. M. Foster, *Christ the King* (Boston, 1894), p. 367; and the third is from William B. Greene, Jr., *PTR* (July 1911):512.

[2]Lyman Atwater, "The Great Railroad Strike," *PQPR* (Oct. 1877):720.

[3]Charles Aiken, "Christianity and Social Problems," *PRR* (Jan. 1892):80.

[4]Louis Berkhof, *The Christian Laborer in the Industrial Struggle* (Grand Rapids: Eerdmans-Sevensma, 1916), p. 10.

[5]See Berkhof, *Christian Laborer*, p. 11; William B. Greene, Jr., "The Church and the Social Question," *PTR* (July 1912):379ff.; Evert Blekkink, "Forward," *L* (Jan. 2, 1907):145-46; David Burrell, *For Christ's Crown and Other Sermons* (New York: Wilbur Ketcham, 1896), pp. 8-16; William Blaikie, "The Influence of the Gospel on Employers and Employed," in *Proceedings: Second General Council* (Philadelphia, 1880), pp. 180-81; James Howerton, *The Church and Social Reforms* (New York: Revell, 1913), pp. 50, 91ff. and passim.

[6]R. H. Tawney, *Religion and the Rise of Capitalism* (New York: Harcourt, Brace and Co., 1926), p. 273. Cf. P. T. Forsyth, "Calvinism and Capitalism," *Contemporary Review* (June-July 1910):82.

[7]Winthrop Hudson, "Puritanism and the Spirit of Capitalism," *Church History* (March 1949):15. Cf. John T. McNeill, *The History and Character of Calvinism* (New York: Oxford University Press, 1954), pp. 418-21.

[8]Forsyth, "Calvinism and Capitalism," *Contemporary Review* (April-May, 1910):733.

[9]John Calvin, *The Institutes of the Christian Religion*, ed. John McNeill (2 vols.; Philadelphia: Westminster, 1960), 2:6, 10.

[10]Lyman Atwater, for example, insisted that the Panic of 1873 taught that these characteristics were essential to economic success. See "The Late Commercial Crisis," *PQPR* (Jan. 1874):123-24.

[11]Charles Hodge, "Thy Kingdom Come," in *Conference Papers* (New York: Scribner's, 1879), pp. 322-24, Aiken, "Christianity and Social Problems," pp. 72, 76; Burrell, *For Christ's Crown*, p. 15; Blekkink, "Forward," pp. 145-46; *CI* (Feb. 17, 1876):2.

[12]Robert Thompson, *The Duty of the Church in the Conflict Between Capital and Labor* (1887), passim. Cf. idem., *Divine Order*, p. 263; *The Social Creed: What the Presbyterian Church Believes About Social Problems* (n.p., Board of Home Missions, 1910), p. 8.

[13]"Work as a Social Elevator," *CI* (March 9, 1876):8-9; Aiken, "Christianity and Social Problems," p. 82; Lyman Atwater, "Our Industrial and Financial Situation," *PQPR* (July 1875):528; Robert Dabney, *Syllabus and Notes of the Course in Polemic and Systematic Theology* (Richmond: Presbyterian Committee of Publication, 1890), p. 415; James Quarles, "Single Tax Upon Land," *PQ* (April 1895):292, 300; "Calvinism in the Business World," *Living Age* (Sept. 3, 1910):635.

[14]Max Weber, *The Protestant Ethic and the Spirit of Capitalism* (New York: Scribner's, 1958), pp. 98-127 and passim; R. H. Tawney, *Religion and the Rise of Capitalism*, pp. 34, 81, 83, 102-32, 199-201, 215-16, 230, 233, 239-54, 316-17.

[15]Fred Graham, *The Constructive Revolutionary: John Calvin and His Socio-Economic Impact* (Richmond: John Knox Press, 1971), pp. 73, 127. Cf. Ernst Troeltsch, *Social Teachings of the Christian Churches* (2 vols.; New York: Macmillan, 1931), 2:903-4; R. M. Kingdon, "Social Welfare in Calvin's Geneva," *American Historical Review* (Feb. 1971):50-69.

[16]See Richard M. Cameron, *Methodism and Society in Historical Perspective* (New York: Abingdon, 1961), pp. 290ff.; Martin Marty, *Righteous Empire: The Protestant Experience in America* (New York: The Dial Press, 1970), p. 146; George Marsden, *Fundamentalism and American Culture: The Shaping of Twentieth Cen-*

tury Evangelicalism, 1870 – 1925 (New York: Oxford University Press, 1980), pp. 13-14.

[17]Berkhof, *Christian Laborer*, p. 17; Charles Aiken, *PR* (Jan. 1887):175-76.

[18]Charles Aiken, *PR* (Oct. 1885):762; R. L. Benn, "Socialism Growing," *PSt* (July 13, 1910):7.

[19]Charles Stelzle, "Presbyterian Department of Church and Labor," *The Annual of the American Academy of Political and Social Science* (Nov. 1907):456.

[20]Aiken, *PR* (Oct. 1885):762.

[21]Louis Voss, "The Old Testament in Its Relation to Social Reform," *PQ* (Oct. 1896):443. Cf. Berkhof, *Christian Laborer*, p. 17.

[22]William Sloane, *Social Regeneration: The Work of Christianity* (Philadelphia: Westminster, 1902), p. 24.

[23]Blaikie, "Influence of the Gospel," p. 181; A. A. Hodge, *Popular Lectures on Theological Themes* (Philadelphia: 1887), p. 330.

[24]Arnold Huizinga, "Social or Individual Regeneration?" *Bibliotheca Sacra* (Jan. 1912):37-38, 49.

[25]George M. Grant, "Progress and Poverty," *PR* (April 1888):177ff.

[26]William Holliday, "Theories of Labor Reform and Social Improvement," *PQPR* (July 1876):432.

[27]Atwater, "Our Industrial and Financial Situation," p. 519.

[28]Adam Shortt, "Looking Backward," *PRR* (April 1891):280. Cf. Holliday, "Theories of Labor Reform," p. 431.

[29]Charles Hodge, *Systematic Theology* (3 vols.; New York: Scribner's, 1874), 3:421-25, quotation from p. 425. Cf. Dabney, *Syllabus and Notes*, p. 416.

[30]Voss, "The Old Testament," pp. 496-97; James McCosh, *Our Moral Nature* (1892), p. 40.

[31]Greene, *PTR* (April 1913):351.

[32]Hodge, *Systematic Theology*, 3:421.

[33]Shortt, "Looking Backward," p. 277.

[34]S. H. Kellogg, "A Tendency of the Times," *PQ* (Jan. 1890):50-51; G. L. Bitzer, "Looking Backward: 2000 – 1887 A.D.," *CO* (June 18, 1890):1.

[35]Voss, "The Old Testament," p. 443.

[36]Sloan, *Social Regeneration,* p. 13; Bitzer, "Looking Backward: 2000 – 1887 A.D.," p. 1.

[37]Atwater, "Our Industrial and Financial Situation," p. 519. Cf. Atwater, "The Labor Question in its Economic and Christian Aspects," *PQPR* (July 1872):479; James McCosh, "Relation of the Church to the Capital and Labor Question," in *National Perils and Opportunities* (New York: Baker and Taylor, 1887), p. 217; George Greene, *PTR* (April 1913):351, who protested that Marxism would paralyze the wholesome ambition, ingenuity, and enterprise of the common person.

[38]Shortt, "Looking Backward," p. 280. Cf. Atwater, "The Labor Question," p. 480; Hodge, *Systematic Theology,* 3:430.

[39]William B. Greene, Jr., *PTR* (Jan. 1915):130.

[40]Quarles, "Single Tax Upon Land," p. 291.

[41]Holliday, "Theories of Labor Reform," p. 435; Samuel Niccolls, "The Duty and Opportunities of the Presbyterian Church in the Twentieth Century," in *Twentieth Century Addresses* (Philadelphia: Presbyterian Board of Publication, 1902), p. 246; A. M. Fraser, "How May the Principles of Calvinism Be Rendered Most Effective under Modern Conditions?" in *Calvin Memorial Addresses* (Richmond: Presbyterian Committee of Publication, 1909), p. 251.

[42]Holliday, "Theories of Labor Reform," pp. 436-38; William B. Greene, Jr., in *PTR* (Oct. 1907):702, protested that if the state became excessively involved in

the marketplace it would "arrogate supremacy in other spheres also." In advocating this position, Calvinists were consistently following the constitutional set of checks and balances that their theology, with its belief in human greed and selfishness, had helped to create. See Richard Hofstadter, *The American Political Tradition and the Men who made It* (New York: Knopf, 1973), pp. 3-4 and George L. Hunt, ed., *Calvinism and the Political Order* (Philadelphia: Westminster, 1965), passim.

⁴³Grant, "Progress and Poverty," pp. 197-98.

⁴⁴Bitzer, "Looking Backward: 2000 – 1887 A.D.," p. 1.

⁴⁵Benn, "Socialism Growing," p. 8; Voss, "The Old Testament," p. 422; Thompson, *Divine Order*, pp. 142-43.

⁴⁶William B. Greene, Jr., *PTR* (Oct. 1913):716-17. Cf. Greene, *PTR* (Oct. 1907):702.

⁴⁷Sloan, *Social Regeneration*, p. 114. Cf. "Labor and Its Compensation," *UP* (April 16, 1885):248: "Sober socialism which speaks through intelligence is entitled to respectful treatment." Cf. also Francis Beattie, *PRR* (April 1806):322.

⁴⁸Sloan, *Social Regeneration*, pp. 13ff., 37. Cf. "Socialism," *PSt* (July 27, 1910):2; "Socialism — a Sure Preventive," *CP* (March 6, 1872):1; Edward Coe, "The Church and Social Questions," in *Proceedings: Seventh General Council*, ed. G. D. Mathews (Washington: Gill and Wallace, 1899), p. 273; Cameron, *Methodism and Society*, p. 291; Marsden, *Fundamentalism and American Culture*, pp. 12, 37.

⁴⁹William B. Greene, Jr., *PTR* (July 1911):512-13. Cf. "The Study of Social Problems," *BT* (May 14, 1914):342-25; Sylvester Scovel, "The World-Wide Meaning and Mission of National Reform," in *Report of the World's Christian Citizenship Conference* (Allegheny, PA: National Reform Association, 1911), p. 15.

⁵⁰Charles Hopkins, *The Rise of the Social Gospel in American Protestantism, 1865 – 1915* (New Haven: Yale University Press, 1940), pp. 15-16; Henry May, *Protestant Churches and Industrial America* (New York: Harper and Brothers, 1949), pp. 83, 193.

⁵¹"The Problem of the Labouring Classes," *Cath P* (June 1879):416. Cf. *PB* (July 25, 1877):1; *PB* (Aug. 1, 1877):1; *PB* (Aug. 15, 1877):1. See also George Swetnam, "All Ye That Labor," in *The Presbyterian Valley*, ed. William McKinney (Pittsburgh: Davis and Wade, 1958), pp. 452-57.

⁵²Atwater, "The Labor Question," pp. 484-85; idem., "Great Railroad Strike," pp. 722-26. Cf. "Labor and Its Compensation," pp. 248-49.

⁵³Quoted by Henry Zwaanstra, *Reformed Thought and Experience in a New World: A Study of the Christian Reformed Church and its American Environment* (Kampen: J. H. Kok, 1973), pp. 241ff. Cf. Berkhof, *Christian Laborer*, pp. 25-28.

⁵⁴Zwaanstra, *Reformed Thought and Experience*, pp. 260-77.

⁵⁵Atwater, "Great Railroad Strike," p. 417.

⁵⁶Atwater, "The Labor Question," pp. 475, 483; idem., "Our Industrial and Financial Situation," p. 523; G. J. Coulson, "Capital and Labor," *SPR* (Oct. 1877):728-29.

⁵⁷Atwater, "Great Railroad Strike," p. 727; idem., "The Labor Question," p. 484.

⁵⁸Atwater, "The Labor Question," pp. 475-77, 483; "The Outcome of Strikes," *PB* (Feb. 13, 1889):1; "Results of a Strike," *PB* (Feb. 13, 1889):1; D. H. MacVicar, "Social Discontent," *PR* (April 1887):275-76; J. M. Foster, *Reformation Principles: Stated and Applied* (Boston, 1890), p. 279.

⁵⁹Alexander McKelway, "Competition, Combination or Cooperation?" *PSt* (Oct. 22, 1902):9-10; *PSt* (Oct. 29, 1902):9-10; *PSt* (Nov. 5, 1902):9-10; *PSt*

(Nov. 12, 1902):10-11; *PSt* (Nov. 26, 1902):12-13. Cf. "The Strike," *PB* (July 25, 1901):6; "The Insolence of Capital and the Mistake of Labor," *BT* (Nov. 1902):74.

[60]George Greene, *PTR* (April 1913):351-52.

[61]McCosh, "Relation of the Church," pp. 216-17. Cf. Hodge, *Popular Lectures,* p. 329; R. V. Hunter, "The Church and the Masses," *PRR* (Jan. 1893):80; Thompson, *Divine Order,* p. 258.

[62]Foster, *Reformation Principles,* pp. 282-84.

[63]McKelway, "Competition, Combination or Cooperation?" *PSt* (Dec. 10, 1902):10; T. W. Chamber, *PR* (1887):763.

[64]MacVicar, "Social Discontent," pp. 275, 281; C. D. Drake, "Christianity the Friend of the Working Classes," in *Proceedings: Second General Council,* p. 191; B. W. Williams, "The Divine Law and the Industrial Problem," *CI* (Nov. 5, 1890):4; "The Churches and the Labor Question," *Pres* (Aug. 31, 1910):5-6.

[65]Atwater, "The Labor Question," p. 477; Foster, *Christ the King,* pp. 368ff.; *POS* (July 6, 1910):819; "Presbyterian General Assembly and Social Questions," *Survey* (June 27, 1914):343; "Social Creed," pp. 9-12.

[66]G. C. Vincent, "Political Economy," *UP* (Feb. 12, 1885):106; Atwater, "Great Railroad Strike," p. 743; B. B. Warfield, *PRR* (Oct. 1893):710-11.

[67]Atwater, "The Labor Question," pp. 471, 488-91. Cf. Holliday, "Theories of Labor Reform," pp. 443-45; McKelway, "Competition, Combination, or Cooperation," *PSt* (Nov. 12, 1902):10-11.

[68]Atwater, "Problem of the Labouring Classes," p. 414. Cf. "One Solution of the Labor Problem," *PB* (Sept. 12, 1888):1.

[69]E.g., Greene, *PTR* (July 1911):514; Holliday, "Theories of Labor Reform," pp. 446-48.

[70]Holliday, "Theories of Labor Reform," p. 448; "One Solution of the Labor Problem," p. 1.

[71]Atwater, "The Labor Question," p. 493. Cf. "The Factory 'Problem,' " *PSt* (June 18, 1902):4; Foster, *Reformation Principles,* p. 284.

[72]Holliday, "Theories of Labor Reform," p. 449. Cf. Greene, *PTR* (July 1911):516; Thompson, *Divine Order,* p. 253.

[73]Martin Marty, *The Modern Schism: Three Paths to the Secular* (New York: Harper and Row, 1969), p. 137. Gail Kennedy, ed., *Democracy and the Gospel of Wealth* (Boston: D. C. Heath and Co., 1949), pp. v-ix; Cushing Strout, *The New Heavens and the New Earth: Political Religion in America* (New York: Harper and Row, 1974), pp. 207-10.

[74]May, *Protestant Churches,* p. 193; Sydney Ahlstrom, *A Religious History of the American People* (New Haven: Yale University Press, 1972), p. 789; Ralph Gabriel, *The Course of American Democratic Thought* (New York: The Ronald Press, 1956), pp. 155-58, 160-61, 164-65.

[75]Shedd, *Orthodoxy and Heterodoxy,* p. 244. Cf. Atwater, "Late Commercial Crisis," p. 126; J. M. Ludlow, "The Art of Being Prosperous," *CI* (Jan. 13, 1876):1.

[76]William B. Greene, Jr., *PTR* (Oct. 1903):705. Cf. Atwater, "Late Commercial Crisis," p. 126.

[77]Quarles, "Teaching of Christ," p. 149; MacVicar, "Social Discontent," pp. 264-65.

[78]"Great Wealth," *PB* (Feb. 28, 1901):6.

[79]"The Twentieth Century Movement," *PB* (Oct. 31, 1901):5.

[80]"Godless and Selfish Wealth," *CI* (March 30, 1876):8-9; "Greed for Wealth," *SWP* (Aug. 21, 1879):1; "A Great Evil," *Pres* (Aug. 21, 1880):7; Coe, "Church and Social Questions," p. 276.

[81]J. A. Quarles, "The Ethics of Trade," *PQ* (Jan. 1889):112.

[82]Atwater, "Late Commercial Crisis," p. 125.

[83]Foster, *Reformation Principles*, pp. 280, 282. Cf. "The Wall St. Whirlpool," *PB* (May 9, 1901):6; "State Control of Public Corporations," *UP* (Feb. 21, 1895):120.

[84]"The End of the 'Boom,' " *Pres* (May 15, 1880):10.

[85]Quarles, "Ethics of Trade," pp. 107-8; Howerton, *Church and Social Reform*, pp. 63ff.; MacVicar, "Social Discontent," p. 276; McKelway: "Competition, Combination or Cooperation?" pp. 12-13; Foster, *Christ the King*, pp. 367ff.

[86]"A Revival of Honesty," *CI* (Feb. 3, 1876):8; "The Leaven of Dishonesty," *CI* (Feb. 17, 1876):10; E. P. Herberton, "Honest Earnestness," *Pres* (Jan. 3, 1880):4; Charles Guthrie, "Morality in its Application to Business," *Proceedings: Seventh General Council*, pp. 265-70; "The Lawyer, the Statesman, the Physician, as Powers for Good," *CI* (Feb. 17, 1876):2.

[87]"Corporate Mentality," *CO* (Feb. 23, 1910):179; Herberton, "Honest Earnestness," p. 4; Guthrie, "Morality," p. 268; "Business Ethics," *PB* (Jan. 17, 1901):5-6.

[88]Dabney, *Syllabus and Notes*, pp. 414-18; the quotation is from p. 415. Cf. Hodge, *Systematic Theology*, pp. 434-36.

[89]Many contemporary observers complained about these trends. See, for example, Edward A. Ross, *Changing America* (New York: The Century Co., 1909), pp. 87-94 and James Bryce, "America Revisited—Changes of a Quarter Century," *Outlook* (March 25, 1905), cited in Allan Nevins, ed., *America Through British Eyes* (New York: Oxford University Press, 1948), pp. 385-86.

[90]"Culture and Work," *CO* (Oct. 12, 1910):2; Blaikie, "The Influence of the Gospel," pp. 187ff.; Coleman, *Social Ethics*, p. 188; Cornelius Dosker, "Christian Stewardship," *L* (Jan. 9, 1907):163; "Helping the Poor," *UP* (Oct. 8, 1885):649; Shedd, *Orthodoxy and Heterodoxy*, pp. 243-44.

[91]John A. Nesbitt, "Facing the Problem," *Pres* (Feb. 23, 1910):6-7; "Cultivation of Thrift," *PB* (Oct. 17, 1888):2; Greene, *PTR* (Oct. 1907):701-2.

[92]Charles Wood, "The Pauperism of our Cities; Its Character, Condition, Causes and Relief," *PQPR* (April 1874):217, 221. Cf. "A Difficult Work," *PB* (April 12, 1881):1; "Helping the Poor," p. 649; "The Poor," *UP* (Nov. 5, 1885):712.

[93]"Social Creed," p. 9.

[94]Shedd, *Orthodoxy and Heterodoxy*, p. 244.

[95]David Breed, "Christian Beneficence and Some New Theories Affecting Property," *PRR* (April 1894):292; J. A. Quarles, "The Teaching of Christ as to Wealth," *The Bible Student* (Sept. 1900):148.

[96]Alfred Yeomans, "The Right of the Poor," *PR* (Jan. 1889):18; "Interpreting Providence," *UP* (April 9, 1885):232; John T. Faris, *The Book of God's Providence* (New York: George H. Doran, 1913), pp. 21, 57. Charles Hopkins, a leading chronicler of the Social Gospel (*The Rise of the Social Gospel*, p. 15) quotes the following statement of Lyman Atwater to show Calvinists' endorsement of the status quo and otherworldliness. In 1875 Atwater wrote, "First lay up treasures in heaven. So doing, in whatever state you are, be content. Even if poor for this world, Christians shall be rich as heirs of God, rich in eternal treasures." Atwater, however, made this statement as a final consideration after attacking ostentatious luxury, denouncing speculation and gambling in stocks, repudiating currency inflation, advocating profit-sharing, and arguing that friends, congregations, and Christian benevolence societies should provide for the poor. See "Our Industrial and Financial Situation," pp. 512, 529; quotation from p. 529.

[97]George Summey, "Thanksgiving for Reverses," *PQ* (Jan. 1904):422-24. Cf. Charles Hodge, "The War," *PR* (Jan. 1863):143-44: "Happiness, abundance of the

good things of this life, health, riches, and honors are not the highest gifts of God. Poverty, suffering, the necessity of labour, disappointment and reproach are often the greatest blessings and evidence of God's special favor."

[98]David Burrell, *The Religion of the Future* (New York: American Tract Society, 1894), pp. 145-53; David Irving, "Systematic Beneficence in the Presbyterian Church," *PQPR* (April 1872):365-70; "Few Pews Not Enough," *PB* (Dec. 5, 1888):1; Jane Denham, "Our Work," *UP* (Sept. 9, 1880):571-72; "Christian Charity," *Pres* (Jan. 14, 1915):3.

[99]Foster, *Reformation Principles,* pp. 439ff. Cf. Breed, "Christian Beneficence," pp. 293, 297.

[100]"Church and the Working Masses," p. 4; "Presbyterian General Assembly and Social Questions," p. 343; Sloan, *Social Regeneration,* p. 69; "Confusing the Issue," *Pres* (Jan. 4, 1910):4. James Howerton protested in 1913 that all of the contributions of "financial giants" to charity "are but a fraction of what has been flagrantly abused for selfish ends, even at the expense of the promotion of sin and vice and misery of every kind." See *Church and Social Reform,* pp. 67, 89.

[101]Charles Hodge, "Preaching the Gospel to the Poor" (Jan. 1871):83. Hodge and others sadly admitted that Northern Presbyterians were not effectively reaching the poor. They blamed this on the denominational requirement that ministers be supported by the congregations they served, and argued for establishing a group of itinerant missionaries who could preach the gospel to congregations of the poor. See Hodge, "Domestic Missions," in *Conference Papers,* pp. 324-25; William Durant, *Preaching to the Poor: A Centennial Test of Presbyterianism* (Albany, NY: Weed, Parsons and Co., 1876), pp. 12-17, 25, 34; "The Gospel for the Poor," *CI* (March 16, 1876):4; "God's Pity for the Great City," *UP* (Dec. 3, 1885):778-79.

[102]Breed, "Christian Beneficence," p. 297. Cf. Scovel, "World-Wide Meaning," p. 14; "Social Creed," p. 8.

[103]McCosh, "Relation of the Church," p. 210; Nesbitt, "Facing the Problem," p. 6; *POS* (July 6, 1910):819; MacVicar, "Social Discontent," p. 264.

[104]Atwater, "Problem of the Labouring Classes," p. 412. Calvinists generally insisted that relief of the poor should be undertaken by private individuals and groups rather than the state because private relief would be more discriminating and personal. See Thompson, *Divine Order,* pp. 214-45; H. Bosma, "Care for the Poor—By State or Church?" *BT* (March 21, 1912):185.

[105]Hodge, "The War," pp. 145-46.

[106]See Donald B. Meyers, *The Protestant Search for Political Realism, 1919–1941* (Los Angeles: University of California Press, 1960), pp. 26-27; Marty, *Righteous Empire,* pp. 149-50; Henry May, *The End of Innocence: A Study of the First Years of Our Time, 1912–1917* (New York: Knopf, 1959), p. 158.

[107]See Blaikie, "Influence of the Gospel," pp. 187ff., and Howerton, *Church and Social Reform,* p. 68, who insisted that economic decisions should be based on "right and justice not utility."

[108]E.g., see William E. Diehl, *Thank God, It's Monday* (Philadelphia: Fortress, 1982); R. C. Sproul, *Stronger Than Steel: The Wayne Alderson Story* (New York: Harper and Row, 1980); Michael Novak, *The Spirit of Democratic Capitalism* (New York: Simon and Schuster, 1982); Patricia Ward and Martha Stout, *Christian Women at Work* (Grand Rapids: Zondervan, 1981); Robert Benne, *The Ethic of Democratic Capitalism: A Moral Reassessment* (Philadelphia: Fortress, 1980).

CHAPTER 9

[1]Charles Aiken, "Christianity and Social Problems," *PRR* (Jan. 1892):65.

[2]George T. Purves, "Problems of the Twentieth Century," in *Twentieth Century*

Addresses (Philadelphia: Presbyterian Board of Publication, 1902), p. 64. Cf. William B. Greene, Jr., "The Church and the Social Question," *PTR* (July 1912):377-78.

³Henry McCook, "Progressive Development of the Presbyterian Church," in *Twentieth Century Addresses,* p. 121. Cf. Frederic Lindsay, *PTR* (July 1908):524; W. H. McMaster, "Municipal Reform," *PSt* (June 14, 1905):10.

⁴James Howerton, *The Church and Social Reforms* (New York: Revell, 1913), pp. 53-54. Cf. Sylvester Scovel, "The World-Wide Meaning and Mission of National Reform," in *Report of the World's Christian Citizenship Conference* (Pittsburgh: National Reform Association, 1911), pp. 12-13.

⁵Charles Erdman, *PTR* (Jan. 1915):133; William B. Greene, Jr. *PTR* (Jan. 1913):166-67. Cf. "The Results of the Movement," *BT* (May 9, 1912):293; "Men and Religion Conservation," *UP* (Feb. 8, 1912):6-7; "Men and Religion at Ashland, Ohio," *Herald and Presbyter* (Jan. 17, 1912):11.

⁶John Hall, "The Future Church," in *Presbyterian Reunion: A Memorial Volume, 1837–1871* (New York: DeWitt C. Lent and Co., 1870), p. 479; "Public Morality," *SWP* (June 14, 1905):4; Arnold Huizinga, "Social Or Individual Regeneration?" *Bibliotheca Sacra* (Jan. 1912):49; William Sloan, *Social Regeneration: the Work of Christianity* (Philadelphia: Westminster, 1902), p. 37; David Water, "Large Cities," in *Proceedings: Third General Council,* ed. G. D. Mathews (Belfast: Assembly's Offices, 1884), p. 499.

⁷Aiken, "Christianity and Social Problems," p. 78; Greene, *PTR* (Oct. 1907):699; S. H. Kellogg, "A Tendency of the Times," *PRR* (Jan. 1890):50-51; Louis Berkhof, *The Church and Social Problems* (Grand Rapids: Eerdmans-Sevensma, 1913), p. 18.

⁸John Dixon, "Aggression by the Churches," in *Proceedings: Fifth General Council* (1892), p. 332; "The True Uplift of Humanity," *Pres* (March 21, 1900):3; Edward Coe, "The Church and Social Questions," in *Proceedings: Seventh General Council,* ed. G. D. Mathews (Washington: McGill and Wallace, 1899), p. 281; Robert Sample, "The Privileges and Duties of the Church," *Pres* (May 16, 1900):8.

⁹Southern Presbyterians and members of the Christian Reformed Church constantly and strongly emphasized this distinction. Many Northern Presbyterians expressed similar views. See Ira Landrith, "The Men of Our Church and Civil Affairs," in *Presbyterian Brotherhood* (Philadelphia: Presbyterian Board of Publication, 1907), p. 240; Greene, "The Church," pp. 378-79, 381; R. V. Hunter, "The Church and the Masses," *PRR* (Jan. 1893):80; "Preaching Peace in Times of Conflict," *Pres* (March 16, 1910):4; Robert Thompson, *The Divine Order of Human Society* (Philadelphia: John D. Wattles, 1891), p. 252.

¹⁰Greene, *PTR* (Jan. 1911):177. Cf. "Missions and Evangelism," *Pres* (Jan. 7, 1915):3; Charles Erdman, *PTR* (April 1911):364; "Three Essentials," *Pres* (March 18, 1915):6; A. F. Forrest, "The Problem of the Down-Town Church," in *Proceedings: Ninth General Council,* p. 174. Forrest cited the Salvation Army as an example of a group that had changed from an evangelistic to a benevolent organization. Cf. "Rev. Chas. Stelzle Resigns," *BT* (Oct. 1913):668-69.

¹¹Coe, "Church and Social Questions," pp. 272-73; Sloan, *Social Regeneration,* p. 60; Aiken, "Christianity and Social Problems," pp. 75-76, 78; Howerton, *Church and Social Reforms,* p. 94.

¹²Thompson, *Divine Order,* pp. 253-54; Greene, *PTR* (Jan. 1911):177; Alexander McKelway, "Moral Issues and Christian Citizenship," *PSt* (Jan. 18, 1905):13.

¹³Howerton, *Church and Social Reforms,* p. 91.

¹⁴J. M. Foster, *Christ the King* (Boston, 1894), p. 434; Coe, "Church and Social Questions," p. 280.

¹⁵"The Country Pastor and Social Service," *PSt* (July 21, 1915):3. Cf. O. A. Kingsbury, "The Social Idea in the Church—The True and False," *PR* (Oct.

1884):685; B. B. Warfield, *PRR* (Oct. 1893):710-11. Southern Presbyterian Moses Hoge argued that the gospel was most effective when it had good allies — "sunlight, pure air, uncontaminated water, wholesome food, abstinence from alcohol, suppression of pornography ... and brothels, and efforts of scientific and philanthropic associations for removal of evils which brutalize the masses." See "City Evangelism: Its Methods," p. 119.

[16]"Law and Order," *Pres* (March 2, 1910):3; "A Pressing Need," *CO* (April 6, 1910):3; "Public Reforms," *CI* (Aug. 10, 1876):8; Willis J. Beecher, "Legislative Restrictions of Evils," *PR* (April 1888):249-57, 262.

[17]John Calvin, *Institutes of the Christian Religion*, ed. John T. McNeill (2 vols.; Philadelphia: Westminster, 1960), 1:348-422. See John Mulder, "Calvinism, Politics and Ironies of History," in *Religion in Life* (Summer 1978):151.

[18]James Coleman, *Social Ethics* (New York: Baker and Taylor, 1902), p. 154; Howerton, *Church and Social Reforms*, pp. 57-79; John Prugh, "The Great Cities of the United States," in *Proceedings: Sixth General Council*, p. 345; Frank S. Scudder, "Social Conscience," *CI* (May 16, 1900):311-12.

[19]Dixon, "Aggression by the Churches," p. 333; Sample, "The Privileges," p. 8; "Preaching Peace," p. 4.

[20]George Greene, *PTR* (July 1912):478.

[21]Quoted by Huizinga, "Social or Individual Regeneration?" p. 47.

[22]Huizinga, "Social or Individual Regeneration?" p. 47; Dick, "The Law of Christ," p. 366; Louis Voss, "The Old Testament in Its Relation to Social Reform," *PQ* (Oct. 1896):443.

[23]Berkhof, *Church and Social Problems*, pp. 14, 23; Charles Hodge, *Conference Papers* (New York: Scribner's, 1879), p. 323.

[24]Greene, *PTR* (Oct. 1908):686. Cf. Thompson, *Divine Order*, pp. 12-14; Cleland B. McAfee, *The Westminster Confession of Faith and the Present Task of the Church* (New York: Revell, 1913), pp. 25-30; George Johnson, *PTR* (Oct. 1911):693.

[25]J. Ross Stevenson, "Calvin's Influence on Civic and Social Life," *Auburn Seminary Record* (July 1909):176; "Christian Participation in Society," *Pres* (April 8, 1891):4; David Burrell, *For Christ's Crown* (New York: Wilbur Ketcham, 1896), p. 15; Evert Blekkink, "Forward," *L* (Jan. 2, 1907):146.

[26]Coleman, *Social Ethics*, pp. 173, 175; Cf. Greene, "The Church," p. 379; Evert Blekkink, "The Spirit of the Age," *L* (Oct. 31, 1906):2.

[27]G. H. Dubbink, "The Church as an Organism," *L* (May 22, 1907):466-67; "Thy Kingdom Come," *BT* (Feb. 1900):121.

[28]Evert Blekkink, "Christ's Everlasting Kingdom," *L* (March 6, 1907):289-90. Cf. Kellogg, "Tendency of the Times," p. 48; Burrell, *For Christ's Crown*, p. 16.

[29]The quotation is from Howerton, *Church and Social Reform*, p. 121. Cf. Coleman, *Social Ethics*, p. 308; Robert Patterson, "The Second Advent not Premillennial," *PR* (April 1883):251-52; Joseph E. McAfee, "Brotherhood: Its Development in the Church," in *Presbyterian Brotherhood*, pp. 169-70.

[30]See Charles Hopkins, *The Rise of the Social Gospel in American Protestantism, 1865 – 1915* (New Haven: Yale University Press, 1940); Henry May, *Protestant Churches and Industrial America* (New York: Harper and Brothers, 1949); Aaron Abell, *The Urban Impact on American Protestantism, 1865 – 1900* (Cambridge, MA: Harvard University Press, 1943).

[31]For examples of basically positive Calvinistic appraisals of the Social Gospel, see W. B. Sheddan, *PTR* (July 1906):425-26; William B. Greene, Jr., *PTR* (April 1915):320; "Social Christianity and Calvinism," *BT* (April 5, 1917):216-17.

[32]Berkhof, *Church and Social Problems*, p. 18. Cf. "Missions and Evangelism," *Pres* (Jan. 7, 1915):3; "Social Christianity and Calvinism," p. 216.

[33]J. C. Dick, "The Law of Christ in Relation to Social Questions," in *First International Convention of the Reformed Presbyterian Church* (Glasgow: Alexander Malcolm and Co., 1896), pp. 359ff; William B. Greene, Jr., *PTR* (Oct. 1907):701.

[34]E. C. Gordon, "Christianity and the Social Crisis," *POS* (March 2, 1910):260; Greene, *PTR* (Oct. 1907):702.

[35]Greene, *PTR* (Oct. 1913):655; Charles Erdman, *PTR* (Jan. 1908):174-75. Cf. *Pres* (Oct. 15, 1890):4; Purves, "Problems of the Twentieth Century," pp. 166-67; James Eells, *PR* (April 1881):438; Benjamin Paist, Jr., *PTR* (April 1912):350-52.

[36]Gordon, "Christianity and the Social Crisis," p. 292.

[37]Waters, "Large Cities," p. 496; Greene, *PTR* (Jan. 1911):176-77; Patterson, "The Second Advent," *PR* (April 1883):250; Burrell, *For Christ's Crown*, p. 15.

[38]Howerton, *Church and Social Reforms*, pp. 16, 50-51. Cf. "Thy Kingdom Come," p. 121; "The Social Creed. What the Presbyterian Church Believes About Social Problems" (n.p., Board of Home Missions, 1910), pp. 6-7.

[39]Berkhof, *Church and Social Problems*, pp. 18-20. Cf. Thompson, *Divine Order*, pp. 253-54.

[40]Waters, "Large Cities," p. 496.

[41]Aiken, "Christianity and Social Problems," pp. 75, 81.

[42]Sloan, *Social Regeneration*, pp. 60-84.

[43]E.g., Coleman, *Social Ethics*, p. 198; Evert Blekkink, "Criminal Silence," *L* (Jan. 9, 1907):161; Dubbink, "Church as Organism," pp. 466-67.

[44]Voss, "The Old Testament," p. 452. Cf. J. E. Fogartie, *PQ* (Jan. 1897):110-11; "Infirmaries and Sanitariums," *POS* (Feb. 2, 1890):130.

[45]See *National Reform Documents* (Allegheny, PA: National Reform Association, 1900) and *Second World's Christian Citizenship Conference* (Pittsburgh: National Reform Association, 1913). See also Moses Hoge, "Christ's Method of Reconciling the Antagonisms of Society," in *Proceedings: Fourth General Council*, ed. William G. Blaikie (London: Presbyterian Alliance Office, 1889), pp. 153-58; James Stalker, "The Influence of our Church on Social Life," in *Proceedings: Sixth General Council*, pp. 144-48.

[46]Hamilton Hymes, "Factors of Hopefulness in American Civilization," *Pres* (July 27, 1910):8; Blekkink, "Spirit of the Age," p. 2.

[47]Howerton, *Church and Social Reforms*, pp. 85-90, 125. Cf. Sloan, *Social Regeneration*, pp. 69-73.

[48]Gordon Russell, *PTR* (Jan. 1914):168; Scovel, "World-Wide Meaning," p. 14; "Social Creed," p. 8.

[49]"Child Labor vs Schools," *SWP* (March 8, 1905):5-6.

[50]E.g., Alexander McKelway, "Some Facts About Child Labor," *PSt* (Jan. 4, 1905):4-5; "The Child and the Golden Age," *PSt* (Feb. 1, 1905):4-6; "Social Creed," p. 9.

[51]E.g., E. C. Wines, "Crime: Its Causes and Cure," *PQ* (May 1878):805-8; "Social Creed," p. 11.

[52]J. B. Bittinger, "Responsibility of Society for the Causes of Crime," *BRPR* (Jan. 1871):22ff., 32-33.

[53]Ibid., pp. 32-33. Cf. J. B. Bittinger, "Crimes of Passion and Crimes of Reflection," *PQPR* (April 1873):231-33; Chaplain Munro, "Applied Christianity in Prisons," *CI* (Jan. 31, 1900):67.

[54]McKenzie Cleland, "Report on Prison Reform," in *Second World's Christian Citizenship Conference* pp. 117, 119ff.; Munro, "Applied Christianity," p. 67; Bit-

tinger, "Responsibility of Society," p. 29; Wines, "Crime," p. 810.

[55] Munro, "Applied Christianity," p. 67; "Social Creed," p. 11.

[56] Wines, "Crime," p. 810; Bittinger, "Responsibility of Society," p. 29.

[57] Cleland, "Report," pp. 115, 122-23.

[58] Ibid., p. 118.

[59] Bittinger, "Responsibility of Society," pp. 25-29. Cf. Cleland, "Report," p. 119.

[60] Bittinger, "Crimes of Passion," p. 236; "Our Criminal Population," *PB* (Jan. 2, 1889):1; Cleland, "Report," p. 124.

[61] Bittinger, "Responsibility of Society," pp. 30-32.

[62] Cleland, "Report," p. 115.

[63] E.g., Munro, "Applied Christianity," p. 67; Munro, "Transformed in Prison," *CI* (May 30, 1900):343-44.

[64] See, for example, Henry Lee, *How Dry We Were* (Englewood Cliffs, NJ: Prentice-Hall, 1963), pp. 238-40; John M. Blum et al., *The National Experience: A History of the United States* (New York: Harcourt, Brace and World, 1963), pp. 612-13; Samuel Eliot Morison et al., *The Growth of the American Republic* (2 vols; New York: Oxford University Press, 1969), 2:438-39.

[65] Paul Carter, *The Decline and Rise of the Social Gospel: Social and Political Liberalism in American Protestant Churches, 1920–1940* (Ithaca, NY: Cornell University Press, 1956), pp. 32-41; James Timberlake, *Prohibition and the Progressive Movement, 1900–1920* (Cambridge, MA: Harvard University Press, 1963), p. 2 and passim.

[66] A. M. Powell, "Temperance Reform in the U.S.," *Cath P* (June 1882):437-38. See *Minutes of the General Assembly of the Presbyterian Church, U.S.A.* (1865), p. 573; *Minutes* (1881), p. 188. By 1910 the General Assembly Committee on Temperance (established in 1881) was spending $24,000 annually, was holding rallies across the nation, and reportedly had distributed eighteeen million pieces of literature throughout the world (*Minutes* [1910], p. 161).

[67] E.g., R. C. Reed, "Church and Temperance," *SPR* (Jan. 1881):49. The PSUSA General Assemblies of 1865 and 1881 affirmed this position. See *Minutes* (1881), p. 188.

[68] D. Stuart Dodge, "The Temperance Cause in the U.S.," in *Proceedings: Ninth General Council*, pp. 385-89, quotation from p. 389.

[69] Mears, "Grounds and Methods," p. 509; David Burrell, *The Religion of the Future* (New York: American Tract Society, 1894), p. 58; "The Corruption of Politics By the Saloon," *PSt* (July 16, 1902):4; "A Sorrowful Record," *PB* (Aug. 17, 1881):1; "Temperance Progress," *PB* (Sept. 26, 1888):1.

[70] Mears, "Grounds and Methods," p. 510. David Burrell, in *For Christ's Crown*, p. 154, pointed out that by 1895 Americans were spending $11,000,000,000 annually on liquor.

[71] Foster, *Reformation Principles*, pp. 156-57.

[72] Sample, "Temperance in America," p. 441; "Corruption of Politics," p. 1; Anderson, "Intemperance," *CO* (May 28, 1890):1-2.

[73] "Prohibition and Crime," *SP* (March 9, 1905):31.

[74] "The Saloon Business," *PB* (Jan. 26, 1881):1; A. M. Wylie, "The Great Evil," *Pres* (Jan. 10, 1880):4; Reed, "Church and Temperance," p. 47; John Dinsmore, "No Government Has a Right to Legislate Vice," *Pres* (May 4, 1910):1.

[75] Anderson, "Intemperance," p. 1.

[76] *Manual of Doctrine*, p. 26; Burrell, *Religion of the Future*, p. 58.

[77] Ben Helm, "The Liquor Question," *CO* (Jan. 22, 1890):4; Foster, *Reformation Principles*, pp. 171-74; Dick, "Temperance Reformation," pp. 423-24.

[78] Sample, "Temperance in America," p. 440. He insisted that Maine, which

had already passed a prohibition law, demonstrated this. Cf. John Hill, "Out in Kansas," *PB* (Feb. 21, 1901):23; W. M. Howie, "Prohibition or License?" *UP* (Aug. 20, 1885):531.

[79]Mears, "Grounds and Methods," pp. 528-29; Burrell, *Religion of the Future,* pp. 62ff.

[80]E.g., J. C. Dick, "The Temperance Reformation," in *First International Convention of the RPC's,* pp. 422-24.

[81]Hill, "Out in Kansas," p. 23.

[82]Dodge, "Church and Temperance," p. 572; "Drunkenness," *CI* (Jan. 20, 1876):8-9; Reed, "Church and Temperance," pp. 58-59.

[83]In so doing, Calvinists typified the approach of the evangelical community as a whole. See Francis Weisenburger, *Triumph of Faith: Contributions of the Church to American Life, 1865 – 1900* (Richmond: William Byrd, 1962), p. 142.

[84]Some, in fact, such as J. Gresham Machen, opposed legal prohibition precisely because they believed that the Bible allowed moderate drinking. See J. Gresham Machen, "The So-Called Child Labor Amendment," *Pres* (Jan. 22, 1925):6-7; *New York Times,* June 7, 1926.

[85]See "Report by the Committee on Industrial Relations . . . ," quoted by Wallace Jamison, *The United Presbyterian Story* (Pittsburgh: The Geneva Press, 1958), pp. 108-9; *Minutes of the General Assembly of the UPCNA* (1911), p. 966; *Minutes* (1912), pp. 180ff.; *Minutes* (1913), pp. 521ff.; Evlyn Fulton, "A History of the Women's General Missionary Society of the United Presbyterian Church of North America" (MRE thesis Pittsburgh-Xenia Seminary, 1949), pp. 116ff.; J. C. Mc-Feeters, *The Covenanters in America* (Philadelphia: Spangler and Davis, 1892), pp. 61-64, 113ff., 147-66, 177-81.

[86]"Vigorous Church Work," *Outlook* (Nov. 30, 1901):804.

[87]Walter W. Moore, "Home Missions," in *Addresses Delivered at the Centennial Celebration of the General Assembly of the Presbyterian Church* (Philadelphia: McCalla and Co., 1888), pp. 184-90; Abell, *Urban Impact,* pp. 155-56; Paula Benkart, "Changing Attitudes of Presbyterians Toward Southern and Eastern European Immigrants, 1880 – 1914," *Journal of Presbyterian History* (Fall 1971):228, 231-32, 235, 242-44. Matthews' church sponsored vocational instruction, English classes for Japanese and Chinese immigrants, a day nursery to benefit working mothers, a center for clothing distribution, and an Anti-Tuberculosis Society. See C. Allyn Russell, "Mark A. Matthews: Seattle Fundamentalist and Civic Reformer," *Journal of Presbyterian History* (Winter 1979):451.

[88]Richard P. Poethig, "Urban/Metropolitan Mission Policies—an Historical Overview," *Journal of Presbyterian History* (Fall 1979):316, 319.

[89]R. M. Patterson, "Church Extension in Large Cities," *Proceedings: Second General Council* (Philadelphia, 1880), pp. 399-400; Patterson thought these four factors made "the defensive and aggressive work of the Church in large cities more difficult than it has been in any age since the days of the apostles" (p. 401).

[90]Waters, "Large Cities," p. 494. Cf. J. K. Wight, "Home Missions and the Presbyterian Church," *PR* (Oct. 1886):618-19.

[91]Samuel Niccoll, "Preaching to the Masses," in *Addresses Delivered at the Centennial Celebration,* pp. 131-33; Bennett Young, "Lay Effort Among the Masses," ibid., p. 145; Patterson, "Church Extension," p. 403; "General Booth's New Scheme," *Pres* (Oct. 15, 1890):4; Dixon, "Aggression by the Churches," pp. 226-332; Thomas C. Johnson, "The Duty of the Church to Quit Robbing the Masses of the Gospel," *PQ* (Jan. 1900):78-84; J. T. Backus, "The Benevolent Work of the Church,"

PQPR (April 1872):246-72; A. T. Pierson, "Organized Christian Work," *Proceedings: Fourth General Council,* pp. 88-93.

⁹²May, *Protestant Churches,* p. 193; Hopkins, *Rise of the Social Gospel,* p. 16. For an extended discussion of this subject, see William S. Barker, "The Social Views of Charles Hodge (1797 – 1878): A Study in 19th Century Calvinism and Conservatism," *Presbyterion* (Spring and Fall 1975):1-2, 20-22.

⁹³See Weisenburger, *Triumph of Faith,* p. 188.

⁹⁴George Hays, "Home Missions," in *Addresses Delivered at the Centennial Celebration,* pp. 148-50; Patterson, "Church Extension," p. 407; Sample, "Privilege and Duties," p. 8; Berkhof, *Church and Social Problems,* p. 23.

⁹⁵Hunter, "Church and the Masses," pp. 84-85. Cf. Hays, "Home Missions," pp. 149-51.

⁹⁶Johnson, "Duty of the Church," pp. 74-79. Cf. Wight, "Home Missions," p. 619.

⁹⁷Hoge, "City Evangelism," p. 121. Cf. Aiken, "Christianity and Social Problems," p. 65.

⁹⁸See Robert Wiebe, *The Search For Order* (New York: Hill and Wang, 1967).

⁹⁹Richard Mouw, *Called to Holy Worldliness* (Philadelphia: Fortress, 1980), p. 35.

¹⁰⁰See Fred Graham, *The Constructive Revolutionary: John Calvin and His Socio-Economic Impact* (Richmond: John Knox Press, 1971) and R. M. Kingdon, "Social Welfare in Calvin's Geneva," *American Historical Review* (Feb. 1971):50-69.

CHAPTER 10

¹James Howerton, "The Hard Doctrines and the Words of Eternal Life," *PQ* (Jan. 1901):134-35. Cf. Samuel Smith, "The Westminster Symbols," in *Memorial Volume of the Westminster Assembly, 1647 – 1897* (Richmond: Presbyterian Committee Publication, 1897), p. 254.

²Frederick Platt, "Calvinism and Criticism," *London Quarterly Review* (July 1909):67-89, quotations from pp. 72, 71.

³Ibid., pp. 85-86.

⁴Ibid., pp. 74-82. quotation from p. 82.

⁵Ibid., pp. 83-84; quotation from p. 84.

⁶Ibid., pp. 86-87.

⁷Ibid., pp. 88-89. Cf. A. Mitchell Hunter, "Has Calvinism a Future?" *Biblical World* (Oct. 1914):231-38.

⁸A. A. Hodge, for example, disputed the claim of the advocates of New Theology that the view of God as immanent and constantly active in the creation was new to Christians. He insisted that Calvinists had "always believed this." See *Popular Lectures on Theological Themes* (Philadelphia: Presbyterian Board of Publication, 1887), p. 27. See also A. A. Hodge, "The Relation of God to the World," *PR* (Jan. 1887):11-12.

⁹James Cothran, "Calvinism and Human Progress," in *Addresses Delivered at the Centennial Celebration of the General Assembly of the Presbyterian Church* (Philadelphia: MacCalla and Co., 1888), pp. 86-90; Henry Beets, "Calvinism and Missions," *BT* (July 29, 1904):273-75; S. L. Morris, "The Relation of Calvin and Calvinism to Missions," in *Calvin Memorial Addresses* (Richmond: Presbyterian Committee of Publication, 1909), pp. 134, 141-42; A. M. Fraser, "How May the Principles of Calvinism Be Rendered Most Effective Under Modern Conditions?" in ibid., pp. 247-53; J. I. Vance, "The World-Wide Mission of Calvinism," in "*Pro-*

ceedings: Ninth General Council," ed. G. D. Mathews (New York: Office of the Alliance, 1909), p. 164; N. S. McFeteridge, Calvinism in History (Philadelphia: Presbyterian Board of Publication, 1882); Lyman Atwater, "Calvinism in Doctrine and Life," PQPR (Jan. 1875):73-106.

[10]B. B. Warfield, Calvin as a Theologian and Calvinism Today (Philadelphia: Presbyterian and Reformed, 1909), p. 23.

[11]Winthrop Hudson's outstanding study of voluntaryism in America, The Great Tradition of the American Churches (New York: Harpers, 1953), is marred by his overemphasis on the churches' complacency and their making peace with the world in the late nineteenth and early twentieth centuries and his depreciation of the strength and subtlety of secularism. See pp. 198-205.

[12]See Paul Boller, Jr., American Thought in Transition: The Impact of Evolutionary Naturalism, 1865 – 1900 (Chicago: Rand McNally and Co., 1969) and Ferenc M. Szasz, The Divided Mind of Protestant America, 1880-1930 (University, AL: University of Alabama Press, 1982).

[13]William Clebsch, From Sacred to Profane America: The Role of Religion in American History (New York: Harper and Row, 1968), pp. 1-2 and passim. Also Harvey Cox, The Secular City: Secularization and Urbanization in Theological Perspective (New York: Macmillan, 1965).

[14]George Marsden, "America's 'Christian' Origins: Puritan New England as a Case Study," in John Calvin: His Influence on the Western World, ed. W. Stanford Reid (Grand Rapids: Zondervan, 1982), p. 256.

[15]See James Skillen, "Public Justice and True Tolerance," in Confessing Christ and Doing Politics, ed. James Skillen (Washington: Association for Public Justice, 1982), pp. 54-62; Martin Marty, The Public Church: Mainline — Evangelical — Catholic (New York: Crossroad, 1981), pp. 3-17, 94-109, 138-39, 168-69; Richard Neuhaus, The Naked Public Square: Religion and Democracy in America (Grand Rapids: Eerdmans, 1984), pp. 156-76.

[16]Gordon Spykman et al., Society, State, and Schools (Grand Rapids: Eerdmans, 1981), p. 39. For an excellent contemporary argument for pluralism, see this book and Rockne M. McCarthy et al., Disestablishment a Second Time: Genuine Pluralism for American Schools (Grand Rapids: Eerdmans/Christian University Press, 1982).

[17]See Cornelius Van Til, Common Grace and the Gospel (Nutley, NJ: Presbyterian and Reformed, 1973).

[18]See Spykman, Society, State, and Schools, pp. 40-43; W. Fred Graham, The Constructive Revolutionary: John Calvin and his Socio-Economic Impact (Richmond: John Knox Press, 1971).

[19]Winthrop Hudson, American Protestantism (Chicago: University of Chicago Press, 1961), p. 131.

[20]John Mulder, "Calvinism, Politics, and the Ironies of History," Religion in Life (Summer 1978):148-61.

[21]E.g., Charles Wood, "The Pauperism of Our Cities; its Character, Condition, Causes and Relief," PQPR (April 1874):226-27; James A. Worden, "Sabbath-School Work in the United States," in Proceedings: Third General Council, ed. G. D. Mathews (Belfast: Assembly Offices, 1884), pp. 422-24; William C. Roberts, "Higher Education in the West," PR (April 1888):210-11.

[22]Abraham Kuyper, Lectures on Calvinism (1898; Grand Rapids: Eerdmans, 1931), pp. 192-93. James Bratt, Dutch Calvinism in Modern America: A History of a Conservative Subculture (Grand Rapids: Eerdmans, 1984), p. 55.

[23]Bratt, Dutch Calvinism, p. 55.

[24]For a succinct statement of this position, see George Marsden, "Reforming a Reformed Heritage, Calvinism vs. Pluralism," *Reformed Journal* (April 1973):15-20. For a discussion of Canadian educational pluralism see Spykman, *Society, State, and Schools,* pp. 136-39. For a discussion of Dutch pluralism see *Society, State, and Schools* pp. 141-44 and Alan Storkey, *A Christian Social Perspective* (Leicester: Inter-Varsity Press, 1979), pp. 268-71. For a discussion of various European forms of pluralism, see McCarthy, *Disestablishment a Second Time,* pp. 107-23.

[25]See Joseph Wood Krutch, *The Modern Temper* (1929; New York, 1956).

[26]Walter Lippmann, *A Preface to Morals* (New York: Macmillan, 1929), p. 3.

[27]Ibid., p. 69.

[28]Ibid., p. 121. See also pp. 84-106.

[29]Ibid., pp. 122-39 and 318-25.

[30]See *Humanist Manifestos I and II* (Buffalo, NY: Prometheus Books, 1973), pp. 7-10.

[31]See *Humanist Manifestos I and II,* pp. 13-23.

[32]See Alfred McClung Lee, "Humanist Strength: Reality," *The Humanist* (Jan./Feb. 1980):5-13, 48. Many Christians today are analyzing and attacking humanism. See, for example, Robert Webber, *Secular Humanism: Threat and Challenge* (Grand Rapids: Zondervan, 1982); Ernest Gordon, *Me, Myself and Who. Humanism: Society's False Premise* (Plainfield, NJ: Logos International, 1980); David Jeremiah, *Before It's Too Late: Crises Facing America* (Nashville: Thomas Nelson, 1982); Tim LaHaye, *The Battle for the Mind: A Subtle Warfare* (Old Tappan, NJ: Revell, 1980); and Herbert Schlossberg, *Idols for Destruction: Christian Faith and its Confrontation with American Society* (Nashville: Thomas Nelson, 1983).

[33]Julian Huxley, "The Humanist Frame," in *The Humanist Frame,* ed. Julian Huxley (London: Allen and Unwin, 1961), p. 19.

[34]See Corliss Lamont, "The Affirmative Ethics of Humanism," *The Humanist* (March/April 1980):4-7; Koristantin Kolenda, "Humanism and Christianity," *The Humanist* (July/Aug. 1980):4-8; F. A. E. Crow, "The Meaning of Death," in *The Humanist Outlook,* ed. A. J. Ayer (London: Pemberton, 1968), pp. 260ff.; Paul Kurtz, *The Fullness of Life* (New York: Horizon Press, 1974), pp. 1off.

[35]Crow, "Meaning of Death," p. 260.

[36]Sidney Hook, "Solzhenitsyn and Secular Humanism: A Response," *The Humanist* (Nov./Dec. 1978):5-6. See also Roy Wood Sellars, "The Humanist Outlook," in *The Humanist Alternative: Some Definitions of Humanism,* ed. Paul Kurtz (Buffalo, NY: Prometheus Books, 1973), pp. 133-35; Marvin Zimmerman, "Aren't Humanists Really Atheists?" in *Humanist Alternative,* pp. 83ff.; Kinsley Martin, "Rock of Ages," in *Humanist Outlook,* pp. 214-21.

[37]Kurtz, *Fullness of Life,* pp. 86-90. Cf. Gora, "Humanism and Atheism," in *Humanist Alternative,* pp. 147-48; Muller, "Human Future," pp. 402-4; Arthur H. Dakin, *Man the Measure: An Essay on Humanism as Religion* (Princeton, NJ: Princeton University Press, 1939), pp. 10-16.

[38]Corliss Lamont, *The Philosophy of Humanism* (New York: Philosophical Library, 1957), p. 18. Cf. Kinsley, "Rock of Ages," pp. 217-21; C. H. Waddington, "The Human Animal," in *Humanist Frame,* pp. 67-79.

[39]H. J. Blackham, "A Definition of Humanism," in *Humanist Alternative,* pp. 35-36; *Humanist Manifestos I and II,* p. 16.

[40]Erich Fromm, *Man For Himself* (New York: Rinehart and Co., 1947), p. 44. Cf. Paul Kurtz, "The Meaning of Humanism," in *Humanist Alternative,* pp. 5-6.

[41]Erich Fromm, *Man For Himself,* p. 45. Cf. Lyle L. Simpson, "The State of Humanism," *The Humanist* (Jan./Feb. 1982):37-40.

[42]*Humanist Manifestos I and II*, p. 9.

[43]Kurtz, *Fullness of Life*, pp. 95ff.; A. J. Ayer, "Introduction," in *Humanist Outlook*, pp. 8-9.

[44]Calvin Wilson, "What Men Have Said of Man," *Pres* (Nov. 18, 1891):12; W. G. T. Shedd, *Orthodoxy and Heterodoxy: A Miscellany* (New York: Scribner's, 1893), pp. 223-25; Smith, "Westminster Symbols," p. 236; John H. Edwards, "The Vanishing Sense of Sin," *PRR* (Oct. 1899):615; Gerhardus Vos, *The Kingdom and the Church* (1904; Grand Rapids: Eerdmans, 1951), pp. 72f.

[45]Vance, "World-Wide Mission of Calvinism," p. 166.

[46]See Jacques Maritain, *Integral Humanism* (New York: Scribner's, 1968); David Ehrenfeld, *The Arrogance of Humanism* (New York: Oxford University Press, 1978), pp. 16-20, 58, 239-53 and passim; Robert L. Johnson, *Humanism and Beyond* (Philadelphia: United Church of Christ Press, 1973); Christopher Lasch, *The Culture of Narcissism: American Life in an Age of Diminishing Expectations* (New York: W. W. Norton and Co., 1979); Thomas Wolfe, "The 'Me' Decade and the Third Great Awakening," *New York Magazine* (Aug. 23, 1976):26-40.

[47]Caspar W. Hodge, "The Significance of Reformed Theology Today," *PTR* (Jan. 1922):13.

[48]D. G. Malan, "Calvinism in the Twentieth Century," *The Evangelical Quarterly* (July 15, 1937):217-25.

[49]Cited in Ernest F. Kevar, "The Re-emergence of Calvinism," *The Evangelical Quarterly* (April 15, 1943):223.

[50]Ibid., pp. 216-23.

[51]Clarence Bouma, "Calvinism in American Theology Today," *The Journal of Religion* (Jan. 1947):34-45. Cf. Paul Woolley, "American Calvinism in the Twentieth Century," in *American Calvinism*, ed. Jacob Hoogstra (Grand Rapids: Baker, 1957), pp. 70-73.

[52]This discussion focuses upon the revival of orthodox Calvinism as explained in the Preface. Another helpful analysis could be made of the renaissance of the essential principles of Reformed dogma or even of the spirit of Calvinism, as John T. McNeill does in *The History and Character of Calvinism* (New York: Oxford University Press, 1954), pp. 432-38.

[53]See Gordon Oesterman, "Evidences and Echoes of Calvin in Twentieth Century America," in *Geneva to Geelong: The Ideas and Influence of John Calvin*, ed. Gordon Oesterman (Grand Rapids: National Union of Christian Schools, 1974), pp. 88-90.

[54]See "Values in the Public Schools: A Prerequisite to Teaching," *Christianity Today* (April 10, 1981):16-18; Reo M. Christenson, "Clarifying 'Values Clarification' for the Innocent," ibid., pp. 36-39; Timothy Crater, "The Unproclaimed Priests of Public Education," ibid., pp. 44-47; David B. Cummings, ed., *The Basis for a Christian School* (Phillipsburg, NJ: Presbyterian and Reformed, 1982); Charles Malik, "The Other Side of Evangelism," *Christianity Today* (Nov. 7, 1980):38-40.

[55]See "We Poll the Pollster—an Interview with George Gallup, Jr.," *Christianity Today* (Dec. 21, 1979):10-12; "The Christianity Today—Gallup Poll: An Overview," ibid., pp. 12-15; "The Religious Personality of the Populace," ibid., pp. 15-17; Andrew Greeley, *The Denominational Society: A Sociological Approach to Religion in America* (Glenview, IL: Scott, Foresman and Co., 1972), pp. 86-107; John Wilson, *Religion in American Society: The Effective Presence* (Englewood Cliffs, NJ: Prentice-Hall, 1978), pp. 395-411; H. Paul Chalfant et al., *Religion in Contemporary Society* (Sherman Oaks, CA: Alfred, 1981), pp. 449-69.

[56]See "Who and Where Are the Evangelicals?" *Christianity Today* (Dec. 21, 1979):17-19; Wilson, *Religion in American Society*, pp. 420-21. Anthropologist

Clifford Geertz suggests that people vary widely in how and to what extent they apply religious teachings to their lives. Some consider religion to be one of many concerns in life, separated into a distinct sphere, having little to do with economic, political, or social behavior. W. T. Jones argues that such persons view reality through "multiple narrow-range vectors"; that is, they see life as having many separate and distinct realms. Gerhard Lenski and others have shown that such a worldview is quite common to Americans. See Clifford Geertz, *Islam Observed: Religious Developments in Morocco and Indonesia* (Chicago: University of Chicago Press, 1968); W. T. Jones, "World Views: Their Nature and Their Function," *Current Anthropology* (Feb. 1972):79-109; Gerhard Lenski, *The Religious Factor* (Garden City, NY: Doubleday, 1961).

[57]E.g., see Daniel Yankelovich, *New Rules: Searching for Self-Fulfillment in a World Turned Upside Down* (New York: Bantam, 1981), pp. 92-94.

[58]Wolfe, "The 'Me' Decade"; Lasch, *Culture of Narcissism*.

[59]Dean Kelley, *Why Conservative Churches Are Growing* (New York: Harper and Row, 1972); David Wells and John Woodbridge, eds., *The Evangelicals: What They Believe, Who They Are, Where They Are Changing* (New York: Abingdon, 1975); Kenneth Woodward et al., "Born Again," *Newsweek* (Oct. 25, 1976):68ff.; Donald G. Bloesch, *The Evangelical Renaissance* (Grand Rapids: Eerdmans, 1973); Richard G. Hutcheson, Jr., *Mainline Churches and the Evangelicals: A Challenging Crisis?* (Atlanta: John Knox Press, 1981); Bernard Ramm, *The Evangelical Heritage* (Waco: Word, 1973); Morris Inch, *The Evangelical Challenge* (Philadelphia: Westminster, 1978).

[60]E.g., William McLoughlin, *Revivals, Awakenings, and Reform: an Essay on Religion and Social Change in America, 1607–1977* (Chicago: University of Chicago Press, 1978), pp. 179-216; John W. Whitehead, "The Boston Tea Party, 1982?" *Christianity Today* (Nov. 12, 1982):29.

[61]Jeremy Rifkin, *The Emerging Order: God in the Age of Scarcity* (New York: Ballantine, 1979).

[62]Richard Lovelace, "Completing an Awakening," *The Christian Century* (March 18, 1981):296-300. Wolfe, "The 'Me' Decade" pp. 26-40; Richard Quebedeaux, *The Worldly Evangelicals* (New York: Harper and Row, 1978); James Barr, *Fundamentalism* (Philadelphia: Westminster, 1978).

[63]See Francis Schaeffer, *A Christian Manifesto* (Westchester, IL: Crossway Books, 1981); Harold O. J. Brown, *The Reconstruction of the Republic* (New Rochelle, NY: Arlington House, 1977); Franky Schaeffer, *Addicted to Mediocrity* (Westchester, IL: Crossway Books, 1981); John W. Whitehead, *The Second American Revolution* (Elgin, IL: David C. Cook, 1982); Charles Peters, *How Washington Really Works* (Reading, MA: Addison-Wesley, 1980); and Jeremy Jackson, *No Other Foundation* (Westchester, IL: Crossway Books, 1980).

[64]See Marsden, "America's 'Christian' Origins," pp. 241-62.

[65]Robert Handy, *A Christian America: Protestant Hopes and Historical Realities* (New York: Oxford University Press, 1971), pp. 95-116; Winthrop Hudson, *Great Tradition of American Churches,* pp. 80-109.

[66]See George Marsden, "Quest for a Christian America," *Eternity* (May 1983):18-23.

[67]Schlossberg, *Idols for Destruction,* p. 296.

INDEX

235